John Ruffini

Vincenzo or Sunken Rocks

Volume I.

John Ruffini

Vincenzo or Sunken Rocks
Volume I.

ISBN/EAN: 9783741198809

Manufactured in Europe, USA, Canada, Australia, Japa

Cover: Foto ©Andreas Hilbeck / pixelio.de

Manufactured and distributed by brebook publishing software (www.brebook.com)

John Ruffini

Vincenzo or Sunken Rocks

COLLECTION

OF

BRITISH AUTHORS.

VOL. 670.

VINCENZO BY JOHN RUFFINI.

IN TWO VOLUMES.
VOL. I.

TAUCHNITZ EDITION.

By the same Author,

LAVINIA	in 2 vols.
DOCTOR ANTONIO	in 1 vol.
LORENZO BENONI	in 1 vol.
A QUIET NOOK	in 1 vol.
THE PARAGREENS	in 1 vol.
CARLINO	in 1 vol.

VINCENZO;

OR,

SUNKEN ROCKS.

BY

JOHN RUFFINI,

AUTHOR OF "DOCTOR ANTONIO," "LAVINIA," ETC.

COPYRIGHT EDITION.

IN TWO VOLUMES.

VOL. I.

LEIPZIG

BERNHARD TAUCHNITZ

1863.

CONTENTS

OF VOLUME I.

		Page
CHAPTER I.	Introduces the Principal Characters	1
— II.	A Vocation	14
— III.	The Castle and the Palace	24
— IV.	Cedant Arma Togæ	39
— V.	Vincenzo goes on a Fool's Errand	49
— VI.	The Day after a Frolic	63
— VII.	Beginning of the Experiences of a Raw Recruit	76
— VIII.	The Signor Avvocato borrows a Stock of Courage from Barnaby	86
— IX.	Fluctuations in the said Stock of Courage	100
— X.	Continuation of the Experiences of a Raw Recruit	114
— XI.	A Colonel Unhorsed	127
— XII.	A New Start	137
— XIII.	An Eventful Day	148
— XIV.	Dangers of Excitement	157
— XV.	The Stray Lamb in the Fold again	165
— XVI.	Tenacem Propositi	180
— XVII.	What shall he be?	194
— XVIII.	Barnaby Pitches into it, and Settles the Question	203
— XIX.	Turiness Silhouettes	212
— XX.	A Pilot in a Troubled Sea	226
— XXI.	Sunshine and Clouds of the First Vacation	238
— XXII.	Spokes in the Wheel	249

		Page
CHAPTER XXIII.	Banished from Eden	262
— XXIV.	Onofrio to the Rescue	276
— XXV.	The Signor Avvocato in his Glory	291
— XXVI.	An Interesting Definition Cut Short	305
— XXVII.	The Interrupted Definition Concluded	315
— XXVIII.	A Happy Pair	331

VINCENZO; OR, SUNKEN ROCKS.

CHAPTER I.

Introduces the Principal Characters.

HALF-hidden behind a tall hedge of roses, which ran round a small piece of artificial water, with a *jet d'eau* in the centre, a peachy-cheeked young girl was busy clipping withered blossoms and dead leaves, singing cheerily the while. When we say that the girl's business was with decayed flowers and dry twigs, we give her credit for a good intention; the doleful fact being that, along with the old and faded ones, perfectly fresh roses, and promising buds, not a few strewed the ground wherever she had passed. But could any one hold her responsible for these trespasses who contrasted the ponderous garden-scissors in her grasp with the plump tiny hands which tried to wield them?

Meanwhile, a quaint-looking figure in a striped cotton cap and green apron, under cover of a row of mulberry-trees, was limping stealthily along towards the pond. Once there, the man — for a man it was, and an old man, and certainly one of the ugliest men alive — well, the man stood waiting a few seconds, then, biding his time, crossed on tiptoe the short open space between the row of trees and the pond; and, when only separated from the girl by the thickness of the hedge of roses, he roared out, "I catch you at it again, Signorina."

The Signorina jumped back in great alarm, and cried, "How rude of you, Barnaby; you have startled me out of my senses."

"I wish I could startle you out of your wicked ways, but that I can't. How many times haven't I told you to let the flowers alone! You have a garden of your own, haven't you, and scissors of your own, haven't you?"

"I have lost mine," pleaded the youthful offender.

"So much the better for these poor things of God. Fine work you have made of it," pursued the old gardener, pointing to the hedge and to the "rosy way" on the ground, with which she had marked her progress; "a hailstorm could not have done worse. And who will have to bear the blame when the whole town comes up for the feast? Why, that old dotard, Barnaby; that good-for-nothing Barnaby. Dotards and good-for-nothings yourselves, confounded ignoramuses."

"You needn't bellow so, I am not deaf," remonstrated the Signorina; "you are always in a rage with some one or other. I don't wonder they call you Radetzky."

This cut on a bleeding wound brought the old man's exasperation to a pitch of fury. He opened his mouth to a frightful extent, stood gasping for a moment; then, probably finding no words adequate to his passion, he made a pull at his cap, threw it on the ground, picked it up, walked two steps away, came back, and said solemnly, "Will you give me my scissors; yes or no, Signora Padrona?"

Whenever he called her "Signora Padrona," Barnaby was in high dudgeon. She did not seem to mind it much, as she only said, "Presently," making in the meantime the most of her short presumed tenure of the scissors. Barnaby, without further parley, turned into the green inclosure, and gave chase. Will-o'-the-Wisp skipped along to avoid pursuit, snipping right and left at random, and laughing heartily. All at once she stopped, gave a faint cry, and lo! the twist of keen merriment in her face gave way to that particular and not over dignified grimace about the mouth which is a forerunner of tears. In her precipitation to do havoc, Miss Rose had caught one of her thumbs between the handles of the scissors.

Here was a piece of poetical justice, which one, even under smaller provocation than our old fellow, might well be tempted to turn to account as a text for a little moral lecture. But Barnaby was a poor hand at moralising, and no amount of poetical or unpoetical justice could ever reconcile him to a consummation which entailed pain on his young mistress. For, be it said to his honour or to his shame, cross-grained and grumbling, and full of sound and fury as he was, the least of the little distresses of this pet of his was enough to make him as chicken-hearted as could be.

The echo of Miss Rose's faint cry had barely died away ere Barnaby was by her side, and, kneeling on one knee, his two arms round her had drawn her close to him. "What is it? where is it?"

"Here," sobbed Rose, showing the injured thumb; and, with the effort of speaking, down dropped two big tears.

"Don't, don't, my darling," cried the good old fellow, raising the small hand to his lips, previous to its inspection. "It's nothing; it will be soon all right. You see the skin is not broken — only a little pinch. We'll rub the pain away in no time;" and he began rubbing with great care. There were coaxing and caressing tones in his voice now, which no one would have dreamed of finding in it a moment before. Even the hotch-potch of grimacing, tumble-down features, which made him a remarkably ugly man, had settled into something almost agreeable to look at, so intense was the gentle and tender feeling which lighted them from within.

"There, the smart is over, isn't it? Not quite yet? but almost — well, we must conjure it away by a little magic;" and, putting the thumb on a level with his mouth, he first mumbled some inarticulate sounds, and then blew noisily over it. "There, it is gone now, and we can smile again." In spite of some effort to the contrary, the corners of the pouting mouth had begun to relax, when a shrill sound, something like a colt's neigh, caught her ear. "Here is Vincenzino," she said, disengaging herself from the old man's arms; "don't tell him I have been crying." And, passing a corner of her long-sleeved pinafore over her eyes, she answered the signal in the same key. Well might Miss Rose be ashamed of being found out to have been crying, for, younger by two years as she looked, she was not the less fourteen years of age.

Presently hove in sight, capering towards the pond, the slim figure of a bare-headed and tonsured lad, in the long and not over-graceful robe of a Seminarist. "Is the rehearsal over?" asked Miss Rose, the moment he was close to her. He did not reply to the question, but, with a sharp glance at her, he said, "You have been crying;" and, turning quickly on Barnaby, added, with a significant stamp of the foot, "it is you who made her cry." Barnaby burst into a contemptuous laugh, and, mimicking the treble and gesture of the young orator most pointedly, repeated word for word the new-comer's address to himself; then, resuming his natural gruff voice, he went on cuttingly, "Of course, it was I who made her cry; who else could it be, I should like to know? Whenever there is mischief done, depend on it Barnaby is at the bottom of it. Barnaby feeds on babies, three weeks' old boys for breakfast, six weeks' old girls for dinner, and so on. Nay, now that I think of it, I had better take to my heels, or for certain I shall be whipped by his Reverence. Ha! ha! ha! confounded brats!" was the *ab irato* winding-up. "Their lips are still moist with mother's milk, and they give themselves airs of authority. I have no patience with them." Having thus delivered his opinion, Barnaby picked up the shears, and walked away in sullen majesty. To avoid misconception, let us here state distinctly that, next to Rose and Rose's father, Vincenzo was Barnaby's greatest favourite. But, by laying at his door Rose's tears, Vincenzo had stung him to the quick, and the old fire-eater had instantly shown fight.

The lad looked after him and said, "Ugly-and-Good seems uncommonly touchy this afternoon."

"To tell the truth," replied Rose, "I have worried him too much;" and she confessed her freaks with the scissors and her mishap.

Ugly-and-Good (*brutto e buono*) is the name given in Italy to an excellent sort of winter pear, having a very rugged exterior. It was Barnaby's legitimate nickname, and, to a certain extent, accepted by him, though with a slight *variante*, viz. the modest addition of a *not* before *good*. It was only lately that a few scamps in the village had taken to calling him "Radetzky." The Austrian field-marshal at that epoch (1848) was acting a very prominent part in the drama of contemporaneous events. This foolish appellation, disapproved as it was by the majority in the village, would have fallen into disuse of itself, had not Barnaby, by resenting it violently, given it the whet that it wanted. Of all pleasures, the one most rarely resisted by young people, especially by boys, is that of working an old man into a passion.

"By-the-by," said Rose, "how did the rehearsal come off?"

"Not come off at all," was the reply. "The musicians are all at the Palazzo, but the bass-viol is missing. The Signor Avvocato has sent out scouts to meet the porters, who are to bring it. Let us go to the Belvedere, and watch for the men."

They skirted the row of mulberry-trees which had masked Barnaby's approach, went down a few steps, then turned to the left into a vine-covered walk, which led them straight to the Belvedere. It looked over the village and the zigzags of the gently rising road, and commanded a pretty extensive view of the plain, down to the red-tiled roofs of the nearest town. Rose sat down, and, producing from her pocket a small box of vari-coloured beads, an unfinished purse, and sewing materials, said, "While we are waiting, I may as well do a row or two of your purse. It's pretty, isn't it, Vincenzo?" She called him Vincenzo without ceremony, speaking to him in the familiar second person of the singular; but he always addressed her in the deferential third, and as "Signora Padrona."

"Beautiful!" replied the lad; "yours are very clever little fingers, Signora."

"And, you may add, very patient ones also," said Rose. "I wouldn't do it for any one but you. Quite extraordinary the work there is in such small things. Shall I do the initials in red or white beads? Which should you like best?"

"Really, I scarcely know," said perplexed Vincenzo; "which should you advise?"

"Red, I should say."

"Then, let it be red," returned Vincenzo, energetically.

"But, remember, you are not to get the purse unless you sing your motet next Thursday to perfection. Do you quite know it?"

"I think I do," said Vincenzo. "Shall I sing it to you?"

"Yes, do." In a clear pleasing mezzo-soprano voice, Vincenzo sang, without once blundering or faltering, the "salutaris," which was his allotted part in the religious festivity appointed for the following Thursday. "Bravo!" exclaimed Rose, clapping her hands. "Papa will be so pleased. You were so slow in learning it, that he never thought you would be equal to it."

"I was very slow," said Vincenzo: "but the fact is, this motet is too high for my voice, which is no longer what it was last year: and then I don't like it as well as I did the other ones."

"Don't tell papa so; he considers this as one of his

best compositions; and, if he knew that you didn't think so highly of it as he does, he would be downright angry; and, as it is, he is not too well pleased with you."

"I do not wonder at that," said Vincenzo, rather sadly. "I have not given him any cause to be pleased with me. When I recollect how miserably I failed in my last examination, I am heartily ashamed of myself."

"But how was it? Had you been idle?" asked the girl.

"No," returned Vincenzo. "Philosophy was the rock on which I was wrecked. I got clear of all other matters with a *bene*."

"Is philosophy, then, so very hard to learn?"

"For me, very; it bewilders me. I can make neither head nor tail of it. It is like reading an unknown language, which, read and read for ever so long, you can never catch the meaning of. And, as to arguing *in formá*, and syllogisms, it is of no use my trying to master them."

"What is a syllogism?" questioned Rose.

"It is a form of argument made to prove white to be black, and black white, in so clever a way that one is at a loss to discover where the flaw lies; at least, I never can. I'll give you an example. Up to this day, you have believed that salt meat makes one thirsty. Well, I am going to prove the contrary, thus — To drink assuages thirst; *atqui*, salt meat makes one drink; *ergo*, salt meat assuages thirst."

"But that is downright nonsense," cried Miss Rose, laughing; "don't you see that the flaw lies in the *ergo?*"

"I dare say it does," assented the lad; "but affirmation is no proof, you know, and you must prove your case *in formâ;* there's the bog."

"My poor Vincenzo," said Rose, looking at the melancholy face, half in merriment, half in sorrow, "I wish I could help you out of your bog, but I can't. However, you must keep up your courage, and try and try till you do succeed. Just think! a lad of seventeen, and only to have got the minor orders. If you go on at this rate, papa says, when will you ever say your first mass?"

"Who knows if I shall ever say one at all?" said Vincenzo, with a doubtful shake of the head. "There are times when I despair of ever being able to acquire the amount of learning necessary for a priest. I am afraid I am naturally dull."

"Nonsense," put in Rose.

"Perhaps," he went on, "the want of early education may have something to do with it. Born a peasant, I was brought up as a peasant — I could almost wish I were one now. When my father — bless his soul! — destined me for the Church, I was already eleven years old, and scarcely able to read or write; so I had to begin at the beginning. I suppose this want of ballast has kept me back in my studies, besides my being, as I said before, naturally thickheaded."

This harsh judgment upon himself, though passed in perfect good faith — who could doubt for a moment the lad's honest face and voice? — was singularly belied by the gentle earnestness with which he spoke — an earnestness beyond his age — and by the accompanying intelligent play of his features. Rose had felt this when she had entered her protest against Vincenzino's first self-accusation of dulness, and ten to one but she would have again protested, if the missing bass-viol had not loomed in sight at this very nick of time. Just turning the corner of the Parish Church Square appeared two men carrying the cumbrous instrument, with a third person somewhat ahead, who had the unmistakeable air of a priest. "Don Natale, I declare," said Rose, springing from her seat. "I wonder if he's come to the rehearsal; let us go and meet him."

And, darting swift as arrows through the vine-covered walk, and along a terrace planted with walnut-trees, the nimble pair cleared the gate in a twinkling, and were scampering down the high road, when a lusty hail from Barnaby made them stop and turn their heads. The old man was running after them, the young lady's straw hat in his hand. "Never mind the hat," laughed Rose; "I suppose I dropped it at the pond."

"Ugly-and-Good means it as a peace-offering," said the lad. "I'll run back for it;" and, suiting the action to the word, he raced away to Barnaby, and was in no time again at Miss Rose's side.

Meanwhile Don Natale, a little ahead of the men with the bass-viol, was jogging on pretty fast, considering his short legs and big round paunch. Don Natale was the *beau idéal* of a parish country priest — fat, broad-faced, double-chinned, red-nosed, good-humoured. Long use had deprived his cassock of all gloss, his three-cornered hat of every, even the last vestige of nap — gloss and nap replaced by a coat of grease. He shouted and telegraphed with his head-gear to the boy and girl, and, when within reach of voice, bellowed out, "Here I am! come in person to explain and make *restitutionem in integrum*. Ouf! Vincenzo knows what that means. What do you think that blockhead of a porter from the town did? Ouf! Why, he took the double-bass to the parish church. And what do you think that goose the clerk did? He shut it up in the vestry, where it has been standing for this hour and a half."

Rose and Vincenzo were close to him by this time, and, as in duty bound, kissed the priest's hand. "Good day, Rosa, Rosetta, Rosettina; good day, Vincenzo — bless my soul, what a sun for the month of May; it scorches one's skin, it does. Hard work to climb up hill at any time, but —"

"I beg you will not call this gentle slope a hill," remonstrated Rose, smiling.

"When you are past sixty-five, and have to carry the weight I do, you'll find it hill enough, my dear child. But, hill or slope, let us move on. By-the-bye, there's a hamper for the palace at Peter the chandler's — a hamper come by post, as big as a babe, and — exhaling such a fragrance! if it were not out of season, I should say of white truffles. Whatever it is, thou wilt smack thy lips at it next Thursday, Vincenzo, thou little rogue — while I — I dine at the castle, you know. It is traditionary that the parish priest should dine at the castle on St. Urban's-day. *Consuetudo est lex*. Not that I have anything to say against the table at the castle; God forbid! — but they hate truffles there, can't bear the smell of them — quite an idiosyncracy. Mine lies the contrary way; I am over-fond of truffles, I confess; perhaps it is a weakness, but there are worse ones, I daresay. Ouf! I am out of breath."

"No wonder you are," cried Rose, laughing; "you do nothing but talk, and talk, and talk."

"Do you hear her? The lamb is scolding the shepherd, I declare," pursued Don Natale, with an arch look at Rose. "You are like Job's friends, fault-finding instead of helping. Come to me, Rosinetta, dear, and be *baculus senectutis meæ* — give me the support of your arm, I mean, and I'll tell you why I go on talking, and talking, and talking."

And, playfully drawing Rose's arm under his own, Don Natale continued:

"I am making up for time lost. I have been gagged these last three-and-thirty years — ever since 1815, my dear — and, now that the gag is removed, thanks to immortal Pio Nono, thanks to magnanimous Charles Albert, thanks last not least to that philosopher of all Christian philosophers, Gioberti" — and he raised his greasy hat in succession to the three names — "now that an honest man, lay or priest, can say his say without hindrance or fear, well, I use and abuse the privilege, and I am rattling on for ever."

To this ingenious theory the young lady might have opposed a sober fact, confirmed by her own experience — namely, that at all times Don Natale had been famous throughout the parish for his superabundance of talkative powers; but she had discretion enough to hold her tongue. They had passed the gate, and were strolling up the long avenue of poplars, which abutted upon the palace, when another little party was noticed, coming down the avenue towards them. It consisted of Rose's father (the Signor Avvocato, as he was called constantly) and four or five of the musicians, who had assembled there for the rehearsal. The two groups, on espying each other, accelerated their pace, and were not long in meeting, when there followed such an explosion of "oh's!" and "ah's!" and "what good wind has blown you hither?" and questions, explanations, and wonderments, as the crows living on the poplars had never witnessed the like of.

However, time pressed; and, after this short halt employed in mutual greetings, and giving and receiving information, the now united column resumed its march in good order. Rose and her father (the Signor Avvocato) headed it, having Don Natale between them; the rest followed by twos and threes. Vincenzo brought up the rear, by chance or by inclination, all alone; and, having no better occupation for the nonce, he kept sedulously kicking out of the way everything in the shape of leaf, root, or stone, which stood in relief enough to allow of its being kicked away.

"What is the matter with thee?" asked Barnaby, sallying suddenly forth from behind a tree.

"Nothing is the matter, Barnaby," answered Vincenzo, with a little surprise.

"Art thou ill, I mean?"

"Not in the least."

"Hast thou had any words with the Signorina?"

"God forbid!" said Vincenzo.

"Why then canst thou not hold up thy head, like the honest lad thou art?"

Upon this, Barnaby went his way, and Vincenzo his.

CHAPTER II.

A Vocation.

VINCENZO had no more been consulted about the profession for which he was being educated than is a bale of goods about its destination. His father was a trusty and meritorious servant of the Signor Avvocato, who eventually came by his death, one might say, in his master's service. He had the management of some pretty extensive ricemarshes which the Signor Avvocato possessed in the environs of Vercelli. A sure and a productive concern this rice cultivation, but very unhealthy! Rice is raised in water, which stagnates and corrupts and begets malaria. Well, it so happened, that, on a certain night, the water was turned off one of the pieces of ground under this man's control — exactly a field that most particularly required irrigation. Upon this, Vincenzo's father, though sadly out of health and spirits (he had just lost his wife), in his zeal to ascertain which of two neighbours was the offender — at all events, to prevent the repetition of the offence — kept watch in the swamps for several nights, and then and there imbibed the germs of the malady which was to cost him his life. He was immediately attacked by ague, which resisted every effort made to overcome it. His master had him removed to a healthier situation, gave him good medical advice, but with little or no benefit. The poor man continued to waste away. As he grew weaker, his mind often wandered, and he had what he and the people about him dignified by the name of apparitions, but which, in fact, were only the common hallucinations of fever. One of the visions which most beset him was that of a beautiful lady with a babe in her lap, sitting on his bed, who said to him, "Devote your Vincenzo to my service, and you shall be cured."

Upon no stronger foundation than this was the poor boy's future career settled for him. There was a smack of the miraculous in the matter which tickled the fancies of the neighbourhood amazingly. The rector of the parish in which the sick man lived took up the case warmly, of course, while the sick man himself clung to his vision with all the instinctive eagerness of self-preservation. A communication was speedily made to the Signor Avvocato; and he, knowing only too well that it was not safe to interfere with real or imaginary calls from on High, said, probably with a shrug of the shoulder, "Why not? Let it be so."

The approbation of the Signor Avvocato was the more important, because, in his double character of Vincenzo's godfather and avowed patron, he was regarded, and was aware that he was so, as the person from whose purse must be drawn the sinews of war; in plain words, as the one who would have to defray the expenses of the superior education necessary to qualify Vincenzo for the priesthood.

While his fate was thus being sealed for him, unconscious Vincenzo was gambolling in the gardens of the palazzo with his little playmate and padroncina, Miss Rose, hunting for birds' nests or chasing butterflies for her — a business he had sedulously pursued for the last two years.

This will serve to explain the familiar style in which we have heard him addressed by Rose, the priest, Barnaby, and the rest. They had known him too long as an urchin in a fustian jacket to change their manners when he changed his jacket for a long black robe. Miss Rose, indeed, on his return after his first year at the seminary, somewhat impressed by the difference of dress, had made an attempt to break through former habits, and had actually in speaking to him used the second person of the plural; but Vincenzo begged so hard that she would still grant him his old privilege, that she had willingly complied. But we must not anticipate.

Well, then, one fine morning Vincenzo was summoned to his godfather's study.

"Vincenzo, my boy," began the Signor Avvocato, "the time is come when you must lay aside childish things and begin to prepare yourself for the profession your father has chosen for you, that of the Church. At his express desire I have written to our Bishop, and made arrangements with the superior of the seminary at Ibella (so was named the small red-tiled town visible from the Belvedere), for your reception there. I shall accompany you thither myself on Monday; to-morrow you shall go and see your father and receive his blessing; next Sunday will be your last holiday here, for the present. So long as you are a good boy and do credit to those interested in you, you may rely on me as a friend. I regret that I cannot myself continue your musical education, but I have expressly stipulated that you shall have singing lessons at the seminary. God knows what sort of a master they have got there; at all events, let him be what he may, he will serve to keep your fine voice and ear from entirely rusting. You understand that on Monday you are to go to Ibella; now you may take yourself off. Go and play."

"Yes, Signor Padrone, thank you, Signor Padrone," and, not slightly bewildered, Vincenzo ran forthwith to break the great news to his young mistress. Now let it be understood that Rose was an ardent little churchgoer, who delighted in the ringing of bells, silvercloth vestments, gorgeously decorated altars, and every sort of religious show. Priesthood was naturally associated in her mind with all these things, and farther with heading of processions, the mighty gold cross and the violet stockings of the bishop of Ibella. In short, to belong to the priesthood was the *ne plus ultra* of glory in her eyes. Had he brought her word of his accession to a throne, Rose would not have been half so elated as she was at the announcement that he was to be a priest. "Only think! why, one of these days he might himself be a Bishop!"

Vincenzo's vanity was not a little inflated by this view of the matter. There was, however, a drawback too close at hand to be overlooked — birds' nesting, chasing of butterflies, all such merry doings were at an end. This ugly side of the medal took the little girl by surprise, and for a time made her hostile even to the dignities of the Church; but, after the first alarm was over, she recovered her spirits and her allegiance, asserting that she would be able to get leave for him often to pay them a visit at the palazzo, and, when they went for the winter to Ibella, what was to prevent his coming to play with her every day? "Papa," she was sure, "would be very glad he should do so." Thus did her eight years' old wisdom dispose of the difficulty.

For the rest of the day Vincenzo was the lion of the household. The servants within doors, the labourers in the fields, vied with one another in complimenting and congratulating him, just as if he had won the great prize in the lottery — with one notable exception, however. Barnaby kept aloof, and looked uglier than ever. At that epoch, he was not yet the victim of lumbago, that relentless foe which had gradually sapped his strength, and reduced him from general manager of the Avvocato's estate, to the honorific sinecure of head gardener, in which capacity he made his appearance in the foregoing chapter.

He was still an active, though not straight-backed man, and on him devolved the honour of driving the youthful catechumen the following day to his father's cottage. It was a pleasant drive, of some two hours' duration, through a gently undulating, rich, maize-growing country; but little joy had Vincenzo of his drive, so outrageously out of humour was his companion. Barnaby growled the whole way, now at the road, then at the tillage and the crops, and, lastly, at the black mare he was driving. "She was an ugly, good-for-nothing beast; a Jesuit."

These opprobrious epithets were the more unaccountable to Vincenzo, as he had always known Blackie to be a favourite with Barnaby. At last, the boy ventured to say, "I thought you liked the mare, Barnaby."

"I?" exclaimed the gardener, with a snap and a snarl. "I! I hate everything that has a black coat, horse or man."

On arriving at home, the lad had a long conference

with his father and the priest of the parish, from which he issued duly impressed with a sense of the high mission confided to him. He thought of nothing else, all the way back to the palazzo, but the miraculous apparition described by his father, every now and then repeating to himself the priest's parting words — "that "he might well feel proud and happy at having been "chosen as God's instrument in a great work." And so proud and happy was Vincenzo at that minute that he felt up to anything and everything, martyrdom included. Barnaby neither growled nor snarled during the return drive; he whistled incessantly instead.

There were many guests at the palazzo on the Sunday following, and Vincenzo had the honour of dining at his patron's table. He sat between Rose and Don Natale — the priest that was improving the occasion by delivering a little speech of mingled advice and congratulation to the priest that was to be. This raised the little peasant into a personage, and drew all eyes upon him. Every one present took more or less notice of the boy during the dinner, and Vincenzo went to rest that night in a flutter of happy excitement. But, when he got up in the morning and saw the padrone's carriage at the door, and was cautioned that he must be ready to start in half an hour, he then began to realize the blank awaiting him beyond that half-hour. No more Rose, no more freedom! The young heart sank; and, had he known of any tribunal before which he could bring an appeal, he would have humbly prayed to be allowed to renounce all hope or chance of ever wearing those violet stockings, so ardently admired by the signorina. Tribunal there was none; Vincenzo stood committed on all sides. Shame and pride drove back the tears which welled up from his full heart as he drove off from the palazzo. Shame and pride kept his eyes dry when, a couple of hours later, he sat down with passive despair, among a number of strange boys, in the great hall of the Seminary of Ibella. But, once safe in his bed, how those fountains of grief flowed! And what a relief it was! Eleven, however, is not the age of despair; so, after the lapse of a few days, the poignant feelings with which he had arrived had subsided into a great yearning after the past, and a great want of interest in the present. Even this state had begun to yield to the influence of time and habit, when an event took place which revived all the pristine keenness of his regrets.

Just three months after Vincenzo's admission to the seminary, his father died. Once the first shock of grief had passed away, the boy could not help thinking and hoping that, along with the object which had dictated the sacrifice — for sacrifice he now confessed it to be — surely all reason for accomplishing it had vanished also. His reasonable anticipations were, however, doomed to be disappointed. When the Signor Avvocato came, as he shortly did, on a visit of condolence, far from making any, the least, allusion to a possible change in his *protégé's* prospects, every word he uttered made it clear that he considered them irrevocably fixed; indeed, so clear was this that Vincenzo lacked the courage to give his patron a hint of what had been occupying his mind. The poor boy called himself all sorts of names afterwards for having been so cowardly, and took a solemn vow to speak out boldly the next time he saw his godfather. But the next time was very long in coming, and, when it did come, alas! Vincenzo's vow remained unfulfilled. He then meditated on the possibility of entering on the difficult subject by means of a letter; he penned many, and sent none. Eleven is as little the age of indomitable resolution as it is of settled despair, and the only result of this contention of mind was, first, a period of renewed despondency, followed, secondly, by one of dull resignation. Yet Vincenzo's lot, as year succeeded year, if not exactly to be set down as happy, could as little be designated as unhappy. His masters were, in the main, humane, even kind; and he received at their hands, as far as his studies were concerned, that easy indulgence which is generally conceded to a pains-taking but naturally deficient boy. His teachers' estimate of his powers of mind was low indeed.

Though Vincenzo had no intimate friends, he was on good terms with the majority of his companions; and, if there was an abundance of lessons, chapel-going, and classes, the allowance for recreation was on a corresponding scale. His visits to the Signor Avvocato, whether in town or country, were much rarer, it is true, than Rose had predetermined they should be; nevertheless, there was the make-weight of that blessed holiday for a whole fortnight spent at the palazzo — to obtain which privilege for his godson, the godfather had had to use all his influence with the reverend professors of Ibella. Blessed holiday, indeed! which renewed the happy past of familiar companionship with his padroncina. Nor was the young seminarist insensible to the figure he cut at church as solo-singer of the mass in music, at Rumelli. It was St. Urban's Feast which brought him this bouquet of delights, and you can fancy, therefore, what an ardent devotee of St. Ur-

ban was Vincenzo. In his morning and evening orisons there was ever a special prayer to St. Urban.

Paradise had its drawbacks; so had these holidays. This was also the established time for the return from school to the castle of the son of the Avvocato's neighbour, the marquis — a bigger and an older boy than Vincenzo, and withal a mischievous sprite. He was for ever plaguing and bullying the seminarist, was for ever inventing nicknames for him, and making him the butt of endless practical jokes; bad enough when Rose was not present, intolerable when she was. This quizzing and joking naturally led to fisticuffs; and out of these scuffles young Church generally came off second-best, with the certainty of a severe lecture from the Signor Avvocato into the bargain.

Amidst such drawbacks and compensations rolled on the course of our hero's clerical preparation, stormless, if not cloudless, until 1848. If there was ever a year calculated to unsettle people's minds, 1848 was pre-eminently that year. Wonders never ceased. A national movement, initiated by a reforming pontiff; constitutions inaugurated at Rome, in Tuscany, Piedmont, and Naples; a republic sprouting forth from the Parisian barricades of February; revolution at Vienna; revolution at Milan; Radetzky driven into the Quadrilateral; the war of Italian independence proclaimed; Charles Albert on the Mincio! Such was the chain of stupendous events, most of them compressed within a few months, with which that extraordinary year startled the world.

Well might grown men's pulses — ay, and those of young lads in priestly schools — beat high and fast with excitement. Vincenzo's enthusiasm bordered on frenzy. How he envied and burned to emulate his heroic brother-seminarists of Milan, who, as fame told, had contrived a moving barricade, fighting under its cover — another Macedonian phalanx! The faint echo of the din and strife of war which reached even the student of Ibella, how welcome it sounded in his ears! The mere word "statuto," as to the meaning of which he knew about as much as he did of the hieroglyphics of Thebes, had a magic spell for him. To watch passing events from near at hand, to mix somehow in the current, to be free — to be free! that became his waking and sleeping dream. If we were to write down all the little plots and contrivances which fermented in the youth's brain of how to reach that ardently desired goal, each and all winding up with his enlisting for a soldier, and going to the seat of war, we should have a long story to tell. But the superiors were more vigilant than usual, and flight became an impossibility. As to an appeal to his godfather and patron, Vincenzo was not up to it. What he had not dared to do at his father's demise, when to do so would have been a comparatively easy matter, he could not muster sufficient courage to attempt, now that six years of acquiescence on his part had strongly rivetted the chain round his leg. Yes, he felt that he wore a chain — a heavy and odious one; he was fain to break it; but how?

It may be as well to mention here that the failure in his last examination, to which we have heard him allude, was mainly due to the excitement of the times. Now, then, the reader understands the frame of mind in which Vincenzo returned to the palazzo, on the occasion of our first meeting him. Had there lurked in the lad's mind any atom of intention to make his godfather the confidant of his thoughts and wishes, it would have been repelled by the frown of displeasure which lay on that honoured godfather's brow.

CHAPTER III

The Castle and the Palace.

The person who told us the story we are about to relate, had, or believed he had, his reasons for keeping back all precise indication as to places and names, and all that we could gather from him about the situation of the village of Rumelli — a name not to be found in maps, we believe — was that it lay in the north of Piedmont proper, at the foot of the hill-country. Were it worth the trouble, we might, by means of deductions, render this description less vague; but we do not see the use of so doing, and leave this easy task to any sagacious reader who may be disposed to undertake it.

Well, whatever its exact whereabouts, Rumelli was a hamlet, with nothing remarkable about it, except that it possessed both a castle and a palace; this last, already mentioned more than once, and neither of which the good folks of Rumelli would have exchanged for all the castles and palaces in Christendom. There was not much to be proud of, though, in so far as the castle was concerned. It was rather a respectable myth than a reality — nothing remaining of its former splendour, save an uninhabitable tower, a bit of the moat used as a nursery for mulberry-trees, and a drawbridge fast stuck in the earth, and serving as a back way to the village. The low heavy lump of bricks, with a sugar-loaf shaped excrescence at each end, which constituted the actual mansion, evidently of comparatively modern construction, had no more character in its architecture than has any substantial farm-house. Such as it was, however, and no living man had seen it otherwise, the castle had lorded it over, and made the rain and sunshine of, Rumelli for God knows how long. In all probability it would have continued to do as much to this day, had not a rival establishment sprung up as if by magic, and advanced and enforced its claim to a share in the sceptre. This is how it happened.

Marquis Amadeus del Palmetto, the present head of the family who owned the castle, in obedience to the traditions of his caste and race, had entered the army at a very early age, and done his part well in the gallant stand made by Piedmont against republican France. When all possibility of resistance was over, and the French occupied the kingdom as masters, the marquis broke his sword, and returned to his Lares and Penates at Rumelli. He had not been there long, however, when it occurred to him that, before settling down definitively as a retired country gentleman, he owed it to the name he bore, first to go and pay his homage to, and take the commands of, his king, whose all of sovereignty at that moment was confined to the island of Sardinia. But Marquis Amadeus had more loyalty than ready cash, and every endeavour to raise money on his already deeply mortgaged estate proved fruitless. The marquis, like most of the Piedmontese aristocracy, was hospitable and open-handed, and, to gratify this amiable disposition, lived far beyond his means.

Could his lordship — so said his man of business

— bring himself to consent to part with some of his unentailed land, and which, indeed, made scarcely any return, there was, as he had already had the honour of informing his noble client, that same Barnaby Mele who had brought home from his wanderings some money, and was on the look-out for a safe investment of his savings.

Besides the numberless objections to parting with land which he had in common with every landed proprietor we ever met, the Marquis had a special one in this case. The castle was, as is the wont of castles, built on a summit, and overlooked the village; but then all the unentailed part of the Marquis's property lay unfortunately on still higher ground, and, to use a traditional phrase of the family, the Del Palmettos wanted no spy over their heads. However, as we know, necessity has no law — money was wanted, money must be had, and could be had in no other way than by selling the hill land; and, after all, there was little danger of this poor devil Barnaby, who had already a cottage of his own, taking a fancy to build. In short, after some demur, the Marquis gave way, a tolerable bargain was made, and the deed of sale signed. Barnaby got a pretty slice of land, the Marquis pocketed the price, and went his journey. On his return, after an absence of only a couple of months, fancy his horror and fury at finding, on the lately-dissevered limit of his estate, the foundations of a vast fabric which would entirely command the castle. This misfortune occurred at the close of the year 1800. Barnaby, it was discovered, was merely a man of straw; the real purchaser was a certain Pietro Stella, a native of Rumelli, about whom the tongues in his native place had been busy more than once during the last twenty years.

Pietro Stella had left his home at sixteen years of age, with no other funds than a strong will and a mason's trowel; had gone to Mexico, and there realized a large fortune, as to the origin of which two stories circulated in Rumelli, each having its sect of believers. According to one version, Pietro had married an immensely rich lady, the daughter of a grandee of Spain into the bargain; according to the other, he had dug out of the ground a stocking full of jewels; whereas we can certify that Pietro had married no one of higher rank than the daughter of a builder, who was far from wealthy, and had never had any other jewels to trade with than a ready wit, an enterprising spirit, and uprightness.

Pietro after a long lapse of years, returned to the place of his birth, accompanied by wife and children. Keeping out of sight himself, he made use of Barnaby, a fellow-villager, whom he had met in Mexico, and rescued from starvation, to bring about the realization of his most cherished scheme — no other than to build himself in his native village a fine house in a commanding situation. A sketch of such a mansion had been lying in his desk for more than ten years. Pietro had set his eyes and heart on that part of the Marquis's land which lay above the castle.

The enriched builder was too well aware of the Del Palmetto crotchet, as to having no one to overlook the castle, not to be pretty certain that never would the Marquis sell a foot of the land in question to any man possessed of the means of building on it, should it so please him. Therefore it was that he had employed Barnaby to make the proposal of purchase, as if for Barnaby's self. The stratagem, as we know, was crowned with success; and no sooner was the Marquis's back turned than Pietro pounced on his prey at the head of an army of workmen. Trees were felled, ground levelled, a terrace raised, materials collected; and in no time, as if by magic, there rose breast-high the walls of what was to be Pietro's dwelling.

High was the wrath of the young Marquis when first he caught sight of what was doing, loud his denunciations of the base conspiracy by which he had been entrapped. Had it not been for a happy sense of his own dignity, he would on the instant have ascended the hill, and given a piece of his mind to the beggarly chimney-sweep, as he called Pietro, who had, in fact, to the perfect recollection of the Marquis, a small boy at the time, once mended one of the castle chimneys. But the swindlers need not calculate on impunity; his lordship would call in the aid of the law, and force them to remove their rubbish with their own hands! On the word of a Marquis, he would have them punished, though he had to go to Turin for that purpose!

No practical result ever followed these and other similar threats. Signor Pietro's position was legally unassailable, explained his lordship's lawyer to his angry lordship. No law could prevent Barnaby from selling what he had bought and paid for to Pietro; no law could prevent Pietro, become the actual owner of the soil, from building on it. As to going to Turin, a form of speech which meant bringing the weight of court favour to bear upon the matter, the Marquis had probably forgotten, when fulminating this menace, that

Turin was for the time being the head-quarters of the French Department of the High Alps, where those belonging to the ancient nobility were far from possessing any preponderant power. So nothing was left to the fiery young nobleman — he was not more than seven-and-twenty — but to champ his bit and wait for the day of reckoning; that is, for the turn of fortune's wheel which should bring him and his class again uppermost, and give him, and such as he, all their own way again, law or no law.

In the meantime, Pietro, like the man of tact and taste that he was, far from manifesting anything approaching to exultation evinced a praiseworthy spirit of conciliation. He never met the Marquis in the road, the only place where a meeting could occur, without raising his hat, and showing, by his manner, infinite respect and deference, and that not a mere pretence, but a sincere reality, Pietro having been brought up in the orthodox faith of the right divine of kings and aristocracies. His mute attentions were ignored; nor did the advances of the curé, the predecessor of Don Natale, who had been prevailed on by Pietro to undertake the part of peacemaker, meet with any more favour. A sharp "Don't mention that man to me," was all that the good priest got for his pains.

It took full three years to complete, decorate, and furnish the new building, which the Rumellians had long before christened the "Palazzo." The appellation may sound ambitious to the ears of the English, who attach to the word Palace an idea of almost royal magnificence. But the title of Palazzo in Italy means something far less, and is, indeed, generally bestowed on all detached mansions which combine with a certain stateliness of proportions taste and elegance of design. In all these essentials, Pietro's new house was certainly not deficient. Pietro was by nature a man of taste, and he had made himself an excellent architect. The palace was three stories high, comprising the attics, built on a raised terrace, which, while enhancing its appearance, helped to dwarf considerably the underlying castle. One access to the palace was by a flight of steps, which led up from the avenue to this terrace; below and around which last ran a carriage-road winding up an ascent to an opposite entrance.

Well, then, in the month of March, of the year 1804, Pietro and his family took up their abode at the palace. Pietro's family at that time consisted of his wife, two children — a boy and a girl — of the respective ages of twelve and ten, and an aged aunt, the only one of his relations he found alive on his return to Rumelli. She, poor soul, died shortly after her removal to her nephew's grand residence. Barnaby, as a matter of course, also went thither, remaining what he had long been, Pietro's confidential servant. The tenour of life at the palace was simple and unostentatious in the extreme. Pietro, his wife, and children, all mixed familiarly with the country folks, and were on excellent terms with their neighbours, always excepting the Marquis, with whom they were on no terms at all. Nevertheless, it had been remarked, with sanguine expectations of a speedy peace, that on the first appearance of the lady of the palace at church, the Marquis, in passing her seat to his accustomed place in his own side-chapel, had slightly bowed to her. Every following Sunday there was a repetition of the same civility, and whenever also the lady and the Marquis met in the roads. But nothing more came of it than just polite salutations. Pietro, who had resumed his business as builder and contractor for public works, was often from home. Years rolled on, and at last 1814 — the year of restorations. Dispossessed sovereigns reascended their thrones, the sovereign of Piedmont among others; and the aristocracy had it all their own way again. Here, then, was the day of reckoning invoked some fourteen years ago by the Marquis. He had waited long for it; here it was, and yet, strange to say, he showed no signs of any wish to avail himself of its advent, at least as regarded the palace and its builder. Perhaps he had never wished to do so; men are often better than they themselves imagine. Perhaps the gentle touch of sorrow had somewhat softened the asperity of his lordship's temper. The Marquis had married in the interval, had become the father of two children, and buried both of them. Perhaps he acknowledged the full force of an accomplished fact, sanctioned also by time, and felt unequal to cope with it. Certainly, many a thing was foolishly done and undone at this epoch in Piedmont and elsewhere, but few would have been more difficult to undo than this one.

The palace had taken root in the hearts and minds of the Rumellians. Public opinion, without abandoning the castle, had adopted the palace, was proud of the palace, was grateful to the palace. The palace had been the Pactolus which had left some particles of gold at the door of each and all of the cottages. And, besides, a stream of a no less precious ore — kindness — had never ceased flowing from thence. Everybody, likewise, found at the palace that which Italians prize above everything — what they, as pithily as originally, style a "dish of welcome" (*un piatto di buona cera*). The needy found ready employment and assistance, the sick relief and medicines; there was a whole apothecary's shop at the palace. The priest, the mayor, and the town council, who had hitherto sworn *in verba* of the castle, now swore also *in verba* of the palace, thanks to which it was that the roof of the parish church had been repaired — that the church could display beautiful silver lamps and copes of cloth of gold — and that the village was endowed with a clean and spacious schoolhouse, instead of the barn which had hitherto served as such. All these benefits had made the position of the palace strong indeed, and difficult to carry. Had the difficulty of the enterprise anything to do with the Marquis's forbearance? We will give him the benefit of the doubt, and hope that he was actuated by less personal and more creditable motives. However this may be, the political change in the kingdom brought along with it a radical one in his lordship's course of life. He was soon after recalled to active service, and left Rumelli to move in a higher and wider sphere. During the succeeding twenty-four years his visits to the castle were few and far between; and it was not till 1838 that he came, as a colonel on half-pay, accompanied by a second wife and an only son, to settle again, this time for good and all, at the family seat. Of all those he had left inmates of the palace, the only survivors were Signor Urbano, Pietro's son, and Barnaby Mele. Signor Urbano had taken his degrees in law at the University of Turin, and from that time forth was known by no other name than that of his title of Avvocato. He was a widower, with an only daughter, Rose — at the period of the Marquis's return, a child of four years old.

Now that the principal offender had gone to his last account, the Marquis felt more disposed to leniency — not to a state however of friendliness with the Avvocato, or any one belonging to him, but to one of neutrality, a cessation in short of all active hostility. Thus he was condescending enough, in a first chance meeting, to return the Signor Avvocato's mute salutation, and to stop and inquire after his little daughter's health. Upon the strength of this courtesy, the Signor Avvocato, a man of ultra-conciliatory spirit, nay pusillanimous turn of mind, had allowed himself to be persuaded by Don Natale, the curé or rector of the parish, into the belief that he was in duty bound to go and call at the castle; and so he did. The Marquis received him graciously, but did not introduce him to the Marchioness, nor did he ever return the visit. Instead of so doing, he established from that day a legal fiction, to the effect that he was soon about to do himself the honour of calling upon the Signor Avvocato — a legal fiction which in the long run the Signor Avvocato also adopted on his own account; and, upon this reciprocation of kindly intentions, the two neighbours never set foot in each other's houses.

The young generation held less to etiquette and social distinctions; and little Rose's calls to Federico to come and play with her, and Federico's inroads into the gardens of the palace, in compliance, were neither of them rare occurrences. But, somehow or other, these merry meetings too often ended, on Rose's side, in red eyes and complaints to Papa of Federico's rudeness. Papa soothed his daughter without remonstrating with the offender; and, by thus putting up with a slight now and then, and accepting on the whole a secondary position, the master of the palace managed to live at peace with his noble neighbour.

This noble neighbour was, it must be confessed, as crafty as an old fox — deeply versed in the art which always put appearances on his side — quite scientific in the process of gilding the bitter pill for the one he meant to swallow it. Thus, for instance, a few years later, when, hard pressed for the means of sending his son to the military academy of Turin, he set on foot a negotiation for the sale of another good slice of the land he still possessed close to the palace, he contrived it so artfully as to make it appear a great concession on his part, and to reap, besides his own price, both credit and thanks.

And yet the Signor Avvocato, rich, kindly, humane to his tenants, open-handed as the day, ought to have been well able to keep his own against any other, let him be who he might, had he had the spirit to do so. For, if less popular than his father — and he was perhaps too much of a gentleman to be equally so — on the other hand he was more looked up to, held in especial reverence on account of his legal knowledge, which he ever willingly and gratuitously placed at the service of those who came to consult him. Illiterate people are apt to make much of a man who understands everything relating to *meum et tuum*, and holds in his hand the guiding thread of the intricate labyrinth called law. But Rose's father was an indolent man, and somewhat of an intellectual sybarite. Strife was abhorrent to his nature; and, so long as he could undisturbedly enjoy his music (his predominant passion

was music), his gardens, his daily gossip, he cared little
or nothing for what went on in the world. Let us
add, in justice to the Avvocato, that a certain passage
of his youth had placed him, politically, in a false
position, and had contributed in a great degree to keep
him down in after life. The fact is, he had been a
Costipato. The sympathizers with constitutional principles were derisively styled *Costipati* by the adverse
party. When, in 1821, a liberal constitution became
for a moment the law of the land, the Signor Avvocato, then a young man under thirty, had, in his father's
absence, illuminated the palace from roof to basement.
This public sign of adhesion to an order of things
shortly after abolished proved a wasp's nest to both
father and son. Signor Pietro had difficulty enough
to clear himself of any participation in the offence.
His son, to avoid being arrested, had no alternative
but to quit Piedmont and take refuge at Geneva. His
exile however lasted only a year; thanks to his father's
interest with influential personages at Turin, he could
without risk return home at the expiration of that
period. A fear however of being called to account for
his unlucky demonstration of opinion had preyed on
him ever since. That a man so clearly designed by
nature to follow and not to lead should awake one fine
morning and find himself mayor of Rumelli, captain of
the national guard (that was to be), and the official
leader of the constitutional party in the village, was
certainly not one of the least extraordinary tricks of
that extraordinary year 1848.

Leaving the path of partial reform in which it had
been for some time creeping, Piedmont, at the bidding
of Charles Albert, began to walk frankly and firmly

in the high road of representative institutions; and one of the first acts of the new government had been to place at the head of municipalities new men known for their attachment to liberty. The Signor Avvocato's wealth, local influence, and political antecedents naturally marked him out to the minister as the most eligible choice that could be made for Rumelli. The newly elected mayor would have gladly declined the honours heaped on him, had he dared; but on one side was the fear of offending the powers that be. and on the other were Don Natale's persuasions and incitements to acceptance. In the end, the Signor Avvocato donned the authority offered to him, though still much against the grain. Not that his self-love was not mightily tickled, or that he was not a liberal at heart. Few had more applauded *in petto* than he had the progressive march of the government, and the grant of a free constitution. It was the national tendency of the movement that made him uneasy; and besides, the attitude of Austria was far from agreeable, and . . . . in short, look where he would, he saw breakers ahead. These and similar misgivings caused him to bear his new honours meekly, nay humbly, with the conciliatory manner of one not at all certain he may not be called on, at no distant time, to answer for himself before some inimical tribunal.

The Marquis was smitten to the heart by what he called the desertion of the Government to the enemy; and, as he measured at a glance all the ground lost to the castle, and consequently gained by the palace, by this change of men and measures, no wonder he inwardly consigned to all the devils the Government, the Statuto, and the new mayor of Rumelli. But, the more bitterly he felt, the more carefully he disguised his rancour under a great assumption of equanimity; above all, he solemnly disavowed all intention of opposition. He confessed he was not a partisan of parliamentary institutions; God did not govern the universe by means of two Houses of Parliament — as far as he had ever heard, at least; however, he would abide by the result of the experiment; if it were successful, so much the better for all parties! In the mean time, as he was, above and before all other considerations, a faithful subject, neutrality should be his watchword! There were not many, indeed, in or out of Rumelli, who courted the perilous honour of being the first to attack an unknown creature, that might bite, and kick, and scratch, for anything any one knew. It was only at a later period, when her peaceful and gentle nature had been ascertained beyond a doubt, that the opponents of Liberty showed fight, when even boys thrust at her with their rattles and wooden swords.

Our acquaintance, the rector of the parish, as indeed the great majority of the clergy throughout the land, frankly adhered to a new order of things, which the popular writings of one of their clerical brethren, the Abbé Gioberti, had so much contributed to bring about, and which furthermore had the sanction of the Head of the Church. To listen to them, was to hear it affirmed that a new era had dawned, that liberty and religion were at last married. Pity that the honeymoon had not been of longer duration! Apart the incoming and the outgoing members of the municipal council — the latter re-actionists, the former constitutionalists by the force of circumstances — the bulk of our small rural community only opened their eyes and ears very wide, and waited for some tangible sign by which to form their estimate of the changes accomplishing. But, when this sign came, in the shape of war, and in a summons to the men on the reserve to join their regiments (men, be it understood, liable by the last conscription to be called into active service if required), when rumours of increased taxation became rife, the good folks of Rumelli began to protrude their lips in ominous fashion, and augur ill of the Statuto. Fortunately their devotion to the king knew no bounds, and their loyalty to his person served as a counterpoise to their dissatisfaction with the Statuto. What his Majesty had willed, what his Majesty had undertaken, must be right! This view of matters was eventually strengthened by the news from the camp, for the most part favourable. Such, then, the posture of affairs, such the state of men's minds in Rumelli on the eve of the fête of St. Urban, the patron of the village. Such the conditions under which the double entertainment given on that day at the castle and at the palace (representatives for the nonce of opposite principles), assumed the importance of a political demonstration.

CHAPTER IV.

Cedant Arma Togæ.

If the bell-ringer of the parish church of Rumelli had hard work of it on this particular St. Urban's day — and he had been ringing away ever since early dawn — at least he could satisfy himself from his elevated position that he was not labouring for nothing.

Not a soul in Rumelli but was abroad by sunrise, and a variegated stream of visitors, most of them from the neighbouring hamlets, never ceased flowing in from hill and plain. Those from the hill were easily recognisable — the men by their breeches, their cocked hats, and the considerable show of pigtails among them; the women by the awkward shortness of their waists. This antiquated costume was no longer that of the inhabitants of the plain — the lowland men had generally adopted velveteen pantaloons and round hats, and their ladies long waists. The head-gear, however, remained the same for the fair sex of both regions. It consisted of a number of large silver pins stuck round the back of the head in a semi-circle, with two larger ones projecting sufficiently to support a red or white veil, or kerchief.

Every available place for such traffic as the day authorized was taken up by six o'clock. Mountains of gingerbread, in all possible fantastic shapes, myriads of strings of chestnuts, heaps of walnuts and hazel-nuts, images of saints and rosaries by the bushel, cheap panpipes, and penny whistles made of the bark of young saplings, solicited the attention of amateurs.

We said that the good folk of Rumelli were astir betimes, and we regret to add that they had another reason for being so, besides that of following the virtuous maxim, that "the early bird gets the worm." The village, in fact, had gone to sleep the night before on a very alarming report, propagated no one knew by whom — a report to the effect that the Bishop of Ibella, who was to have officiated at the parish church next day, was ill, and would not be able to attend. This would be a disaster, indeed, if it turned out to be true, and what bad news does not? as the good folks learned by experience in this very instance.

So late as ten o'clock of the previous evening, an express from Ibella had brought word to the rectory, and to the castle, that his Reverence was slightly indisposed, and would not be able for his clerical duties. This confirmation of the distressing rumours of the day before was a thunderbolt to the castle, which had thus lost its most illustrious guest. The whole parish was under a cloud of disappointment, which did not, for all that, prevent an observant eye being kept on the rival establishments. The interest in their proceedings, especially in those of the castle, was, however, languid in comparison to what it would have been had the bishop been coming. What mattered it who did or did not come, now that the great gun was missing!

Nevertheless a sharp reckoning was made of the visitors to the potentates. At a quarter to ten — the service was to begin at ten — the state of the poll was as follows: — For the castle — three carriages, eleven people; big fishes among them, a retired general (in regimentals) and his lady, a half-pay major (also in regimentals) with a wooden leg, Count what's-his-name, a civilian and brother to the Marquis's lately deceased wife, two canons from the cathedral of Ibella — plus, three cavalry, viz. the Marchesino, son of the Marquis, one of his brother officers, and the Commandant of the Carabineers stationed at Ibella.

For the palace — six carriages, one-and-twenty people; big fishes among them, the Intendente (first civil authority of the province) of Ibella, with lady and sister, the first President of the Court of Appeal, the Attorney-General, the advocate of the poor of the same place, a canon, the preacher for the occasion, a young friar of the order of the Barnabites, an order in odour of liberalism, three gentlemen from Turin, relations of the late wife of the Signor Avvocato — plus, one horseman, the Commandant of the National Guard of Ibella in uniform.

While notes were thus being compared out of doors, and auguries *pro* and *con* drawn from the number and quality of the respective guests, Vincenzo and Barnaby were watching from the Belvedere the movements of the castle, with the view to ascertain and let the Signor Padrone know, when the Marquis and his party set out for the church. The Signor Avvocato had his reasons for wishing to be the second to start. It was an established custom at Rumelli, that the ten o'clock mass, which the family from the castle were in the habit of attending, should not begin until the Marquis, or his lady, when there was one, or some representative of the family, should be in their place in their own chapel. Don Natale, when he was appointed to the parish, had found this custom established, and had seen no cause to interfere with it. Truth to say, the persons who enjoyed the benefit of this privilege had never abused it; on the contrary, they were generally of a laudable punctuality to the hour. But, somehow or other, this good quality had suddenly failed them, when a mass in music with orchestra, under the auspices and management of the Signor Avvocato, had been substituted for the usual high mass with accompaniment of organ, on the day of St. Urban, the patron of Rumelli.

The fact is, that on the first year of the innovation no one from the castle was in the chapel at the appointed hour, and the Signor Avvocato, *pro tem.* conductor of the orchestra, had the mortification of waiting, roll of music in hand to beat the time, for full twenty minutes. In his capacity of leader of the band, he might have taken the law into his own hands, and, by giving the signal to the orchestra, compelled, in a certain way, the beginning of the service; but we know that he was not the man for any bold measure. He took, as his nature prompted, a middle course; that is, swallowed the bitter pill for the present; but, to prevent for the future any possible repetition of the same slight, he had the castle watched, so as to make sure that its inmates were gone to church before he went thither himself. Thus when Vincenzo, out of breath, rushed from the Belvedere to announce that "the castle was *en route*," then, and then only, did the Signor Avvocato give the signal for the setting out of his party.

He headed the march with the Intendent's lady on his right arm, and holding his daughter with the other hand. If we were to say that he was not a little elated, we should not be telling the exact truth; but he tried only to look benignant and happy. No great effort was necessary for this, for nature had unmistakably intended him to be the one and the other, if the Government and his neighbours would permit him to be so. Rose's father was a tall, florid-complexioned, still very handsome man, with but a slight inclination to corpulency. Had he not stooped a little — the result of habit and not of age — few men could have been seen who wore their fifty and six years more lightly than he did. Well, had he not stooped, and had his gait been more in proportion to the bulk of his body, in other words, had his step been longer, his would have been a very commanding presence. As for his smile and address, none could be pleasanter.

In glaring contrast to his was the bearing and manner of the leader of the other party — "the storming party," as the Signor Avvocato could not help whispering to the lady on his arm. Stiff, erect, and as martial-looking as his undersize, his loose regimentals, and rather ludicrous *codino* (pigtail) would allow, the Marquis led on his train as if to battle instead of to mass. A spare old man, very thin, very shrivelled, and, as a rule, looking daggers at mankind in general, such was the Marquis. Hanging on his arm was Madame la Generale, the only specimen of the fair sex among the castle guests, and who was supported on the other side by one of the canons. "Beauty between army and church," remarked some profane joker in the opposite ranks. Certainly, if glitter and noise could carry the day, the castle might cry out victory beforehand — such a blaze of epaulets as it sent forth, such a jingling of spurs and swords as accompanied its procession.

The Black Coats — "the undertakers," as the Marquis quizzically denominated them — looked tame indeed in comparison. They had, at any rate, the advantage in numbers, which is something; and then, black coats, when on the back of a procurator fiscal, or an advocate of the poor, not to speak of intendentes and presidents, have a close connexion with sundry practical results, which give to the said black coats a serious importance in the eyes of rustics. Any one, for instance, might have, some day or other, a son, or nephew, or friend, implicated in a Sunday brawl, and there was no saying how far the severe or lenient view taken of the matter by the public prosecutor might influence the fate of son, nephew, or friend. Or, a poor devil might have a clear legal case, and no money to support it in court; in which predicament a good word from the advocate above named could do much towards the poor devil's being admitted to the "benefit of the poor," as the phrase is — that is, to have the benefit of his suit cost free. These and such-like considerations had, probably, their share in the warm reception given to the Black Coats throughout their passage; even warmer, some said, than the one bestowed on the glittering epaulets, especially when, issuing from opposite sides, both at the same moment entered the church square, where the majority of the local population had long before taken their stand.

But how was it that the castle party, which had had a good ten minutes' start of the other, and a good third less of road to traverse, should only reach the square half a minute sooner than the palace party? There were more reasons than one for this delay. First of all, the sun being very hot, the Marquis, in compliment to the Lady Generale, had struck across some fields of his own, that she might have the benefit of the shade of trees and vine-covered walks — an act of gallantry which necessitated a great deviation from the straight road; then the Lady Generale was very fat, the general asthmatic, the major had a wooden leg, and the marquis himself, full of fire for his age (seventy-five), had, in Hamlet's words, "most weak hams." To all these combined causes of slowness add an acceleration of speed of the palace party, afraid of being behind time, and the simultaneity of arrival is readily accounted for.

At sight of the rival column, the Marquis, who was perhaps fifteen feet nearer the church door, slackened his pace, and put on a gracious grin. The Signor Avvocato, of course, could do no less than quicken his step, and smile in his turn. Another twenty seconds, and there they are face to face — a position which two well-bred gentlemen and close neighbours cannot, even if wearing hostile colours, decently prolong without exchanging salutations and polite inquiries. Consequently, there ensued a general full stop. Cocked hats were raised to the ladies, a finger, military fashion, laid on shakoes. Round hats were not slow in answering the compliment. The general and intendente advanced towards each other; acquaintances left their respective sides to shake hands and greet each other; and, every one knowing every one, the two groups soon coalesced into one.

Taking advantage of the momentary confusion, Federico, the young Marchesino, stole behind the unwitting Vincenzo, who was staring with all his might at the row of crosses on the general's breast, and, watching his opportunity, suddenly sent both his knees into the back of Vincenzo's legs, exclaiming, "How fares it with you, Abbas Mirza!" This was one of the hundred nicknames with which he pestered the young abbé, who thus taken unawares would have lost his balance, had not his tormentor, unwilling to push the joke too far, held him up by the waist. The seminarist turned round as red as a turkey-cock, and, forgetting in his wrath that embryo priests must not swear, sent after the retreating offender, convulsed with laughter, a sonorous "D— the fool!" Fortunately for Vincenzo's self-love, this little episode, as far as he could perceive, had escaped notice in the general press. Miss Rose, most surely, had seen nothing of it.

By this time, the Signor Avvocato had made his condolences about the untoward event, which had deprived the castle, and indeed the whole community, of the brightest ornament of the day; the Marquis, in his turn, had expressed his regrets, and a hope that his reverence's indisposition was not a serious one, and nothing remained to do but to enter the church. But the Marquis drew back, and would not hear of going in first; the advocate mayor on his side, persisted that not for his life would he take precedence of the Marquis, and the scene was verging on the ludicrous, when three words of Latin — the only words of Latin his lordship knew — cut this gordian knot. *Cedant arma togæ* was the shibboleth with which the Marquis conquered the scruples of his opponent. For truth's sake we must add, that an impatient jerk, given by the Lady Intendente to the Signor Avvocato's arm, came to lend weight to the laconic Latin sentence. The Signor Avvocato, with a last apologetic flourish of his hand, bowed his head, lowered his shoulders, and passed on with his two fair companions.

In despair of our ability to do it justice, we renounce any attempt to describe the splendour of the service, and the perfect arrangement of all its parts. It outshone, by universal consent, all the former displays on the same festival. Nothing was left to desire in all that appertained to the musical department, and Vincenzo's execution of the famous motet was so excellent as quite to restore him to the good graces of his godfather and patron. Let us hope that the culinary efforts at palace and castle were equally successful, and that the respective guests fared the better for the rivalry of the dinner givers. All Rumelli knew beforehand what was to compose the *menu* at both places, as most of the dainties, coming from a distance, had passed through Peter the chandler's shop, the post-office of Rumelli, and had been discussed by a competent jury, and pronounced upon, before they had reached their final destination. The general feeling inclined towards the dinner at the palace.

At the proper moment, both factions repaired again to the church, and from church back to head-quarters, each making it a point to take the longest road through the village, stop here and there to make small purchases, or to converse with the bystanders; in short, to mix in some way in the merry-makings. And everywhere, palace and castle, met with a respectful and warm welcome. So far, popular favour seemed resolved to keep the balance pretty steady between the two parties. No signal advantage could be boasted of by either. But as the day wore on, the star of the castle paled, and that of the palace was decidedly in the ascendant. The absence of the bishop, in the end, turned the scale, and the wherefore is easily explained.

The grounds of castle and palace were always thrown open to the public on St. Urban's day, and after vespers crowds were used to congregate in both, though undoubtedly those of the palace attracted the greater multitude. The palace grounds had a right to the preference, seeing that they were by far the most tastefully laid out, had ornamental pieces of water, and *jets d'eau*, brilliant *parterres*, and above all, "bosky shades and cool, mossy retreats." No wonder such charms made it a favourite resort, even before the time when a band played on the terrace; but when, some ten or twelve years ago, to all its other attractions was added that of music, for one loiterer in the castle alleys, ten might be found in those of the palace. Still a certain number of people, sufficient to maintain a show of competition, haunted the castle grounds, principally peasant women from the hills, who had never, perhaps, seen a bishop, or were in particular want of the episcopal benediction. Now, as it was well known beforehand this magnet would not be forthcoming, those piously-inclined individuals deserted the castle, and in the evening solitude reigned undisputed there, even long before the usual display of fire-works at the palace.

All the Marquis's guests left at dark, save the Count and Marchesino Federico; all the guests of the Signor Avvocato but three — the canon, the special preacher, and the intendente — remained over the night. Long after the castle was plunged in obscurity, lights gleamed from every window of the palace. Thus ended the proceedings of a day which might wear for its appropriate motto the Latin quotation of the Marquis, *Cedant arma togæ*.

CHAPTER V.

Vincenzo goes on a Fool's Errand.

About three o'clock in the afternoon of the next day, Rose was sitting in the Belvedere, her favourite place at that hour, busy at work with the purse which we have once before seen in her hands. The excitement of the festa had fatally interfered with the progress of her intended gift, the completion of which was the more pressing as he for whom it was destined was to leave the palace early next day to return to the seminary at Ibella. Let us note here that the Belvedere was the boundary of her father's estate on this its eastern side, and beyond it began the castle grounds, sloping gently down to the castle itself, a distance, perhaps, of two hundred paces. Debouching into the road, which ran below the Belvedere, after traversing some of the Marquis's fields, was a beaten track, which had served to connect the lower and upper land, when both still belonged to the Del Palmetto family. This will explain how it was possible for Rose in her retreat to be startled by the tramp of a horse. On looking up, she saw the Marchesino riding along the footpath just mentioned towards the road.

This young gentleman had left the Turin Military Academy not long before; and, having got a cornetcy in a light cavalry regiment, stationed for the last three months at Ibella, he had been able often to give Rumelli in general the benefit of a sight of his dashing uniform and red shako, and to Rose, in particular, that of his tender glances and gallant attentions. Not that he was or professed to be in love with her; but, as a spirited youth, and an officer, he considered himself in duty bound to flirt with all the pretty girls who came in his way — and Rose was very pretty indeed. Frederick was of a good height, with a well proportioned active figure — nevertheless, far from handsome. He was red-haired and freckled, and had no trace of the bloom of youth on his countenance — a disadvantage which often attaches itself to the offspring of elderly parents. The Marquis must have been full fifty-five, when his second wife presented him with this boy.

The moment he perceived he had attracted the young lady's attention, Frederick waved his foraging cap to her; and, putting his horse to a brisk canter, he brought him up close to the wall of the Belvedere.

"How do you do, Signorina? I was on my way to the palace to bid you good-bye."

"Thank you, Signor Federico," returned Rose. "Are you going away?"

"Yes, this very instant; have you any commands for Ibella — or for the camp?"

"What! are you going to the camp?" asked Rose in surprise.

"Yes; we start to-morrow for Vigevano, to join the rest of our regiment there, and from thence we shall march into Lombardy. Have you no talisman, no keepsake, to bestow on a poor soldier going to the wars?"

"You have my best wishes, Signor Federico," said the girl.

"A precious gift, indeed; but which would be enhanced still, if supported by some tangible proof of your good will — that ribbon round your neck, or this purse, for instance;" and he took up the purse from the window sill, on which Rose had mechanically laid it when he first accosted her. It must be understood that, by raising himself a little in his stirrup, the young officer could bring himself on a level with the window of the Belvedere.

"No, not that," said Rose, thrusting out her hand to seize her work. "I have promised that to some one else."

"So I see," said Federico, scanning the initials upon it; "promised to Priest-in-the-bud. But such as these are profane gifts, unsuited to holy Churchmen— better give Vincenzo a rosary, and allow me to keep this."

"Oh, no!" cried the girl, eagerly; "give it back to me, pray, sir."

"Well, well, if it must be so," said the young hypocrite, holding out the purse, but at the same time slyly spurring his horse, which, obeying the hint, so widened the space between the two hands as to baffle the gentleman's kind intentions. Every apparent attempt to get the animal close to the wall had no other result than of making him more and more restive.

"You see, I am doing my best," called out the youth, shaking in his saddle in an ominous way; "indeed, it is not my fault if I do not succeed."

"Throw it to me," urged Rose.

"So I would, but I cannot — it is all I can do to manage Moretto with both hands." Moretto, indeed, with his forelegs in the air, seemed bent on executing a pirouette. "I feel he is getting the better of me," exclaimed the Marchesino. "I must let him have his way — farewell, Signorina;" and off the rogue set at

4*

a gallop down the road, Rose screaming after him in every key of her voice to stop and listen to her.

"What is the matter?" asked Vincenzo, coming up out of breath.

"Marchesino Federico has taken away your purse," replied Rose, with a half sob.

"Taken away my purse! — how? when?" inquired the seminarist.

"This instant, he rode away with it;" and Rose gave a hurried account of the whole transaction.

"It is too bad!" cried Vincenzo, white with anger; then, looking at her earnestly, he added, "Am I to understand that he took it against your express wish, Signora?"

"Yes, indeed, in spite of all I could say."

"Then you shall have it back again," affirmed the little man, with a stamp of his foot by way of emphasis, and turned away.

"Where are you going, Vincenzo?" asked Rose, rather frightened.

"To Ibella," answered Vincenzo, without, however, stopping.

"Oh! pray, pray, don't!" entreated the girl, running after him; "it is of no use. He will not give it up for the mere asking, and you cannot take it from him by force; for he is the stronger of the two. Besides, he is an officer; and, if papa should find out that you were gone, and alone —"

But Vincenzo's blood was up — he was past every consideration of prudence. All that Rose obtained was a promise that he would be back at eight o'clock, the supper hour at the palace. He picked up his hat, which lay at the foot of a tree, and jumped over the gate. Rose, hurrying to the Belvedere, was just in time to catch sight of him as he turned down the road. Once more she called on him to stop, but this appeal was as unheeded as the rest; so she had nothing to do but to sit down and watch his progress down the hill through her fast-falling tears.

It might be half-past three in the afternoon; the sun was high in the heavens, and broiling hot; but our Paladin was indifferent to that fact, being too much occupied with the young lady's grievance to have perceptions for aught else. He had no settled plan as to how he was to achieve the recovery of the stolen treasure; or, to speak more correctly, the wildest schemes towards that end flitted across his brain — such as calling out Federico, applying for aid to the intendente, or asking redress from the colonel of the young officer's regiment. In this state of excitement, he strode on with such a will that in one hour and a half he accomplished a distance which was considered handsomely done by the best of pedestrians in two hours.

The sight of houses and people somewhat sobered him. It brought with it the consciousness of the danger he was in, of being interfered with by the authorities of the seminary, were they made aware that he was parading the streets alone — a feat strictly forbidden to Seminarists. Fortunately, the house he was in search of, one on which he had kept his eye for the last three months, was on his road, being in those outskirts of the town he had to pass. He went there at once; but, his loud knocking at the street door, which was closed, not being attended to, he came to the conclusion that there was nobody at home. A neighbour, who was standing at a window opposite, confirmed him in this belief, informing him officiously that the Marchesino del Palmetto was probably, as this was his dinner hour, at the café of the Post in the Piazza d'Armi.

Vincenzo knew perfectly well — indeed, too well — where the Café della Posta and the Piazza d'Armi were situated; that is, at the further end of the town, and in quite an alarming proximity to the Seminary. But, far or near, thither he must proceed, and thither he did proceed, looking straight before him, and avoiding as much as possible great thoroughfares. He reached his destination without hindrance; and, after poking his nose into three or four wrong rooms, at last stumbled upon the right one. Del Palmetto and two brother officers were playing at billiards. Frederick, bending over the table, was in the act of striking the ball, when he caught sight of the new comer, and exclaimed:

"Wonders will never cease. *Sacerdos secundum Melchisedech*, I declare. Here is a distich for thee, Priest-in-the-bud; see if I scan it rightly —

> Presbyter in sylvis tendebat retia grillis
> Et tantum fecit that at last he got unum."

"Can't you talk and play at the same time?" asked the Marchesino's adversary.

"Then here's a cannon dedicated by special permission to his reverence," wound up Del Palmetto, playing. The stroke failed, and the bungler was made sport of by his brother-officers.

"The intention was good, at all events; and good intentions help us on the way to Paradise, do not they, Abbas?" asked the Marchesino, walking up to Vincenzo.

"Will you allow me to speak two words ... to you in private at your leisure?" said Vincenzo, sinking down exhausted on a bench, and wiping the moisture from his face and brow. The sentence, short as it was, came forth broken in half, owing partly to the emotion of the speaker; still more so to the parched state of his lips. Vincenzo's tongue literally clove to the roof of his mouth.

"Not before you have had something to drink," replied Federico, taking a glass full of some liquid off a table. "Here, try this; it was meant for me, but I have not touched it."

"What is it?" inquired Vincenzo, glass in hand.

"Orgeat," said Frederick, with a wink to his companions. Vincenzo swallowed the contents of the glass at one gulp. He was aware the instant after that he had not drunk anything so simple as orgeat, but he took good care to say nothing of his discovery, from the fear of exposing himself to further mortifications.

"Good, is it not?" asked Federico, who had again returned to his game. Vincenzo could only nod assent; the beverage, whatever it was, had cut short his respiration.

The success of his trick had driven away the first impulse — they say all such are good — which had moved the Marchesino at sight of the lad's heated face and troubled looks. Guessing the errand on which the seminarist had come, Del Palmetto had had half a mind to draw the messenger aside, put the purse into his hand, and so end the matter; but, now that he saw a chance of fresh sport, he gave up as tame and absurd the better course he had for a moment contemplated, and instead manœuvred to gain time; so, turning to Vincenzo, he said, "You are not in a hurry, are you?" There was that in the tone of the question which prompted an answer conformable to the wishes of the questioner. Vincenzo returned a laconic "Not in the least," accompanied by a grand toss of the head.

"Because, you must know," continued the Marchesino, "our stake is a dinner; and I hope — nay, I insist — that you make one of our party. We are all of us as hungry as hawks; and, truth to say, I have a superstitious objection to any interruption of a game when the luck is on my side, as it evidently is now."

These and such like explanations met with nothing from Vincenzo but monosyllables of consent, or significant nods and smiles, implying that he was ready for anything and everything. He was too much engrossed by his own novel and unaccountable sensations to have any attention to spare for other topics. His being seemed to have expanded into an engine of ten thousand horse-power, and to be soaring through space with the speed of a winged dragon — withal, a delicious consciousness of unlimited strength, and, along with this, a great inclination to be merciful. If he did not pound into atoms the little puny Marchesino and Co., it was only that he was a good fellow, and they were good fellows also. Give an abstemious and imaginative boy of seventeen a strong dose of extract of absynth and water, such as our Vincenzo had had, and you will see that self-exaltation is the characteristic of the intoxication it produces. It is in this self-elevating action that the great danger and attraction of the liquor just named lies, scarcely inferior to the attraction and danger of opium.

It was lucky for Vincenzo that the game did not come to a conclusion before the room had done spinning like a top; he was able to rise without any accident ensuing; and, at the friendly invitation of Del Palmetto, who passed his arm under that of the seminarist, to walk steadily enough to the end of a passage, where there was a washhand-basin stuck in the wall, and a very big and very dirty jack-towel hanging by its side. Here the young Marquis, while washing his hands, said to Vincenzo, in a confidential whisper, "You are sent by Miss Rose for the purse, I know — all right — I have left it at my lodgings. Let us have a morsel to eat first, and then we'll go together and fetch it."

"Very well," said Vincenzo, "provided I have not long to wait."

"I won't keep you long," said the other; "so now wash your hands, and let us join our friends and have dinner."

"But I have dined already, and I am not hungry," objected Vincenzo, as in his turn he washed his hands.

"Never mind that; you needn't *eat;* only sit down for form's sake. The lieutenant, who gives the dinner, would take it amiss if you refused."

Upon this understanding, the two newly made friends walked out of the passage into a spacious court-yard, in which were set, here and there, tables of various sizes. At one, where the cloth was laid for four, were already seated Del Palmetto's two brother-officers. "So here you are at last!" exclaimed he who had lost.

"Your pardon for keeping you waiting," said the Marchesino, as he and Vincenzo took their places.

Vincenzo had spoken the truth in saying that he had dined, and also spoken what he assumed to be the truth when he had stated that he was not hungry; but, at sight of an engaging sausage, a fascinating cold roast chicken, and a lovely fresh salad, spread out before him, he discovered that he had been under a mistake, and that he should prefer doing something more than merely sitting down to table for form's sake. In fact, he had dined as early as one o'clock, and now it was past six. Besides, his long walk, not to mention the *extrait d'absinthe*, was rather calculated to sharpen a naturally good appetite. Accordingly, he did not require much pressing to be induced to try a leg of the chicken, the very first mouthful of which he was tasting, when, lo and behold! a slovenly-looking individual in shirt sleeves and slippers, appeared in front of the table, and addressed him familiarly in these words, "So I have caught you at last! Come home this instant." Signor Vincenzo raised his head haughtily, and said, majestically, "Who art thou that comest to give orders to me?" The functionary, who was no eagle, took this apostrophe *ad literam*, and replied accordingly, "Who am I? why, don't you know me, Bastian, the porter of the seminary?" To which the quick rejoinder was, "If that be thy unworthy trade, go back to it, thou filthy gaoler." The porter shook his fist threateningly at the speaker, as much as to say, "You dare speak thus to me, do you? Wait a moment!" and decamped.

"Bravo! well done!" cried Del Palmetto, filling all the glasses; "here's to the bravest spirit ever hid in a cassock!" One cannot decently decline a toast in one's own honour; at least so thought Vincenzo, and therefore he drank off the bumper at his side. "I wager anything that some of the black robes will be let loose on you before five minutes are passed," said the Marchesino.

"Let them come," said Vincenzo, with a motion of the head full of meaning, and then once more turned his attention to the leg of chicken. He was excited, and felt equal to any contingency. He ate heartily, drinking, however, in moderation; but even three glasses of wine — and he had had no more up to that time — began to tell upon one so unaccustomed to take any at all — witness the twinkle in his eye and his fast-growing talkativeness.

Things were at this pass, when the waiter who brought in the dessert also brought in word that one of the reverend prefetti of the seminary was waiting without, and wished to speak to Signor Vincenzo. A long-rooted habit of deference, asserting its right even at this moment of excitement, prompted the young Abbé to rise and obey his superior; but Del Palmetto interfered, saying, "Why should you disturb yourself? why couldn't his Reverence favour us with his company, and say what he has to say to you here?"

"Why not, indeed?" said Vincenzo, reseating himself; and, addressing the waiter, he added, rather pompously, "Have the goodness to tell the Signor Prefetto, with my compliments, that I am at this moment at dinner with some excellent friends of mine, and that I should take it as a favour if he would come to me, instead of my going to him."

The waiter departed, and almost immediately returned, ushering in a tall and good-looking ecclesiastic, who must, doubtless, have been a man of the world, for he showed no symptoms of displeasure at the scene before him; but, raising his hat to all present, he addressed the Marchesino by name, and then said to Vincenzo, with great amenity of manner, "How are you, Vincenzo? I am glad to see you again, and in such excellent company."

"And heartily happy am I to see your Reverence looking so well," said Vincenzo, standing up; "and I shall be still happier if you will take a glass of wine with us."

The prefetto thanked him, but excused himself by saying that it was one of his rules never to eat or drink except at his regular meals.

"If so," resumed Vincenzo, with much coolness, "we at least may have the honour of drinking to your Reverence's continued good health." And, smacking his lips after drinking the toast, he added, "Now that this preliminary is over, may I beg to know on what business you wish to speak to me?"

"Oh! business. There is none I know of," replied the priest, carelessly. "I heard you were here as I was passing by, and came in to give you a good day. But, as it is getting late, I think we might as well walk home together."

"Suppose I had all the inclination in the world to do so, I could not. I am not here merely for the sake of pleasure, as superficial observers might take for granted. I am here on a matter of importance; a matter connected with; — never mind whom; a matter which admits of no delay, as the gentlemen present can tell you — that is, not all the gentlemen present; but my

excellent friend, the young Marquis del Palmetto, can.
And so, this point being also satisfactorily settled, I
beg permission to sit down; but, previous to doing so,
I shall once more drink your very good health;" and,
having swallowed another bumper, with infinite composure, Vincenzo reseated himself.

"Then I'll leave you to transact your business,"
said the priest, turning away. "Should you feel disposed to come home by-and-bye, you will find Bastian
waiting for you."

"D—— Bastian!" shouted the youth, springing
to his feet. "I'll have no turnkey dogging me, do
you hear? Thank God, I am a free citizen of a free
country;" and he roared out at the top of his voice,
"Long live the Statuto!" The prefetto shook his head,
bowed, and departed.

"Bravo, Hector!" cried Del Palmetto, who was
himself a little heated. "Only, if you take the Statuto in earnest, let me warn you to make the most of
it while you can. The moment we come back from
the war, we'll put your Statuto into limbo."

"Into limbo?" echoed Vincenzo, staring vacantly
at Federico. "Then, are you not also for the Statuto?"

"Not one of us," affirmed the young nobleman.
"Do you think the army is going to submit to a batch
of advocates, whose only merit is their gift of the
gab?"

Vincenzo, after pondering a little, hit the table
with his fist, crying, "Have I, then, been consorting
all this while with *Codini*, with Jesuits, with traitors?
I shake the dust of this vile place from my shoes;"
and, upsetting his chair in his precipitation, rushed
away.

Del Palmetto and his brother-officers were not slow in pursuing and overtaking the fugitive.

"Don't you see it is a joke?" cried Frederick. "Come along, and let us drink to our eternal friendship."

Vincenzo, easily pacified, allowed himself to be taken back to the dinner table. The poor youth had now drunk too much to stop short of any extravagance. So, when Del Palmetto proposed that they should go into the passage where the washhand-basin was, and exchange clothes, Vincenzo declared it was a capital idea, and immediately complied. It is easy to imagine the bursts of laughter elicited by the appearance of the seminarist in the uniform of a cavalry officer, and of the cavalry officer in the garb of a seminarist; this latter scamp improving the occasion to deliver, in a nasal twang, a short and most risible sermon. An organ-grinder was next called in, and a ball improvised; in which, as may be expected, the hapless hero of the *fête* cut a prominent figure.

All this passed in the presence of a crowd of people. The spectators, at first, had been only the customers of the establishment; but presently, as the rumour of the wild doings at the *café* got wind, people flocked thither from all quarters of the town. The scandal was as great as it could be; and those having any interest in the seminary who witnessed it, Bastian among others, were not likely to make light of it in their reports. All this time, Vincenzo was haunted by an indistinct notion of having something to do, with which, in some way or other, Miss Rose was concerned; but what this something was, do what he would, he could not remember.

By dusk, the poor lad being past making sport for anybody, Del Palmetto and his companions had him removed from the public gaze, and conveyed to a room in the *café*, where he found the only accommodation he stood in need of for the present — a bed; and there they left him snoring.

CHAPTER VI.

The Day after a Frolic.

VINCENZO awoke late next morning, in a lamentable condition of body and mind; giddy, sick, aching from head to foot, and thoroughly disgusted with himself. He sat upon his bed, took his poor throbbing temples between his hands, and tried to recollect. Bastian and the prefetto were the only images which came out clear and distinct from the nightmare of the last night. That he had misbehaved to both, he had not a shadow of a doubt; but he had no clue by which to discover in what manner, or to what extent. All the rest, from the eclipse of the prefetto, down to the present moment, was a pell-mell of indistinct scraps, of which he might have only dreamt, for aught he could tell; and as to the part he had possibly played in this misty interlude, if not a dream, it was a perfect blank.

One thing alone was certain — that he had shamefully disgraced himself. What would the Signor Avvocato say, when his godson's misdeeds came to his ears? What would Miss Rose ... and the purse! Oh, heavens!! The recollection of the purse, forgotten to that moment, went like a shot through his heart and brain. Lost past hope of recovery. It was just what he deserved — he was not worthy of it, or of any kindness from such an angel as Miss Rose.

The small room, or, rather, closet, in which he had passed the night, was stiflingly hot and close. He got up and opened the only window. A bit of glass hung beside the window. He looked into it, and started. What a hideous face he saw! All the lower part of it besmeared with the burnt cork, which had given him a moustache and chintuft. A jug and basin were on the table, but not a drop of water in either. He looked for some signs of a bell — there was none. No other resource for him but to open the door and call; which he did, after flinging on his cassock.

His summons was answered immediately, by the same man who had waited at dinner the day before.

"How do you feel this morning, sir?" asked the waiter, without the least attempt to hide the smile called up on his broad countenance by the rueful figure before him.

"Like one who has made an ass of himself overnight," answered the penitent lad.

"A little headache, probably? A strong cup of coffee will remove that in no time."

"First of all," said Vincenzo, "I want plenty of water, so that I may wash myself. And, if I could also have some soap to get rid of those stains on my face, I should be obliged to you."

The waiter promised he should have what he required, and soon returned with a large jug of water and a fine new cake of soap. Vincenzo eyed the soap with some perplexity, and said —

"I am afraid that soap won't do for me, my friend;

for, truth to say, I have not a farthing of money. Can't you give me some old common bit?"

"You may use this all the same," said the obliging waiter. "First of all, the soap belongs to me, and you are welcome to it; and then, the Marchesino left orders that you were to have whatever you asked for, and he would pay all expenses. When you are ready for your coffee, be so good as to call Battista."

Vincenzo was touched by Del Palmetto's thoughtfulness — more touched than he would have deemed himself capable of being by any attention from such a quarter. But, indeed, Del Palmetto's behaviour to him, as far as he could remember the events of the preceding day, had left on Vincenzo's mind an impression altogether to the credit of his late foe.

The waiter's double declaration having now removed all his scruples about the soap, he used it unsparingly in his ablutions; and, having put as much order as he could into his attire, he called for Battista, who presently brought him the promised coffee.

"Has any one come for me from the seminary?" asked Vincenzo.

"Not that I know of," replied the waiter. An answer which confirmed Vincenzo in his preconception, that his sins must be so entirely past forgiveness in that quarter, that the sinner himself was deemed unworthy of any notice. This issue had nothing very appalling in it to one who had yearned after it with all his soul for the last two months.

"No; nobody has called save the Marchesino," went on Battista. "He has been here twice, but you were asleep both times; and he would not allow you to be disturbed. He said he might call again, but he could not be sure, as he had much to do, in consequence of the regiment having received orders to leave the town before noon."

"And what o'clock is it now?" inquired the lad, swallowing his coffee.

"Half-past eight."

"And what time was it when ... I went to bed last night?"

"It was still daylight," said Battista; "a little past eight, perhaps."

"I was very unruly downstairs, was I not?",

"Not so very bad; rather funny, and a little noisy, to be sure; but your friends were not far behind you, I can tell you."

"If I recollect right," said Vincenzo, "there was some music after dinner."

"Yes, a fellow with his organ came and played in the court, and you took a fancy to dance, and so did the other three. The Signor Marchesino — oh! he is a merry gentleman — went and fetched Margaret, the cook, and oh! dear, it was as good as a play to see you, in the Marchesino's uniform, whirling her round and round like a top." The scene must have been droll enough in reality, for Battista burst into a laugh at the mere recollection.

"Were there many people looking on?" asked Vincenzo, with a long face.

"Many people!" repeated Battista. "Bless you, the yard was as full as it could hold;" then, noticing the deep blush on his listener's face, Battista's eloquence of description came to a full stop; and he added, good-naturedly, "there's no disgrace, you know, in taking a glass too much once or so in a man's life. Such a thing may happen to the best of us."

Vincenzo, left to himself, had an intense longing to go out and inhale a little fresh pure air; that which came in from the courtyard was neither fresh nor pure; on the other hand, he was afraid of missing Del Palmetto's possible visit, and with it all chance of recovering the purse. In this state of perplexity he mechanically took up the two new rolls, which the waiter had brought with his coffee, and had had the delicacy to leave behind; and, as he was thrusting them into the pocket of his cassock, he felt an obstruction, which had not been there the day before: he turned the pocket inside out, and lo! what should appear but the purse which he had been so anxiously pursuing?

The lad cut a caper of childlike delight, kissed the treasure; then, wrapping it carefully in the piece of paper in which it had already been enveloped, he hid it in the deepest corner of the pocket of his cassock, wondering all the while how it had come there. Had the Marchesino willingly returned it? Vincenzo, in thinking so, judged that young man too generously. The fact admitted of a more common-place explanation. At the time Del Palmetto exchanged clothes with the seminarist, he still possessed recollection enough to take the disputed article out of his uniform pocket, and transfer it to that of the cassock he assumed; but later — that is, when he took back his coat, and restored the black robe to Vincenzo — Del Palmetto had left the clearness of his memory at the bottom of many succeeding bumpers, and so the purse remained in the cassock-pocket. Vincenzo had proved more lucky than wise.

Feeling now almost elated, and with no further reason to wait for Federico, our lad sallied forth into the street; and, keeping as close to the houses as possible, took the shortest way out of the town; that is, went out of it at the end opposite to that by which he had come. Leaving Ibella behind him, he followed the main road for a little; then struck to the left, into a well-known meadow, and stretched himself at full length on the thick soft grass, under the shade of some wide-spreading walnut trees. It was happiness to breathe the pure air, to feel the cool grass beneath him, and to look at the blue canopy of heaven above. It seemed as though the immensity of the azure dome reduced his troubles to very small proportions. He tried hard to think and deliberate upon some course of action; but he was not equal to any mental exertion, he felt too lazy; all that he could do, was to enjoy the agreeable sensation of physical well-being which stole over him.

After a time, this sweet heaviness resolved itself into a sound sleep, from which he was suddenly startled by a blast of trumpets, accompanied by an outburst of loud shouts. It was the squadron of Del Palmetto's regiment leaving Ibella, amid the hurrahs of a considerable portion of the population, cheering and fraternizing with the soldiers. Vincenzo would fain have joined in the cheers and the good wishes, at least said farewell to Del Palmetto, but the crowd deterred him. In his present circumstances, he knew that the safest course for him was to avoid attracting notice. He ensconced himself behind the large trunk of one of the trees; and, from that hiding-place, saw the whole troop defile, Del Palmetto on his beautiful Moretto, his big sword drawn. Lucky Del Palmetto! How Vincenzo envied him! What would he not have given to be in the Marchesino's place, at least to be one of those brave fellows going to the war.

When the last of them had passed, the youth resumed his horizontal position on the grass; and, following up the new train of thought called up by the sight of the soldiers, he asked himself, why he should not enlist also, and fight for his country? Why not, in fact? Enlisting and going to the seat of war had been the *dénouement* of all those schemes for liberty he had been weaving during these two last months. But how was he to enlist? to whom apply? these were practical difficulties which could only be solved, if solved at all, by application to such acquaintances as he had in the town — the obliging waiter, for instance — but, at that moment, such a step was impossible. After the little enviable notoriety he had acquired, to parade the streets of Ibella, in broad day, in search of such information, was out of the question. He had, indeed, already made up his mind, should he be driven to the dire extremity of returning to the palace, not to traverse the town until he could do so unseen — that is, after dark.

Like many another older and wiser person, Vincenzo's cogitations ended with a resolution to trust to the chapter of accidents. Some one might pass — a military man, for instance — with the look of one able to give the information required, and from whom Vincenzo would feel inclined to ask it. While thus keeping watch for such an individual, Vincenzo drew forth one of the fresh rolls he had pocketed, and munched it leisurely. It was the hottest hour of the day, and passers-by were rare — a labourer now and then, or an artisan going to his work; a tardy market-woman, trudging behind her donkey; or dusty muleteers driving a string of dusty mules.

As the shades of the trees began to lengthen, the townsfolk who had accompanied the troopers began to return; and, for a whole hour there was plenty of movement, and of dust in clouds, on the highway. They were all people belonging to Ibella, whom Vincenzo had best let alone. Later, and later still, when the sun's rays struck the road aslant, some pertinacious promenader from the town ventured as far as the meadow in which our skulker lay — an old lady with her maid, a paterfamilias and his sons, a couple of priests, a merry set of young men — none with a face in which Vincenzo could descry any knowledge of military matters.

Two uniforms at last loomed in the distance. The seminarist's heart gave a great thump — two sergeants, arm in arm, by Jove! They came up opposite to the lad's hiding-place, stood there a moment, as if undecided whether to go on or not, and then turned back. Vincenzo sprang up, and was about to cross the meadow, when he spied dangers ahead, and had to squat down in a hurry. Three priests — one known to him but too well, and to whom he was known but too well, the prefetto of last night — were sailing down the road, cutting him off from the sergeants. Crouching on all fours behind a tree, he had the pleasure of watching the soldiers gradually dwindle down to mere specks in the distance.

He had probably lost his last chance. Vincenzo's heart began to misgive him, that he should be obliged

after all to swallow the bitter pill of taking refuge at
the palace, and becoming the laughing-stock of all
Rumelli. To be an object of ridicule to one's acquaintances is a heavy punishment at any age, particularly
so to a boy; but Vincenzo, to do him justice, quailed
less at the thought of his own humiliation than at the
idea of the Signor Avvocato's anger, and Miss Rose's
disgust and displeasure. Little exhilarating as was the
prospect, it did not prevent his feeling hungry, or eating his last roll; after which he set himself to wait
patiently for the now not very distant moment when
twilight would make it easy for him to steal into Ibella
unnoticed, and ask a word of advice from Battista as
to enlisting. Should that hope fail him, then there
would be nothing left for him to do but turn his steps
towards Rumelli.

Presently the tramp of a horse, and the sound of
a deep bass voice singing a popular air, attracted his
attention; and, looking in the direction of the highway, he saw a man on a tall horse, riding leisurely
along. The song, no other than the, at that time
hackneyed, hymn of Pio Nono, augured well for the
inquiry Vincenzo was meditating. He accordingly
crawled to the side of the road to get a closer view of
the horseman, that he might judge whether the singer's
physiognomy kept the promise held forth by the choice
of the song. There was not much that was prepossess-
ing in the little that could be seen of the rider's looks:
a hawk nose, and a pair of hungry grey eyes, being
the only features that emerged from the wilderness of
black hair, and double-pointed beard, in which his face
was framed. His appearance, indeed, vividly recalled
to Vincenzo those similitudes of brigands, which he

had seen doing duty at the entrance of waxwork exhibitions: they were not a whit more forbidding than the man before him. The Calabrese hat, encircled by a broad green band, in which was stuck a plume of cock's feathers, finished the resemblance. To complete the stage effect of the costume, a large red cross was embroidered on the left breast of the short military tunic he wore; and a long cavalry sword dangled from a white leather belt buckled round his waist.

The red cross was encouraging. Vincenzo had heard that the volunteers in the present holy war of independence had adopted that sign in imitation of the crusaders of old. The red cross outweighed the ill-favoured countenance — and, therefore, ere the rider passed, the lad stood up, and, raising his three-cornered had most respectfully, said, "Good evening, sir; will you allow me to ask you a question?"

The horseman halted, surveyed the speaker, then answered, "Certainly, my young reverend; put as many queries as you like. Pray, what may it be you wish to know?"

"Can you tell me what it is necessary to do, in order to enlist for a soldier?"

"Enlist!" repeated the horseman, in surprise; "is it for yourself, or for some friend, that you want the information?"

"For myself," replied Vincenzo.

"Where do you come from?" asked the stranger.

"From the .... from a seminary," stammered Vincenzo.

"Oh! oh! I see how it is," said the rider, dismounting, and leading his horse to the edge of the road, that it might have the benefit of some mouthfuls of grass during the colloquy. Vincenzo stared in amazement at the tall, long-legged, lanky figure striding towards him: the very figure of a Don Quixote — but Vincenzo had never read Cervantes.

"I see how it is," repeated the man, sitting down, and looking his young interlocutor full in the face; "you are a victim of the Jesuits."

"Indeed, I am not," protested the youth.

"No use denying it; I read it in your eyes," insisted the other. "They tell me that you are an innocent boy driven to desperation by that wily sect, but who won't admit it, so great is the terror they have managed to inspire him with. I know their ways; but never fear; the reign of the Jesuits is over. Pio Nono and Colonel Roganti are too many for them. Surely, you have heard of Colonel Roganti, haven't you?"

Vincenzo confessed in all humility that he had never heard of Colonel Roganti.

"Is it possible?" cried he of the double-pointed beard; "never heard of the man who has filled the world with his name, who has fought Austria and the Jesuits all his life long? Then, what do they teach you in your seminary?"

"They don't teach modern history there," pleaded the youth.

"I thought so; just like them," sneered the colonel. "Well, I am the man," (with a great thump on his chest,) "I have already got together six thousand picked men at Novara, my head-quarters; I want six thousand more before I begin operations; and, to find them, I ride about rousing the country, preaching the holy war, enlisting, recruiting, playing the very devil. You are a lucky dog to have met me; that you are. I have just the very thing for you — a vacant chaplaincy in one of my regiments."

"Thank you very much," said the lad, overflowing with gratitude, "but I am no priest; I have only got the minor orders."

"What does that matter?" said the colonel; "you have got the tonsure and the cassock; that is enough and to spare."

"But I can't say mass; I can't confess, or preach; I can't do one of the things that a chaplain is expected to do. Let me be a soldier, will you?"

"Be it so, then," assented the colonel, whose sense of fun was so greatly tickled by the naive earnestness of the youth that he had much ado not to laugh.

"Which shall it be — infantry or cavalry?"

Vincenzo meditated for an instant; then modestly said, "Infantry."

"Very well — now let me give you a word of caution. A soldier, understand, has no will of his own — passive obedience is his motto, blindly to do what he is bidden, his duty. For instance, suppose you see me act, or hear me speak, in a way that may seem questionable; well, your duty is to hold your tongue, and take it for granted that all I do or say is for the good of the country. Otherwise, farewell discipline; and, this being a time of war, discipline must be strictly enforced. It would cost me a pang to have you put in irons or shot; but I would have it done, if necessary, for the sake of discipline. I am for fair play, and so I warn you."

"Thank you," said Vincenzo, full of a deep, almost solemn emotion; "I may sin through ignorance, but not from want of good-will. I know that the first duty of a soldier is self-abnegation, and I am determined to do my duty to the best of my power. Indeed, my wish will be to give you every satisfaction, sir."

"Sensibly and honourably spoken," observed the colonel; "now then, nothing more remains to be settled between us than that you give me your hand, and repeat after me the form of your engagement. I, ... your name and age, if you please?"

"Vincenzo Candia, aged seventeen," prompted the youth, adding, "Perhaps I ought to make known to you that I have no money."

"Never mind the money," said the colonel; "we shall find plenty at head-quarters. Now, repeat carefully after me — I, Vincenzo Candia, seventeen years old, engage myself, of my free will, to serve as a soldier all through the present campaign, under the orders of his Excellency Colonel Roganti." Vincenzo repeated this formula word for word. There, you are enlisted, and now *en route*," said the great man, rising and throwing his long legs across his Rosinante. "We shall not go far this evening, and a morsel to eat and a bed wait for us at the first resting-place." Vincenzo was quite ready to proceed, and followed his new commander in silence.

CHAPTER VII.

Beginning of the Experiences of a Raw Recruit.

The day was on the wane, and in another half hour it would be dark enough to shelter Vincenzo from observation. After all, he cared little now whom he might meet; he was in the service of H. Majesty, and under the protection of one who would not allow him to be molested. In his candour and inexperience, the imaginative boy had no more doubt of the reality of his enlistment than if King C. Albert had enlisted him in person. And, had any one come and told him at that moment that the man whose every word he had listened to, and believed to be true as Gospel writ, was no colonel, but a quack and a cheat, bent on drawing capital from the boy's honest face, and evident respectability, the odds are that Vincenzo would have laughed to scorn accuser and accusation, and acquired new faith in the charlatan.

Vincenzo felt and looked grave, as a conscientious youth well may, and ought to do, who has taken the first important, nay, decisive step, in life, and is fully alive to its responsibilities. His thoughts dwelt long and fondly on the inmates of the palace. Perhaps he should never look on their faces again — a knot formed in his throat at such a possibility — perhaps he was destined before long to fall in battle! Well, let it be so; *they* should have no cause at least to be ashamed of him. In the meantime, he must not leave them any longer in the dark as to his present fate: he was sure they must feel uneasy about him — Miss Rose in particular, aware as she was of the errand on which he had gone to Ibella. He would write the first opportunity that offered — beg them to forgive him, tell every thing, not forgetting to say that he had found the purse, and had it safe in his pocket; that would please Miss Rose — and, as he walked, he began mentally to indite his epistle.

"Vincenzo," called the horseman.

"Sir," replied the youth, as if awakening.

"Now that you are a soldier, and that I am your colonel, you must address me by the title of my military rank."

"Yes, colonel," said the recruit.

"What are you thinking of?" resumed the elder.

"Of many things," answered Vincenzo, in some embarrassment.

"Of home, perhaps?"

"Yes, sir ... colonel, I mean; at least, if not exactly of home — for I am an orphan, and have no home — of that which stands me in lieu of one."

"A disheartening subject for a soldier to dwell upon," remarked the colonel; "but, if you cannot help thinking of home, think of it in connexion with the day of your return, wearing a great star on your breast, and alike the pride and envy of all your old intimates."

"I will try to follow your advice," said the lad, submissively.

"Do you know the hymn of Pio Nono?"

"Yes, colonel."

"Can you sing it?"

"Yes, colonel."

"Well, then, let us sing it together." They did so, and the colonel, after expressing great satisfaction with Vincenzo's voice and performance, added, "I never begin operations — recruiting operations, I mean — without first singing this composition, and in future I shall always expect you to join me. It draws the audience up to the proper pitch for my purpose. Men, my good boy, must be taken as they are. The peasants I have to address, the best stuff for my corps, are most of them ignorant, material creatures, and must be dealt with like children. I shrink from no means, however personally unpalatable to me, so long as they are honest, by which I hope to attain my aim, my sole aim — the deliverance of my country. For this end, of which I never lose sight, I distribute, wherever I go, copies of Pio Nono's hymn, and portraits of him printed on cloth, that can be worn round the neck, like scapularies. I give you this explanation, not alone to prevent your possible misconception of my actions, but also to let you know that it will be part of your duty to assist me in the dissemination of both these articles; trifles in themselves, but having a weighty effect, I assure you, on the simple mind of country folks. I charge a penny for the hymn, and twopence for His Holiness's portrait — less than the first cost; but those who are able and willing, may, of course, be asked to give more. My commission includes the power to receive offerings for the benefit of the country. The country, I need scarcely inform you, is equally in want of money and men. Is not money the great sinews of war?"

There was in these, and such-like confidence something jarring to the lad's feelings, something degrading in the notion of having to go about, and, as it were, beg, even though the good of the country was the motive. But then, if a man of the colonel's importance, station, and experience (near at hand he looked full fifty), saw no objections to such proceedings, why should a youngster, who was nobody, be more squeamish? Add to this argument, that the general propositions laid down by his chief, seemed, to Vincenzo's judgment, fair and sound. There was no denying that men must be taken as they are, and no means be shrunk from, provided they were honest, by which the salvation of the country might be wrought out. Neither was there any denying, that the country was in want of money, nor that money was the great sinews of war. These were truisms that no one could impugn. Vincenzo came out of this debate with himself with a strengthened conviction that he had a clear duty before him, and that, the greater his antipathy to that duty, the more reason for his discharging it conscientiously, and like a man.

An opportunity of testing his *bonâ fide* conclusion was not long in presenting itself. Ten o'clock was striking at some town, or village, or whatever it was, near at hand. They had long left the highway for a cross-road, and Vincenzo was entirely out of his depth as to local geography, when the colonel stopped at an isolated house, a roadside inn, in full activity; that is, full of light, and sound, and bustle — "the tail of a wedding," as the hostler graphically explained. Having, with his own eyes, seen to the proper accommodation of his nag, and himself removed the saddle, the long-legged man put a small valise, hitherto unremarked by Vincenzo, under his arm, and then led the way to a large room on the first-floor, which had an open gallery stretching along the full length of its front. There was a great gathering of people there, most of them farmers and peasants, eating, drinking, and talking.

After giving his instructions to the waiter, the colonel stationed himself at one of the empty tables in the centre of the room, the small valise by his side, filled a glass for himself, and one for his companion, brimful with wine, stood up, and, waving his glass, cried, in a stentorian voice, "Here's a bumper to Pio Nono; long live the Pontiff Reformer!" Nearly every head in the room turned to look at the speaker. He, with another flourish of his hand to the company, disposed of the contents of his glass; then, profiting by the half silence produced by his toast, he struck up the hymn, Vincenzo joining in it, as in duty bound.

The singing, it must be allowed, was capital; it was listened to in relative silence, and with evident pleasure. That it was a seasonable diversion, reviving the flagging spirits of many a guest, was certain from the salvo of bravos, and loud clapping of hands, which saluted its conclusion. The experienced colonel struck the iron while it was hot; he bowed, and made the following pithy speech: —

"Gentlemen desirous of procuring the hymn that has just been sung, also scapularies coming direct from Rome, bearing the likeness of His Holiness, and blessed by him, can be supplied with them very cheaply. My young pupil and friend here will hand the one and the other round for inspection." (Vincenzo, on hearing these words, felt the blood rising to his face.) "No one is obliged to buy; but those who do, will be doing a good turn to their own souls, and also to their country. The times, gentlemen, are difficult, and money is the great sinews of war. Offerings to be appropriated to the equipment of volunteers will be received with gratitude!"

A mist rose before Vincenzo's eyes as the colonel consigned to him the valise, with its lid now thrown open, and directed him to carry it round. He set his teeth fast, and resolutely performed the task. Meanwhile, the tall man was favouring a limited, but select, circle of admirers, who had gathered round him, the hostess foremost, with a few choice scraps of a fancy biography. "A most interesting boy ... a victim of the Jesuits; it required all *my* energy to rescue him from their grip. No father, no mother, no relations. You can have no conception of what he has had to endure. I found him starving, literally starving. I'll stand by him; protect him to the last. I am not rich, but never mind; so long as I have a morsel of bread he shall have the half of it. No lack of benevolent people, thank God, to help me in my charitable undertaking."

These broken confidences serve to initiate us into the secret motives, which had induced the *soidisant* colonel to attach Vincenzo's fortunes to his own — namely, to endorse his own roguishness on the lad's youth and honest looks, and turn the interest aroused by them, and by a forged tale of persecution and destitution, into a well-supplied mint for himself.

Presently the unconscious object of this puffing returned to his large associate with a handful of small coin; and, pale and worn out with emotion — what he had been doing was so very like begging — he sank into a chair in a corner. But the colonel, with a covetous glance at the money, desired the youth to come by him, and have something to eat. A plentiful supper by this time was served on the little table in the centre of the room. Vincenzo felt faint and hungry enough to need but little encouragement to eat; but, much as he relished his meal, he would have relished it still more without the exaggerated parental fondness lavished on him by the colonel, and the obtrusive marks of sympathy and interest showered on him by the landlady and company — a sympathy and interest so pointed as to be scarcely justifiable, even in the case either of a convalescent, or of one who had had a very narrow escape from some great peril.

These attentions were the more puzzling and unaccountable to Vincenzo, for being interspersed with hints and references to something which the speaker clearly took for granted had happened — such as, "Cheer up, my boy, and don't think of the past; it is all over — they won't come now, and take you from your friend — you are quite safe with him; he will protect you — don't spare the chicken, have another leg — the supper is *gratis et amore Dei*, you know — would to God we could do more!"

Such snatches of speeches as these were Sanscrit to Vincenzo, and made him feel ill at ease. However, he turned to account the good will of his hostess, to ask her to procure him writing materials — a commission which she readily undertook, but which must have had its difficulties from the time it took to accomplish. Pen, ink, and paper, were found at last, and carried by the obliging hostess to the little room allotted to Vincenzo, next to that of his chief and guardian.

The youth felt dizzy, wearied, and sleepy; the bed looked very tempting; but he roused himself valiantly, and resolved not to go to rest until he should have achieved his epistles. Who could tell whether he might find time to write them on the morrow? The task proved easier the further he advanced in it; the rising tide of feeling, as he poured out his heart on paper, helped him on wonderfully. The letter to the Signor Avvocato proved rather long, that to Miss Rose consisted of but a few lines. They ran thus:

"DEAR SIGNORINA, — For all that relates to my late disgraceful conduct, my sincere repentance, and my present prospects, I must refer you to my letter to your good father. I venture to write to you only to say that the purse is safe with me — not, however, through any merit of mine; for I must confess, with sorrow, that its recovery is due to a mere lucky chance. I keep it as a precious deposit, to be returned to you at our first meeting, if God grant me so much happiness, when I hope to have so behaved as to deserve your forgiveness, and the confirmed possession of the promised dear gift. Should I never see you again I feel sure that your kind heart will not disapprove of the way I shall have disposed of it; that is, should the knowledge ever reach you."

To make this last phrase clear to the reader, it is necessary to add that, as he finished writing it, Vincenzo drew the purse from his pocket, and wrote, in his clearest hand, on the outside of the paper on which it was wrapped, "May 27th, 1848. Should I fall in battle, I, the undersigned, beg, as a last favour of those who may find my body, to bury with it the inclosed purse. VINCENZO CANDIA." This done, he put the note for Rose, open, into that for the Signor Avvocato, directed and sealed this last, placed it under his pillow, and went to bed.

The colonel was no early riser, fortunately for Vincenzo; who thus had a pretty long sip of the Lethean waters, even till seven in the morning, when a twofold summons, from the knuckles and the double-bass voice of the occupant of the next room, came to warn him that it was time for him to rise and make ready for departure. The night had not cooled the landlady's interest in the youth, as shown by the substantial breakfast she had provided for him, her constant exhortations to eat heartily, and be of good cheer, and also by sundry greasy parcels, with which she crammed his pockets. Vincenzo was a good deal touched by all this great demonstrativeness, but also a little bored. Of course he did his utmost to veil this, while he gave full vent to his really grateful feelings.

"By-the-by," said Vincenzo, as he was bidding adieu to her, "can you inform me where is the nearest post-office?"

"At the next village," replied the hostess, naming it, "a short quarter of an hour's walk, the third shop after you pass the baker's; you can't help seeing the baker's; it has just been fresh painted. Though, now that I think of it, why not leave your letter with me? The letter-carrier for Ibella passes this way at eleven o'clock every day, and always calls in here. It will be a saving of time, if your letter goes at once to Ibella."

"Thank you very much," said Vincenzo; "but —"

"You may trust it to me, I assure you," insisted the warm-hearted woman. "I would rather go on foot with it to Ibella myself than disappoint you of its being forwarded."

Vincenzo gave her the letter, though with a lingering reluctance; even had he been sure that the letter would be lost, he could not have had the heart to hurt the good soul by any appearance of distrust. By this time Rosinante was at the door, and Don Quixote in the saddle — a few more last thanks and good wishes, and the travellers disappeared in a cloud of dust.

"A thoroughly kind-hearted woman, and a staunch patriot to boot," said the colonel; "I have taken a note of the house and the innkeeper's name; both shall be mentioned to his Majesty the first time I see him. No one does a good turn to Colonel Roganti, but finds, sooner or later, his due reward."

Vincenzo wondered how his chief had managed to discover the landlady's patriotism. As to the goodness of her heart and kindness, no one was better able to bear witness to both than Vincenzo, or more disposed to give her all the credit she deserved.

CHAPTER VIII.

The Signor Avvocato borrows a Stock of Courage from Barnaby.

When, at the close of day, on the Friday of Vincenzo's ill-fated expedition to Ibella, supper-time arrived at the palace, and no Vincenzo was forthcoming, Rose had no other alternative than to state candidly, and unreservedly, the nature of the errand on which the seminarist had gone.

"A fool's errand," observed the Signor Avvocato. "Del Palmetto will only laugh at him and very likely give him a good drubbing into the bargain. I am sorry, Rose, that you are mixed up in this silly affair. How was it you came to think of so absurd a present as a purse for a boy who has no money and wants none?"

"But you see, papa, it isn't always so easy to find out something new to give. Last year I made him a pair of velvet braces, the year before I worked him slippers, and the year before that I embroidered his initials on a pocket-handkerchief, this time I was fairly puzzled what to do."

"Well, well," resumed the father, "I dare say it would have been all the same had you taken it into your little head to provide him with a pair of gloves. It was very wrong and rude of Federico. I have told you more than once not to encourage his familiarity."

"I never have, papa, but you also bid me be civil to him; and when a person you have known all your life, comes to wish you good-bye, before he goes away to fight, it is difficult not to be good-natured."

"Of course, of course, you were right," returned papa, dutifully; "but now, about Vincenzo, we must hope that, having probably found it difficult so see Del Palmetto, he thought it too late to return here, and has been wise enough to go back to the seminary at once. As he had to be there by mid-day to-morrow, he does not lose much of his holiday. He must lay his account, however, to a good lecture for having gone out alone. I am not to blame. I have repeatedly forbidden him ever to do so; he knows, as well as I do, that it is against rule; but I see very well that young fellow will end by getting me into hot water with the authorities. He is beginning to be unsteady, I am sorry to say, very unsteady."

Misgivings about his godson did not apparently weigh much on the godfather's spirits. He ate an excellent supper, slept an unbroken sleep the night through, enjoyed his early walk in his garden, his early chat with his labourers next morning, with as easy a mind as though Vincenzo had been the pearl of seminarists. The owner of the palace was a methodical man, a piece of choice clockwork. He rose every day at seven; walked out till eight, when he had a cup of coffee, which constituted his breakfast; then walked out again till nine. From that hour till eleven he transacted business, received visitors, and gave legal advice. The two hours remaining between that and one o'clock, the dinner hour, he devoted to music, his ruling passion; and any interruption of his musical studies was always peculiarly unwelcome. This regular distribution of his forenoons had undergone some slight modifications of late, since he had been promoted to the honour of being Mayor. Nevertheless, with few exceptions, he had managed so as to banish all the duties of his municipal office until the afternoons. Well, then, the amateur musician had not been ten minutes at his piano, on this particular Saturday, when a tap at the door of his retreat, and an entreating call from Rose, put a stop to the sonata he was trying over.

"Bless my heart! Rose, my dear, come in; what is it?"

"A messenger from the seminary with a letter," said Rose, thrusting in her curly head.

"Well, where is it?"

"The man says he must give it into your own hands, papa," replied Rose.

"Holy patience!" grumbled the Signor Avvocato, going into the passage. The messenger was waiting on the top of the first landing of the stairs that led to the Signor Avvocato's private rooms; the man was a servant belonging to the seminary, and well known by sight to the mayor.

"What news? good, I hope," said the gentleman.

"I should be sorry to be the bearer of any but good, Signor Avvocato," answered the messenger, rather sentontiously, as he delivered the letter. "The reverend principal of the seminary charged me most particularly to place this myself in your own hands. So I hope you will excuse my intrusion; and, if there be any answer, I am here at your service."

"Very good," said Rose's father. "Just step into the kitchen and take some refreshment, while I read the contents of this despatch. Rose, you had better see if the cook is below; if not, send for her."

The style of living was very homely and primitive in the palace, whose inmates abundantly put in practice the hackneyed axiom, that "one is best served by oneself." A host of servants were kept; but they were rarely within reach when wanted — all and each of them having the habit, when not engaged in some special duty, of giving a hand either in the garden, laundry, or dairy, in short, wherever there was at the moment most to do.

The Signor Avvocato returned to his seat before the piano to read his letter, flattering himself that he should be able to resume his sonata in a minute or two; but any such hope died within him, when he beheld the unusual length of the epistle. He rose from the music stool, and, with a jerk of impatience, threw himself on the sofa to master the contents of the despatch, with, at all events, more comfort to his body. The reader needs not be told that the letter contained a summary of Vincenzo's trespasses of the day before, the narration coloured of course by the narrator's opinions. "I see how it is," groaned the Signor Avvocato. "It is written in the book of fate that I am never to have a moment's peace;" and, having thus protested against the interruption, he again fixed his eyes on the catalogue of sins he held in his hand. The last paragraph ran as follows —

"Our spiritual head, the bishop of the diocese, has already had laid before him all the facts, which it has been my painful duty herein to detail for your information. Any ultimate decision rests with his grace; and, in the present state of the affair, it would be presumption in me to enter into conjectures as to the impression his grace is likely to receive, or as to the sentence he may deem it fit to pass on the offender. Still, I feel it almost a Christian duty to prepare you for what (to me) seems inevitable under the circumstances. I allude to the uselessness of any application for the re-admission of your *protégé* into an establishment, which, I regret to say, he has done all in his power to disgrace. You will remark, sir, that I do not even hint at a possible formal decree of expulsion; which, but for the high regard I entertain for your worthy self, would be only a just punishment for so aggravated a fault. One more observation and I have done. Political enthusiasm was the trait we were least prepared to meet with in young Candia's character; but that he is tainted with the newfangled notions of the day can be proved, beyond a doubt, by abundant evidence. Where can he have contracted a bent of mind, pernicious to all, most especially to youth? Not here assuredly, not in our well-ordered peaceful community. But where then? I shall not seek to know; suffice it to say, that those who have fostered and encouraged such a tendency in the lad, have assumed a heavy responsibility. I have the honour to remain, sir, with the highest consideration, etc. etc. your most devoted humble servant."

"*In caudâ venenum,*" said the Avvocato, aloud, and with a bitter smile. "Could I only make sure that *old times* would never return!" The passionate tone in which the words were pronounced, the arm menacingly stretched forth, and the closed fist that struck the empty air, intimated, with infinite clearness, that the Signor Avvocato's blood was up at boiling point. "But I cannot be sure," he added, and the threatening arm fell supine upon the sofa. He pondered a little, went to the window, and called out, "Barnaby — some one send me Barnaby directly." Nor did the Signor Avvocato again seek the comfortable corner of the sofa, but paced uneasily up and down the room. As the staunch confidential servant, or rather faithful friend of his father — as one who had the honour and interests of the family more at heart than even the family themselves — Barnaby was *de jure* the adviser to whom the Signor Avvocato turned in all his difficulties. But it was less for the sake of the old gardener's clear good sense and trustworthiness, than for that of his combativeness, that his master wanted him at this moment. Just as the coward instinctively has recourse to the bottle for courage, so did the master of the palace, stung to the quick, seek the person of all others most certain to spur him on to the system of retaliation, which the feeble-minded gentleman longed to adopt, yet shrunk from. Barnaby, by temperament and habit the despiser and hater of all compromise, ever the prompter and supporter of extreme measures, was the very man for the occasion. Barnaby unfortunately was missing. Barnaby, early that morning, had set out in the open cart and gone nobody knew where. This was what Roso came to tell her father; and so struck was she by his look of disturbance that she asked him if he had had any bad news.

"About as bad as can be," he replied, testily. "Insubordination, drunkenness, riot, profanation, and what not; these are the noble deeds of that precious favourite of yours. You may stare, but I am speaking of no one else than your friend Vincenzo — you have cause to be proud of having such a friend — he is expelled the seminary, as a matter of course. Didn't I tell you, that one of these fine days he would get me into a scrape with the authorities of that nursery of priests?

Well, he has done it now, to his satisfaction, I hope For the sake of that saucy scapegrace, I am bearded, insulted — yes, your father, a gentleman and a magistrate, is made a target for the most injurious imputations — yes, yes, yes, all true; read that, if you are curious to know more of the business;" and, hitting the letter angrily with his knuckles, he gave it to his daughter.

Rose, after she had looked over the obnoxious missive, exclaimed, in great agitation, "And where is Vincenzo now?"

"At Jericho, for aught I know or care," was the testy answer.

"And you really think, papa, that they will not take him back into the seminary?"

"Of course not; they have had enough of him."

"And so he will not be a priest after all," gasped the poor girl in sincere distress.

"There will be no lack of priests, my dear, though he be none. What's the use of crying, child? it won't mend the matter."

But Barnaby, what had become of him all this time? Shortly after eight that morning, he was pruning the ivy and honeysuckle overgrowing the entrance to his young mistress's favourite summer-house, when Lucangelo, the dairy-lad, who went always at dawn of day to Ibella with the surplus milk from the palace, happened to pass in the road beneath on his way home.

"Good day, Lucangelo," said Barnaby; "any news down there?"

Lucangelo was brimming over with news, which he was longing to pour forth. We are already in possession of the staple of it. Signor Vincenzo had been seen the day before making merry with three officers at the Caffè della Posta; and, dressed up as an officer himself, had been drinking and singing, and had finished off by dancing with the cook *coram populo.*

Barnaby pooh-poohed the story as a hoax — there must be a mistake as to the identity, some good-for-nothing wretch had personated Vincenzo. But Lucangelo stuck to his own version of the story as the true one, and gave as his authority a *de visu* witness, one of the maids of the caffè, who had helped to carry the culprit to bed. Notwithstanding which, Barnaby maintained a stout incredulity, and cautioned Lucangelo of the danger of spreading false reports, which might make him liable to be prosecuted for a libel against a member of so powerful an establishment as the seminary.

The moment the dairy-boy disappeared, so did all Barnaby's assumed indifference. He hurried to the stables; in a trice had Blackie in the shafts of the light open cart, and *en route* for Ibella. On reaching the town he drove straight to the Caffè della Posta; and there Battista, an old acquaintance of his, soon made him acquainted with all the particulars of Vincenzo's misadventure.

"A mere boyish frolic, and which ought not to be considered as any serious disgrace to the youth," concluded Battista, too philosophically disposed not to treat the matter lightly, and wishing at the same time to humour the desire of his friend Barnaby to see it lightly treated.

"And where may the young scamp be now?" asked Barnaby.

"More than I can tell," was the answer. "Half an

hour ago he was upstairs in the room where he slept; but now the bird is flown."

"Returned to his penitentiary, do you think?"

"To his what?" asked Battista.

"I mean, do you suppose he is gone back to the seminary?"

Battista shook his head, adding, "My opinion is that he was too down in the mouth for that. However, there's no saying what he may or may not have done. You had better go and see."

Barnaby followed the advice, and, instead of Vincenzo, found the porter, who assailed him with a terrific and graphic description of the missing lamb's trespasses. Barnaby treated the porter and his description with undisguised contempt; and, on the porter concluding his harangue by a declaration that he would rather give up the keys of the establishment than disgrace them by using them to let in that young sinner again, Barnaby clenched his fist, and retorted that he, the porter, was a disgrace, and his infernal jail a disgrace, and the Jesuits who had made it their nest, were a disgrace. Whereupon the two old men were within an ace of coming to blows, when such a catastrophe was warded off by an opportune reflection of Barnaby's — a reflection he duly communicated to his adversary — that vermin such as he was not worthy of a licking from the hands of a Christian.

Barnaby next went to his master's town house, in the faint hope that Vincenzo might have sought a refuge there. Again disappointed, the sturdy old fellow proceeded to call on the commandant of the National Guard, one of the Signor Avvocato's most intimate friends. Finding no tidings of Vincenzo there, he inquired at some of the largest shops to see if any information of the runaway could be obtained in those marts for gossip as well as wares; but no one had seen or heard of the boy. Beaten on all sides, and loth to prolong his own absence, the gardener at length made up his mind to drive back to the palace. No sooner was he within the gates than at least a dozen voices were raised to warn him that the Signor Padrone had been wanting him most particularly for the last hour and a half.

"I thought you were lost too," exclaimed the Signor Avvocato at sight of the familiar bottle-nose and goggle-eyes. "Do you know that—"

"I know everything," said Barnaby, dropping, without ceremony, into a chair, and wiping the sweat-drops of heat and agitation from his face and bald pate, with a bright orange cotton handkerchief; "I am just come from Ibella."

"Has he gone back to the seminary?" asked Rose, anxiously.

"He had wit enough not to do that," answered Barnaby.

"Is it all really true, Barnaby?" questioned Rose.

"True! what?" retorted Barnaby in his crabbedest tone.

"That he has behaved very badly."

"All nonsense and humbug. Pray who says so?" asked Barnaby, standing up and looking defiant.

The young lady was about to speak, when her father stopped her by an admonitory, "Rose! perhaps you will allow me to explain." Then, turning to Barnaby, the Signor Avvocato said, "The fact is, I have had a letter from the principal of the seminary, a letter which contains most serious charges against Vincenzo—of drunkenness, riot, and rebellion to his superiors."

"It is all false," shouted Barnaby; "false, I tell you, from beginning to end. Vincenzo was not drunk — a little excited perhaps, and if he was it was all the Marchesino's doing. Vincenzo's behaviour to the Signor Prefetto was from first to last respectful and dignified. I have had all the particulars from Battista, who waited upon the party. You can go and question him yourself if you please. Vincenzo never spoke one word louder than another. He put on the Marchesino's uniform, it is true; only for a few minutes though, and he was as good as forced to do so. After all, there was no great harm in that. As Battista says, what was it but a mere boyish frolic, and no disgrace to anybody? Now you have the truth, whatever may be in your principal's letter."

"But he mentions there was dancing also," here put in the Signor Avvocato.

"Well, and suppose there was," said Barnaby, "you are not sure that Vincenzo danced, and if he did — Lord, dancing is not murder, is it?"

The Signor Avvocato chose to overlook the lameness of the argument, and said —

"As far as I can make it out, the whole affair is no bigger than a mole-hill; but, looked at through certain glasses, is magnified to the size of a mountain. And it is *à propos* of such a silly matter that the house of a respectable father of a family is to be denounced as a school of anarchy (not a muscle of Barnaby's ugly face stirred; anarchy was not within the circle of his acquaintance), that a man of honour is bespattered with mud!"

This was plain enough, and Barnaby bristled up immediately.

"Who bespatters you with mud?" he asked with an effort to be calm.

"Who? Why the writer of this letter," said the Signor Avvocato, taking it up and reading aloud the offending paragraphs already quoted.

Barnaby tried to speak, but the excess of his emotions choked him, and he spun round and round like a dog running after its tail; at last, when he recovered utterance, he exclaimed —

"And you have not torn that paper to shreds and sent it back to the writer with a damn as big as a house upon it."

"I will not permit you to use such unbecoming language, especially in the presence of my daughter," said the Signor Avvocato, authoritatively. "Rose," and he nodded towards the door. Rose obeyed the mute injunction.

Barnaby, abashed for a second, soon recovered both his anger and his free speech.

"St. Anthony himself, I declare," said he to his master, "would lose his patience with you. I never saw your equal for offering your left cheek when you have had a slap on the right. It's your way to put up, and put up everlastingly, with any kind of treatment, and pray what is the upshot? Why, that you are not respected. Oh! shake your head as much as you like, you are not half as much thought of as you ought to be. Signor Pietro, bless his soul in glory, never sat quiet under an affront, not he indeed; but you! you are not your father's son, you must have been changed in the cradle."

"You talk an infinite amount of nonsense, Barnaby," said the Signor Avvocato. "How do you know I am not going to resent this insolent attack?"

"Well, do it at once, and strike hard while you are about it," said Barnaby, with a partial clearing of clouds from his ugly face; "send a verbal message by me, that's your best way."

"No such thing," replied the master. "With the clearest case of right on our side, you would infallibly manage to put yourself and me in the wrong. You are far too vehement and intemperate of speech, Barnaby. I shall write an answer. Forms ought never to be overlooked between gentlemen."

"I don't pretend to know much about forms," observed Barnaby, his features collapsing into gloom, as he watched the Signor Avvocato sit down to his desk and begin to write. "What I do know is, that a rogue is a rogue, and I call him a rogue. Write strongly at all events; they hit you through Vincenzo, remember, and, form or no form, let them see that you are aware of the fact."

The Signor Avvocato wrote as follows: —

"MOST ILLUSTRIOUS AND REVEREND SIR, — I hasten to acknowledge the receipt of your honoured letter of this day's date. The sad and unlooked-for intelligence it contains about my godson Vincenzo occasions me an astonishment to the full as great as that you express. It seems scarcely credible that a boy, whose conduct hitherto has been rather praiseworthy than otherwise, should of a sudden so egregiously misbehave. However this may be, rest assured, reverend sir, that I shall do my duty by him — I mean, visit him with my severest displeasure. It is due to myself to state, once for all, that I was ignorant of his having left my house for Ibella unaccompanied — a violation of the rules of the seminary against which I have warned him over and over again. As to the extent to which the lad's present prospects may be injured by his offence, I wait with confidence, not presuming to prejudge it, the decision of the competent authority in whose power that decision alone rests. With reference to the charge of political enthusiasm, which you bring against the young pupil in question, allow me to say that I have never perceived in him any bias of the sort, unless you mean by political enthusiasm that sentiment of personal dignity which is becoming in every free citizen, whatever his age, joined to a proper respect for the fundamental laws of his country. In either case it is quite possible, and I am unable to regret that it should be so, Vincenzo may have imbibed some of the notions above mentioned under my roof — the more lucky for him, as such ideas do not apparently form part of the various and highly-useful instruction imparted in your distinguished and respectable establishment.

"Be pleased to accept, most illustrious and reverend sir, the assurance of the high consideration with which I have the honour to be, &c."

The Signor Avvocato read over his letter as if to himself, but yet sufficiently loud to allow Barnaby to learn the contents, sealed it, addressed it, and then consigned it to the messenger from Ibella, with directions to deliver it into the hands of the principal of the seminary, with Avvocato Stella's compliments.

"Only a bit of paper," observed the master, rubbing his hands with satisfaction; "only a little bit of paper, Barnaby, but it carries weight enough to fell an ox."

Barnaby said nothing, but shrugged his shoulders, as if dubious as to that conclusion. Evidently he would have preferred, to the long rigmarole he had just heard read over, to have been allowed to carry a message by word of mouth; he would have taken care to make it more than metaphorically heavy enough to fell an ox.

CHAPTER IX.

Fluctuations in the said Stock of Courage.

The Signor Avvocato sat down to his dinner in high spirits, ate and talked a great deal, and even cut one or two jokes at his daughter's expense. Her rueful looks and pensive demeanour betrayed, indeed, some painful preoccupation. He bade her cheer up. Vincenzo was not likely to play the truant long; people without money could not travel far. He would lay a wager with her that Vincenzo would make his appearance by supper time at latest. Unimaginative Rose was quite of the same opinion as her father. She did not feel the least alarm at Vincenzo's absence, not the least doubt as to his speedy return. She did not even care much how far he had deserved to incur the displeasure of his superiors. What preyed on her mind was the fact that he had incurred it, and the direful corollary of that fact, his being expelled the seminary, and therefore never being a priest. "As to that," observed her father, "nobody could say what the future held in store; the devil was never so black as he was

painted, and then, priest or no priest, Vincenzo would
not lack a friend so long as — ah! well, no use to say
more at present." After this kindly hint the good-
natured gentleman went to his own room, to enjoy his
usual siesta of an hour or so, and then, refreshed by
his nap, he took his hat and cane and sallied forth to
Rumelli. A motion of much importance, to which he
anticipated opposition, and for which he himself would
not have voted but for his official capacity, stood on
the books for that day. The motion was to be that of
sending an address to the king, expressive of the
Rumellians' warm admiration of his Majesty's gallant
conduct at the head of his troops. This, of course,
was tantamount to an approval of the war, which in
his heart of hearts the Signor Avvocato disapproved,
and he was cognizant besides, that the marquis, in
spite of his boasted neutrality, had been actively canvassing against it some of the more timorous councillors.

The Signor Avvocato was still revolving in his
mind the best arguments wherewith to silence the opponents, when he came in sight of the Town Hall, and
descried at the entrance the marquis and three members
of the council in close conference; the marquis, a paper
in his hand, was talking and gesticulating with great
animation. On the mayor's nearing the group, the
marquis strode up to him, saying, "Here is the mayor;
perhaps he has received official news."

"None of any consequence," replied the mayor.
"Are there any new rumours abroad?"

"Yes, indeed, and let us pray God they may not
be true," replied the marquis, "though the channel

through which they have reached me is unexceptionable."

"Well, but what have you heard?" asked the mayor anxiously.

"Nothing less," said the marquis, reading a paragraph from the letter in his hand, "than that an unexpected attack from a body of Austrians issuing from Verona, combined with a vigorous sortie of the garrison of Peschiera, has forced the besiegers to raise the siege and retire in disorder upon Lonato, leaving all their artillery and a number of prisoners in the hands of the enemy."

"Is your letter from the camp?" asked the mayor in as steady a voice as he could command.

"Why, no; but it is from Turin, and I am assured it is a faithful copy of a letter come direct from Lonato."

"Then it is not worth anything as proof," said the mayor reassured; "such news is too unlikely to be true. At the date of the last official bulletin, that is at nine o'clock last evening, all was going on favourably on our side at Peschiera and elsewhere."

"Very true," said the marquis; "but in war, my good sir, and I ought to know something about it, in war a moment suffices to turn the scale."

"The wish is father to the thought," mumbled the mayor to himself as he went up the town-hall steps.

But the marquis's intelligence, authentic or not, had not the less secured the defeat of the address. The councillors were not more willing to discuss it than the mayor to carry it under the circumstances; it was therefore adjourned *nem. con.* Business being thus unexpectedly at an end, and plenty of time at his disposal, it occurred to the Signor Avvocato that he might as well drive to Ibella, and investigate whether there were any grounds for the tidings communicated by the marquis. He accordingly despatched a messenger to the palace with orders for the gig to be sent down to him immediately, and in as short a time as possible the Signor Avvocato was driving to Ibella. "This report," thought he, as he held the whip suspended over Blackie, "though not likely to be true, may prove so, and, if it should, farewell to statuto and mayoralty; we shall have the Austrians instead. I have just hit on the right moment to write that bitter letter to the reverend principal. It was written to be sure under great provocation, but what of that? Not the less shall I have the seminary, and the chapter, and the bishop about my ears, let alone the marquis. A precious fool I was to allow that old firebrand Barnaby to get the better of my judgment. There is nothing for it, if that cursed news be true, except to try and compromise the matter, explain away and soften down somehow or other what I wrote. A bitter pill to swallow it will be; nevertheless, for extreme evils extreme remedies. How that stiff-necked magnate will chuckle in his sleeve! I wish I had more of the devil in me than I have. What can they do to me after all — they can't kill me, nor hurt my daughter, nor take away my estate, nor my money? Ah, who can be sure of that? I am old enough to have seen some pretty proofs of what such people can do when they have the power. At all events, they can rob me of my peace of mind, and what is life worth without peace? No, no struggling; I was not born for it. But the reports may be false." And such, fortunately, was the case.

The account of the raising of the siege of Peschiera was only one among a multitude of hoaxes and falsehoods with which the so-called Austriacanti (Austrian sympathizers) endeavoured to alarm the country, and throw discredit on the Government.

The intendente laughed the mayor out of his fears; they had not an atom of foundation to rest on; nothing could be more cheering than the news from all sides. Peschiera was daily expected to surrender, &c. Whatever might be the issue of the war, the mayor might depend on this, the old regime was for ever annihilated, and so on. The Signor Avvocato breathed freely again, and mentally reconfirmed every syllable of his famous, yet lately deplored, letter. If he had come to make inquiries of the Signor Intendente, it was not that he had been gulled by that arch-codino of a marquis, but simply that he might have some tangible support to deny with authority rumours that unsettled people's minds, created distressing agitation, especially in rural districts like his own. And the droll part of the affair was, that the Signor Avvocato, basing his belief on that one particle of doubt harboured in his mind with which he had reached the Intendenza, was now fully persuaded that he had from the first entirely disbelieved the marquis's information.

"By the bye," said he, when the topic of public news was exhausted, "have you heard of my godson's escapade, and of the ridiculous fuss that has been made about it at the seminary?"

The intendente had heard the story, but told in a

loose unconnected way. The Signor Avvocato, desirous of making the intendente perfectly acquainted with the subject, gave Barnaby's version of the matter, and mentioning the principal's letter, concluded by reciting his own answer, accompanied by a little good-humoured swagger.

"Capital!" said the intendente, laughing; then added, "however, the sooner you make it up the better."

"Catch me doing anything of the kind," said the Signor Avvocato, with a knowing wink.

"Ah! you will have to do so in the end."

"Not so," persisted the Signor Avvocato, glad for once in his life to play the *inexorabilis acer*.

"My dear sir," resumed the Signor Intendente, "he who has to live side by side with a punctilious neighbour had better not be over-punctilious himself. The clergy, my good friend, can do us much good; there's no gainsaying it; also an infinite amount of harm. Make up the quarrel, I say, and do not let personal pique interfere with the boy's career, and with your own comfort. Ten to one the principal is ready to meet you half way. Follow my advice; go and see him."

"Not for worlds," replied our sulky Achilles, who, however, had bethought himself that, as his being in the town would be known to everybody in it, he could not decently avoid paying a visit to the authority on whom Vincenzo's fate depended. "I'll tell you what I will do. I will go and pay my devoirs to his grace."

"That's right," said the intendente, "and pray offer his grace my best respects. If he had us all in an egg, how he would smash us; but, as he is a man of the world, he knows how to adapt himself to circumstances. Tell me first, do you wish me to take any steps with regard to your runaway?"

"Not for the present, thank you. I make sure of finding him at the palace when I return; if not, I will have recourse to you."

The reception given to the Signor Avvocato by the head of the diocese was gracious in the extreme; he was treated with that mixture of amenity and gravity, which is the peculiar accomplishment of the high dignitaries of the Church when they are also men of the world. The bishop said he had had no time as yet to give the case of Vincenzo the full attention it required; the investigation was incomplete, and there were precedents to be consulted. His grace admitted that his first impressions had been strong, and contrary to the culprit; he now hoped, indeed believed he was on the track of some extenuating circumstances — extenuating, he meant, to a certain degree. The best course for the moment, the best for all concerned, particularly for the young Seminarist himself, seemed to his grace — and perhaps the Signor Avvocato would take the same view — the best course seemed to be not to hurry forward any decision, to allow the matter to rest, allow the scandal, for scandal there had been, to die away of itself. The Signor Avvocato might depend on it, that no final sentence would be pronounced without all proper consideration being paid to the personal feelings and personal claims of the lad's worthy patron and godfather.

All that the Signor Avvocato could extricate from this maze of compliments, hints and reticences, was, that there was no intention of proceeding to extremities, and that after a little more see-sawing, Vincenzo would be received back into the seminary. A belief which sent the good gentleman home in very high spirits, so greatly elated indeed, that he drove straight to the Town Hall of Rumelli, and then and there made the town-clerk write and send orders of convocation to the councillors, for eight o'clock the next morning. On which occasion, after a spirited speech from the mayor, the motion for the address to his Majesty was carried unanimously by storm.

It was in the frame of mind incident on such a victory, followed, first by an excellent dinner, and then by a full hour of sound sleep, that Vincenzo's epistle found his godfather; and certainly no letter, especially one containing a confession of guilt, ever arrived with better chances of a favourable reception.

"Ha! ha!" exclaimed Rose's father, seating himself comfortably in a capacious arm-chair; "the dutiful runaway condescends at last to give us some news of his important self. Let us see what he says; here's an inclosure for you, Rose, some mighty serious communication, no doubt; there take it, my dear; ah! dated midnight, the goblin hour; place unnamed. So the young man is skulking, is he — we'll see who tires first."

"Papa! papa!" cried Rose, clapping her hands; "only think the purse is found — he has got it; I am so glad."

"Delighted for your sake, my dear;" said papa, reading aloud. "Most illustrious sir, and revered godfather —"

"But I don't understand what follows," interrupted Rose.

"Nor I," assented papa, after having perused the passage, alluding to the possible ultimate disposal of the purse, in the note to Rose. "Some down-right nonsense to which I have not the key, Rose."

"Why does he say," continued Rose, "if I am to meet you no more? Does he mean to stay away for ever?"

"Who knows?" said the Signor Avvocato; "but now, Rose, my child, let me go on with my own letter;" and, having obtained silence, he read on, every now and then giving vent to his varied feelings by such comments as these: "Ah! truth will out; a little excited forsooth — beastly drunk he means; why, he even allows he was so far gone as to have no distinct recollection in the morning of what had taken place the evening before. *Habemus reum confessum*, as we say in law; most repentant, of course, heartily ashamed, of course, and well he may be." Here came another dip into the letter, and then another annotation; "It is only fair to say that no one could accuse himself with a better grace or in a better style. I had no idea, upon my word, that the boy could write so well. I hope he had no prompter." Here, he stopped and read on a few lines. "Ah! we are coming at last to the kernel of the affair — here's an open declaration that he will not take orders."

"Not take orders!" repeated Rose, with something like a groan.

"No; he flatly refuses to do so. He says, he studied for the Church, out of obedience to his father; but that he never felt any decided vocation, and the little inclination he had is now gone; and he shrinks from the awful duties and responsibilities of the priesthood. Well, sir, I understand, and appreciate your scruples; but why not have made them known sooner — when your father died, for instance? No one wished to force you to enter the Church; now it seems to me too late to change — what else can you do to earn an honest penny, unless you go back to the spade, and your hands are grown too soft for that sort of work. Let us see what he says next: hm! hm! hm! By heaven! the boy is gone crazy," all at once shouted the Signor Avvocato. "Can you guess what he has done, Rose?"

"What is it, papa?" cried Rose.

"Why, enlisted as a soldier, and is off to join the troops before Peschiera."

"Off to fight? And suppose he is killed," exclaimed Rose, in blank terror.

"Well, if he is killed, if he is killed;" kept on muttering the elderly gentleman, sorely tempted, yet unwilling to wind up his phrase with a "serve him right." He did refrain, however, and said instead, "First of all, Rose, all who go into battle are not killed; and secondly, some time must elapse before he is sent into action; he must go through some amount of drilling, and we may be able to get him back before the worst happens."

"Oh yes! do, dear papa, send after him directly;" was Rose's eager answer.

"To send is easy enough, my dear; whether he will be given up to us is not so certain," returned the Signor Avvocato. "In a legal point of view, to be sure, he being a minor, and unauthorized by me, his guardian, so to say, the enlistment ought not to stand good; but at a moment like this, when soldiers are so much needed, legality is a poor shield. Whatever else is doubtful, one thing is as clear as daylight to me, and that is, this dear godson of mine is born to be my plague. Do what you will to do to your neighbour as you would be done by, be liberal to your tenants, respect the laws, it is all in vain as far as your own tranquillity is concerned. Turn which way you will, some new buffet is ready for you. Rose, give over crying, like a good girl, and go and send Barnaby here."

While Rose was away on this errand her father continued his reflections in the form of a monologue. "Much depends on what sort of a man this Colonel Roganti is; in all likelihood, a martinet, who has but one idea in his head, discipline, swears by discipline, knows of no other reason except discipline, can't follow any argument save one that enforces discipline. Fancy that hop o' my thumb taking it into his head to turn soldier, as if he were a man! Why, one of those big Croats could swallow the whole of him at one mouthful. Be a soldier, indeed! you'll soon find out to your cost what soldiering means, my fine fellow, if I don't succeed in extricating you from this scrape. And try I must, for I should not like any harm to happen to the boy; I can't help caring for him, though he does worry me to death with his vagaries! I never dreamt of his having such a spirit, not I. What pluck in a boy of seventeen! of all things in man or boy, I admire pluck most, perhaps, because I haven't an overplus of it myself. He comes of a brave stock, Master Vincenzo; his father, before he fell ill, was the boldest man alive; he would have faced the devil himself."

Here Rose again made her appearance, bringing with her Barnaby.

"Ah! well, Barnaby, you have heard the news, I suppose. What may be your opinion of this new freak of our scapegrace, eh?"

It formed an essential part of Ugly-and-Good's philosophy never to evince surprise at any occurrence, nay, to take for granted that, whatever happened, he had foreseen it; a power of divination which dwindled away in the present case, under a vigorous cross-questioning from his master, into his having for a length of time past conjectured that Vincenzo had something on his mind.

"Yes, the determination to plague us all to death, that's what he had on his mind," said the Signor Avvocato, fretfully. "I can see that clearly enough now myself — but that is nothing to the purpose; the question is, what is best to be done to remedy the evil? What do you advise, Barnaby?"

"Advise, indeed! What's the use of advising when one is sure the advice won't be taken?"

"How do you know that?" asked the Signor Avvocato, in a persuasive tone. "Speak out, man."

"Well, then, my advice is," answered Barnaby, roughly, "let him go and be a soldier."

"Oh! Barnaby," cried Rose, half-reproachfully, half-entreatingly. "Or," went on the old gardener, "send after him, and get him back; but only if you mean to give up that nonsense of making him wear a black robe."

"Oh! Barnaby," again cried Rose, this time in the tone of a child deprived of a favourite toy.

"Allow me to tell you," said the Signor Avvocato, "that you are wandering from the question."

"Not a bit, not a bit," stoutly affirmed Barnaby.

"Really," said the master of the palace, "there is no discussing any subject with you, Barnaby. You are too despotic."

"Of course I am, when I see but one right way," retorted Barnaby. "I tell you that Vincenzo is not of the stuff of which priests are made. I tell you he has been pining these six years to confess as much to you himself, and has never dared to do so. You are not bound to follow my advice, you know. You are master, and I am man. Send him to the seminary again, and see what will come of it:" and so saying, with a grotesquely awkward flourish of his right hand, Barnaby walked towards the door.

"Be so good as to send Giuseppe to me," said the Signor Avvocato. Barnaby stopped, turned round, and asked almost defiantly, "What for, sir?"

Giuseppe, be it known, was a very intelligent young man of the neighbourhood, now in the Signor Avvocato's employ, and who had *de facto* superseded Barnaby in the management of the estate. Barnaby was extremely jealous of Giuseppe.

"What for?" repeated the Signor Avvocato. "I intend to send him to Novara. Vincenzo must not be forsaken."

"Nor shall he, so long as —" gasped forth the irascible old gardener, who had recourse to his usual panacea of two or three circles — dog-fashion, to recover his utterance; "nor shall he, as long as Barnaby Mele has a leg to stand upon. No one goes to Novara, mind that, sir, but me." The goggle eyes, twisted towards his nose, were full of threats. "I'll have Blackie in the cart in a moment;" and the old fellow, waiting for no answer, limped briskly away.

"Holy patience!" bawled the Signor Avvocato. "Where are you going? Stop, I tell you."

"Do you mean to prevent my going to Novara?" roared back Barnaby.

"You shall go, you shall go, but not in such a hurry, before one has had time to think of what is best to be done. Let's suppose you reach Novara safely, and find this Colonel Roganti — Vincenzo says the colonel has his head-quarters there — well, how can you make sure of gaining access to him, unless you have some letter of introduction?"

"Never you fear," said Barnaby; "let me alone for managing that."

"Wait a little," said the master; "granted that you do make your way to the colonel's presence, what authority will you be able to produce, so as to make good your claims to Vincenzo?"

"Authority!" repeated Barnaby, scornfully; "I'll show him authority enough, I warrant me."

"Old goose, I'll tell you what you will do — pick a quarrel, make a mess of the business, and get sent to prison for your pains."

Barnaby laughed outright. "Let them try, that's all."

The Signor Avvocato pondered a little, then said, "I have it. I'll give you a letter to the Intendente of Ibella; the Intendente of Ibella will give you a line or two to the Intendente of Novara; and, when you arrive there, go straight to the Intendenza, and do nothing until you receive directions from the Intendento himself, and abide entirely by what he advises, and no mistake, mind. Now you may go and get the horse ready while I write my letter."

Half an hour after this stormy debate, Blackie was trotting at a round pace to Ibella, with Barnaby and the Signor Avvocato's despatch.

CHAPTER X.

Continuation of the Experiences of a Raw Recruit.

To judge by the employment of his first day's pilgrimage with his young recruit, Colonel Roganti was in no hurry to bring his corps up to the effective force of twelve thousand men, nor did he even seem very well to know what he was about, so ambiguous and contradictory proved his movements. Contrary, in fact, to the programme he had himself arranged, of stopping and addressing an audience at the next village — the village of the baker's newly painted shop, if you remember, he hurried through and past it, alleging as a reason for so doing, the scanty number of people to be seen out of doors (an allegation broadly belied by the evidence of Vincenzo's eyes), and the consequent advisability of making for another place, not far off, which he named, and where their exertions were likely to have more success.

They accordingly pushed on towards this new station, and had not gone far, when the sound of horses' hoofs made itself heard in their rear, and on looking back they saw two mounted carabineers, riding slowly in the direction they were themselves going. Vincenzo recollected having noticed, in the village he and his leader had just left, these two personages, conspicuous by their tri-coloured plume — for, being Sunday, they were in full uniform — and he wondered why, in passing, they should give the colonel so broad a stare. They said nothing however, and went their way. Probably, the two police-soldiers had their reasons for taking so close a survey of so queer looking a figure as Colonel Roganti was; and only a few months previously they would not have rested contented with only bestowing on him a look of curiosity, but infallibly demanded his papers, or otherwise constrained him to give an account of himself. As it was, the police had received such strict injunctions to avoid giving cause for complaint by any unnecessary interference, that now, in nine cases out of ten, where there were grounds for interfering, they chose to abstain, to the great convenience and gratification of swindlers and humbugs. A change of political system inevitably brings with it a slackening in the action of the police; when a worn-out lock is being replaced, the door must perforce remain open a while.

The meeting with the carabineers either coincided with, or was the occasion of, a new modification in the colonel's plans. After some remarks as to the great heat of the day, he turned out of the road into a plantation of mulberry-trees, and, leaving Rosinante to graze in peace, laid himself down in the shade, and bade his young comrade do the same — the sun was overpowering, he observed, and he was unwilling to overtask the strength of his young chaplain. Vincenzo protested alike against this carefulness and the appellation conferred on him — he was not afraid of the sun, and he was both able and willing to go on, he replied; and, further, he had enlisted as a soldier, and not as a chaplain.

"True," said the colonel, "and the more's the pity — such a comfortable berth as I had in my eye for you; little to do, high pay, and the most dainty feeding."

"Those are not the things I am in search of," said Vincenzo, a little piqued.

"Very well; you shall have your own choice. Nor do I contest your willingness or ability for a further march — only permit me to regulate the use of your powers to the best of my experience. I ought to know something of what men can do. I have trained more soldiers than I have hairs on my head and chin — and you see I am neither bald nor beardless," wound up the speaker, with a pull at his thick beard.

Without being absolutely true in so far as the present halt was concerned, neither was the plea of its being made out of regard for his young companion absolutely false: the degree of rascality to which the *soi-disant* colonel had attained did not exclude a certain dose of considerateness for other people, especially when useful to him. Truly the man was more of a bungler than a villain; and, had there been more equilibrium between his very capacious appetites and his means of satisfying them, there are many chances that he would have turned out a harmless, if not a reputable, member of society. Whereas, having been born poor, and lacking the industry or the good luck to raise his means up to the height of his wants, and likewise the inclination to bring his wants down to a level with his scanty means, he had had to draw upon his wits to fill up the deficit; and, after an adventurous career both in his own country and abroad, now a soldier in Charles Albert's army, now a partisan of Dom Pedro in Portugal or of Queen Isabella in Spain, here he was, neither richer nor wiser, taking advantage of the war of independence to make out of it a dishonest penny.

The colonel in a few minutes was snoring gloriously; and Vincenzo, tired of keeping watch over the uncouth form stretched by his side, yielded little by little to the influence of example and of the hour, and fell soundly asleep — for how long neither he nor his companion, on awaking, could exactly determine, neither of them possessing any more precise guide to go by in the computation of time than the position of the sun, which was unluckily just then concealed by a dense mass of black threatening clouds. "We shall have rain before long," said the colonel, getting into his saddle, "so let us push on briskly; a hospitable roof will be welcome, and I think I know of one not far distant."

They went on at a smart pace, Vincenzo most determinedly keeping up with the horse, even occasionally getting a-head of Rosinante, and drinking in with delight the gusts of cool wind which precede a storm. By and bye, large drops of rain began to fall, which in another quarter of an hour thickened into a downright pour, and soon turned the ankle-deep bed of dust on the road into an adhesive compound, out of which our poor pedestrian had no small difficulty to pull his feet. Seeing this dilemma, the colonel bade Vincenzo mount behind him and take hold of his belt; and then the sorry nag was urged to its quickest canter, and in less than half an hour deposited his double burden, wet to the skin, under the porch of a large house. The hospitable roof alluded to by Roganti, who, it seemed, knew the country well, proved this time, contrary to Vincenzo's expectation, not an inn, but a mansion of good appearance.

The hymn of Pio Nono, which the two men began immediately to sing, attracted into the porch a bevy of children, whose joyful shouts and noisy footsteps had already given notice of some merry game going on within the house. At sight of the hirsute man there was a hush of the busy tongues, and unmistakable signs of uneasiness were manifested by the little band, especially when the object of their incipient fear motioned towards them with his hat, and gave a most winning grin. Indeed, this pantomime determined the speedy retreat of the foremost members of the infantine troop, and would in all likelihood have cleared the porch of them all in a twinkling, had not a young lady, probably an elder sister, made her appearance in time to reassure the troubled spirits, and afford a rallying point to which the little ones flocked, like a brood of chickens to a mother-hen.

The colonel bowed low, the palm of his right hand on the red cross on his left breast, in token of allegiance to the young chatelaine. "Caught in the rain, I see," said the lady; "come in, and dry your clothes. Is that — your horse?"

She put the query with a little hesitation, as if at some loss to reconcile the possession of such a luxury with the humble mien and more than modest accoutrement of the persons before her. The reader must be aware that an abundant fall of rain on the thick coating of dust, gracing the original not very brilliant apparel

on the back of our wayfarers, would stamp on tunic
and cassock a variety of zebra-like arabesques, not
at all improving to their appearance. The Calabrese
hat and the three-cornered one, battered in and dripping
like sieves, looked pitiful and ludicrous in the extreme.

"My old and faithful companion on many a battle-
field," answered the colonel, patting the animal. "I
am an old soldier, covered with scars, almost a cripple,
as you may perceive," continued the speaker, limping
along with difficulty after his conductress, "and I could
not do without his help."

"We'll see presently that your faithful companion
is properly taken care of," said the young lady, ushering the colonel and Vincenzo into a large parlour
on the ground-floor. "Louis, run for Janet, and tell
her to bring some faggots." The curly-headed boy
entrusted with the message galloped away, astride of a
walking-stick, and presently Janet appeared with a
bundle of faggots, which in a few seconds were blazing
and crackling on the wide hearth.

"Sit down here and dry yourself," said the young
lady to the elder of the two travellers, placing a chair
for him in front of the fire, "there's nothing so bad for
old wounds, I know, as getting wet."

Colonel Roganti, offering a profusion of thanks,
did as she bid him. Vincenzo went and stood by him,
and the young lady disappeared, followed by all the
little fry — to return shortly after with a bottle of
wine and two glasses on a tray, and all the little fry
at her heels.

"Take a glass of wine, it will do you good," she
said, handing one to the colonel; "and you also," she

added, offering another to Vincenzo. The colonel rose up with a tottering movement — he had become strangely shaky since he had mentioned his old wounds, and the being a cripple — flourished his glass to his gracious hostess, and emptied it at a gulp. Vincenzo scarcely put his lips to his.

"Now I'll go and see that your horse is stabled and fed," said the young lady; and away she went, the children clattering after her. The zeal and the little self-importance with which she played her part of mistress of the house clearly indicated that the duty had but newly devolved upon her, and that probably only for a time. The travellers availed themselves of this moment of privacy to give their clothes the benefit of the drying action of the fire, and to rub off tunic and cassock as much of the compound of dust and water which encrusted them as the means at their disposal, viz. their hands and handkerchiefs, allowed. Janet, bringing in wherewith to lay the table for their dinner, caught them thus employed, and compassionately invited them to follow her into the next room, which proved to be the laundry. There they found all that was necessary for their own ablutions, and the cleansing of their clothes.

The table was spread when they returned to the parlour, and a plentiful repast was shortly after served, to which they both did ample justice. A curly black head reconnoitred now and then their doings from the open door, but infallibly vanished at the slightest attempt of the long-bearded guest to entice it to his side by bland smiles and words. The meal had been ended some time, when a handsome pale-faced lady, about forty years of age, entered the room, leaning on

the arm of the young girl who had hitherto done the
honours of the house. The pale lady immediately sat
down, and her young companion, evidently her daughter
pouring into a plate the contents of a small basket full
of cherries, distributed some among the little flock in
her train, and placed the rest before the colonel and
Vincenzo.

"I hope you have not far to go," said the elderly
lady, addressing the colonel.

"No," replied he, "only to —," naming a place
which was not Novara.

"I am glad to hear it," resumed she; "for your
companion seems very young and delicate to travel on
foot in this heat. Your son, I imagine?"

"Yes, my — adopted son," answered the colonel,
adding something in so low a voice that Vincenzo
could not catch what he said, but which elicited from
the lady a sympathetic ejaculation of "poor boy!" and
a look full of interest at Vincenzo.

"Do you belong to the army?" inquired the lady.

"Why, yes — and no. I am now on the retired
list," said the colonel, in a faltering voice.

"My husband is in the army," went on the lady,
with a little pride; "he is just now under the walls of
Peschiera. It is rumoured that the surrender of the
garrison is about to take place. Have you heard any
later news?"

"I have no doubt of the surrender," said Roganti;
"it is an infinite sorrow to me not to be there; alas!
the spirit is willing, but the flesh weak; I am but the
shell of a man, a cripple," and, as if to give evidence
of the fact, he rose and began a tottering walk. Vincenzo blushed to the whites of his eyes.

"Poor man! don't fatigue yourself," urged the lady; "pray sit down again."

"Thank you, madam, but we must be moving; the weather has cleared up, and it is growing late; we have still a good bit of road to get over before sunset."

"Take another glass of wine, while the horse is getting saddled," pressed the kind lady. The colonel complied with alacrity, and then offered his thanks for the hospitality he and his companion had received, in somewhat bombastic phrases. Vincenzo modestly and simply expressed the gratitude he felt. "A good journey, and God bless you," said the lady to him, as, at the colonel's bidding, he walked away first. Roganti loitered behind a minute or two in close and confidential conference with the lady, received something from her, which he put into his pocket with another flowery speech, and then hopped to the porch, where, with no end of grimaces meant to express acute pain, he, by the help of a stable-boy, succeeded at last in perching himself on the tall Rosinante, and set off, stared at by the crowd of urchins.

The horseman with Vincenzo following, had not gone forty steps down the avenue, when a clear young voice called to them to stop, and the young lady, running up to them out of breath, slipped a tiny parcel into Vincenzo's hand, saying, "This is for you, from mamma," and darted away again. The act had been so instantaneous, and Vincenzo taken so by surprise, that he had neither the time nor the presence of mind to ask for any explanation, or even to say "thank you."

"What may that be?" asked the colonel, with an eager look at the small round packet.

"Money," said Vincenzo, taking off the paper, and turning scarlet as he saw a five-franc piece.

"All right; give it to me," said the colonel, stretching forth his hand; "it is intended as an offering to the sacred cause."

"But the signorina said it was for me from her mother," observed Vincenzo; "what could make her say so? To me, the gift seems rather like an alms-giving."

"How obtuse you are, my lad; the lady's wish that her contribution for the holy war should pass through your hands, only marks her appreciation of your youth and gentle bearing; it is as much as to say, I give this mite in consideration of that brave boy; it is a highly complimentary act, don't you see? Give it to me, I say."

"Here it is," said Vincenzo, handing the piece of money to his chief. "I never for a moment thought of appropriating it; I don't like compliments of a certain sort; I am a soldier and not a beggar."

"What nonsense you talk," said the colonel. "Instead of being thankful to those two ladies —"

"My heart is full of gratitude towards them," interrupted the youth; "they meant it all in kindness, and God bless them for it; but I say it is unfortunate that anything in your tone or bearing should have led them to such a misconception of our situation, as to suggest or encourage alms-giving."

"I encourage alms-giving!!" cried Roganti, putting both his hands to his temples. "I, Colonel Roganti, the most independent man in the world!"

"Why, then," pursued Vincenzo, with increasing animation; "why, then, not state frankly who you are, and the mission in which you are engaged? Why, instead of doing so, deny your belonging to the army, and say that you are on the retired list? Why describe yourself as a cripple, and walk like one —?"

"Stop, sir, I must call you to order," cried the man on the horse, in a would-be authoritative tone. "Subordination is the first requisite in a soldier; I have told you that already, explained to you that, without subordination, you can never make a soldier worth his salt. I have already warned you, sir, and I warn you again once for all, you must take it for granted that all I say or do, however it may sound or look according to your unripe judgment, is for the good of the country, and for the triumph of the great cause. What can you know of the motives of a man like me; you, a stripling, without a hair on your chin? How dare you scrutinize, still more criticize, the behaviour of one, your superior in age, station, and experience? Suppose my mission is not only a military, but a political one? Suppose that I have a part to play, and must appear what I am not, in order to watch and confound treason? Suppose that I am on the track of a conspiracy, to break the neck of which I must for a while put aside the boldness of the lion for the cunning of the serpent? Suppose all this, and then say who is right and who is wrong? Well for you, my dear boy, that I have taken quite a fancy to you, and that I condescend to afford explanations where I could, and ought to give orders; well for you, I say, or the words you spoke just now might have cost you dear, very dear." And the crafty humbug, after this tirade, wrapt himself in a cloud of offended majesty.

Vincenzo was too young and too imaginative not to be imposed upon by those eternal rulers of even grown-up mankind, big words; and the political mission, the treason, and the cunning of the serpent, fell on his ears and mind with the weight of mighty arguments. Besides, his organ of veneration, which was particularly developed, ill accommodated itself to, nay, shrank from, the supposition of deceit in one so much his elder; the more so as, in his innocence, Vincenzo saw no plausible motive for that deceit. What possible interest, in fact, could the colonel have, so reasoned the youth, to drag after him an expensive incumbrance in the shape of a friendless, penniless boy, unless it was, as he had affirmed from the first, to befriend a victim of the Jesuits, as he wrongly assumed the boy to be, and to secure one more arm to fight for the liberty of the country?

With these and such-like reflections Vincenzo strove to rub off his mind the stratum of distrust created by the late occurrences, and to reduce his misgivings *ad absurdum* — a task in which he succeeded but tolerably, the colonel's mysterious whisper in the ear of the pale lady, and the "poor boy," together with the look which followed that exclamation, standing in the way of a complete acquittal. Yet, disturbed in his mind as he was, Vincenzo was far from feeling unhappy — could not feel so; quite the contrary. The keen interest he took in all he was seeing, the agreeable excitement he derived from the novelty of his situation, and of the scenery, left him no leisure or disposition to dwell upon his causes of uneasiness. The azure expanse of the sky, the wide horizon, the setting sun tipping with gold the tall elms bordering the road, the verdure, the song of the birds, the cows in the pasture, the mere fact of moving freely about, proved to the young wayfarer so many sources of lively enjoyment.

The landscape through which he journeyed had no pretensions to be picturesque — an immense plain with scarcely perceptible undulations, giving the idea of a green and yellow sea, with fleets of innumerable mulberry-trees at anchor, and bounded to the north by a very rocky coast, the Alps. But then the vegetation was so vigorous, the shades of green so rich and various, every leaf, every blade of grass gleamed so fresh and glossy in the sun after the shower, the festoons of vine hung so gracefully from tree to tree, the newly-mown hay scented the air so deliciously, that the looker-on must be fastidious indeed, and happily for himself Vincenzo was not so, whose heart did not dilate at the sight of such smiling plenty and luxuriant vegetation.

The night was fast closing in, when, after a stage of three good hours and a half our pair of travellers stopped for refreshment and rest at a small inn at the entrance of a village. Here the hymn to Pio Nono was again sung, the toast and the patriotic speech again delivered, the sale of prints and scapularies attempted as usual, with little or no change from the programme of the previous evening, but with a very different result in so far as related to the collection of money. The company was scanty, and, worse than that, unsympathising; the landlord surly and taciturn, and, to judge from appearances, anything but inclined to become the recipient of those charming confidences about a young orphan, victim of the Jesuits, those confidences which had melted the heart of that model landlady of yesterday, and had been requited with excellent accommodation for the love of God. So, after smoking a pipe in silent dudgeon, the colonel went early to bed, and so did his acolyte.

CHAPTER XI.

A Colonel Unhorsed.

VARIETY not being the *forte* of Colonel Roganti, and indeed his present trade admitting but of little change, we give up the ungrateful task of following him step by step, and of registering his tricks during the interval which separated the Sunday when we left him from the Tuesday, when we find him again. We will only note *en passant*, that twenty-four hours more of partnership with and close observation of his long-legged leader, had intensified to an alarming degree Vincenzo's surmises that the man was not playing fair, and was not what he gave himself out to be. Even green and inexperienced Vincenzo had come at last to feel, that the obsequious, nay, beggarly ways of the *soi-disant* colonel, were irreconcilable with the character of a true soldier. And as to the recruiting scheme, it was evidently a sham, a something used as a blind; how otherwise explain the fact, that not once had the man, either by word or deed, made any allusion to it before any of the audiences he always managed to collect round them both? How was it to be known that he was desirous of enlisting soldiers, unless he said so? All that he seemed to care to be understood was, that he had scapularies for sale, and thankfully received voluntary contributions for the war. All this looked like imposition, like sheer begging under pretence of patriotism, a begging to which Vincenzo had no inclination to lend himself.

Such were the thoughts fermenting in the ex-Seminarist's young brains on the Tuesday morning. Why then not part company at once with the man he so strongly suspected? Was he afraid of throwing himself on the world, far from his home, penniless amid strangers? Not in the least. Vincenzo was perfectly aware that he was not yet so far from Rumelli as to be out of range of his godfather's influence; he was perfectly sure, that he had only to pronounce the Signor Avvocato's respected name, to procure for himself both protection and the means of returning home. Had the case even been different, Vincenzo had self-reliance enough to have set forth alone, trusting to Providence to raise up help for him.

What deterred him from immediately quitting Roganti, was the not being quite certain that Roganti was an impostor; it was the fear of wronging a man who might be innocent, and who had been kind to him in his way; in a word, it was conscientiousness, that great weak point of honest people, and which puts them at such an enormous disadvantage in their transactions with the wicked, who have none of that incommodious appendage. To extricate himself from the dilemma of either giving offence without any due cause, or countenancing fraud, Vincenzo, after long meditation, lighted upon a *mezzo termine*, and this was that he would submit his difficulty to the intendente of the first town they should enter. (Up to that day, whether from chance or design, Vincenzo's leader had never even passed through one.) Any intendente would probably know, or, if he did not already know, would have the power at once to discover, whether or not there was indeed a Colonel Roganti in the army, whose head-quarters were at Novara, etc. Vincenzo would decide according to the result of the inquiry.

The question might be put, it was true, to the mayor of the first village they came to; but with less chance of obtaining a solution than from an intendente, who is a central authority, with plenty of *employés* about him, and a police under his orders. Another reason for Vincenzo preferring the latter course was, that knowing, as he did, the intendente of Ibella, he could make use of that gentleman's name as a sort of introduction, and thus gain admittance more easily to the great man's presence. There still remained the knotty point of how to elude the colonel's strict surveillance. As to that, no course of action could be planned beforehand; all must depend on circumstances. Vincenzo must be ready to take advantage of them.

Having thus eased his mind, our young man prepared himself with a lighter heart for the labours of the day. It was only seven o'clock in the morning of the said Tuesday, when the colonel took up a position on horseback, in front of the inn where he had passed the night, and began operations. To account for a crowd of people thronging the village at so early an hour, and on a week day, we must say that a cattle fair was to be held there. The colonel was not the man to neglect so good an opportunity of letting the hymn be heard, or of making a little speech and puffing his scapularies. The hymn, the speech, and the scapularies succeeded so amazingly well with the numerous throng they attracted, and the harvest of pence proved so encouraging, that, forgetful, or maybe ignorant, of Horace's *non bis in idem*, the speculator yielded to the obvious temptation of trying his luck once more; that is, giving such well-disposed individuals the benefit of a second performance. Accordingly, a couple of hours or so later, he presented himself in front of another inn, or rather wine-shop, at the other end of the village, and was soon the centre of attraction to another numerous gathering.

Now, as the colonel's evil star would have it, there happened to be among the crowd a horse-dealer, one who furnished the neighbourhood with horses, and accommodated his customers by allowing them to pay by instalments. Well, to see Rosinante, and to identify him as the very same animal he had not two months back sold to a brother-in-law, who lived up in the hills, was for this horse-dealer one and the same thing. So, without preamble, he elbowed his way through the throng up to the colonel, and apostrophised him thus —

"By your leave, my good fellow, I should like to know how you came by that animal."

The colonel looked daggers at the questioner, and retorted angrily, "What business is it of yours?"

"Softly, my friend," said the horse-dealer, in a quiet voice. He was a stalwart man of about forty, and of very conciliating manners; but with an eye which told plainly enough that he might be a dangerous customer on occasions. "Softly, my friend; you needn't put yourself in a passion, nor be insolent neither, my good sir. My business with the horse is clear enough, and here it is in two words. I sold the horse you are on, a very short time ago, to my brother-in-law who lives at Racorno. I saw him only last Sunday, and he was then well contented with his bargain, and had no idea, I am sure, of parting with it; and that is the reason why I wonder to see you bestriding it. It may be that my brother changed his mind, and that you came by the beast honestly enough; but it may be also that you came by it otherwise — and —"

"'Take care how you impeach the character of an honourable man;" interrupted the colonel, in a loud voice, and looking as big as he could; "if you do, you must take the consequences; there are laws to punish defamation, sir."

"I know that," replied the other, without losing his composure; "and if I am wrong, I shall be ready to make you all possible amends. But one thing at a time. Just now have the goodness to come with me to the mayor; if you are a true man, you can have no objection. Do you know if the mayor is at home?" asked he, turning to the bystanders. Being answered in the affirmative, the horse-dealer grasped Rosinante by the bridle, and said to the rider, "Now then, let us go and settle the matter before the mayor; I just ask to be satisfied about the horse, nothing more. What do you say, good folks," continued he, addressing the crowd; "do I require anything unreasonable?"

Of course the crowd shouted with one voice that he was right. Besides being generally respected, the speaker had many a personal acquaintance among the present, not a few of whom, by the way, were in arrears with him, and naturally anxious to propitiate him.

The colonel, who had by this time doffed a portion of his arrogance, here said, deprecatingly —

"Would there be anything very extraordinary in my having hired the animal?"

"Why not?" said the other; "you may also have paid well for the loan of it; but excuse me for saying, that as I haven't the honour of knowing you, I must decline believing you on your unattested word. You can explain it all to the mayor, and if the mayor decides in your favour, well, I will abide by his decision, and make you an apology for distrusting you. I will even do more, I'll pay you a compensation. Can I offer more fairly?" added he, appealing to the chorus.

A volley of "Yes," "True," "Fairly spoken," and so on gave an unmistakable intimation that the chorus shared the sentiments of the horse-dealer.

"Well, let us be moving," said the plaintiff to the defendant, giving a shake to the bridle by way of a gentle hint. Thus driven to the wall, the colonel had nothing for it but to dismount, and with an escort more numerous than agreeable, proceed to the mayor's. Vincenzo, who had anxiously watched the various phases of this incident, silently accompanied his leader, trying now and then, by sidelong glances at the face of that personage, to anticipate the probable issue of the approaching investigation. The colonel caught one of these furtive glances, and said in an undertone, as if in answer, "I am the victim of a plot, artfully contrived by my enemies, who are also the enemies of my king and country; you slip away quietly and get out of the scrape — do, follow my advice."

Vincenzo hesitated for a moment, but the chivalrous part of his nature asserted itself, and he replied, "I'll stand by you if you are innocent. I have done no harm, and I have nothing to fear."

"You can do me no good; go," was the hasty rejoinder, as they were entering the mayor's house.

The mayor was an intelligent-looking farmer, a man probably of fifty years of age, who no sooner heard the nature of the charge than he recollected having that very morning received from the intendenza two letters relating to two cases of horse-stealing. "Go, some one of you, and fetch them," said the mayor; "the town-clerk is at the town-hall, and knows where they are." Ten messengers started at once, and the letters were produced in no time. One of them, in fact, referred to a horse, the description of which tallied exactly with Rosinante; the said horse had been hired for twenty-four hours by a tall long-bearded man, etc. etc., so long ago as the Monday before the last, and never returned to its owner, Paolo Sappi, of Racorno, the identical brother-in-law of the horse-dealer.

Roganti admitted the fact, but stoutly denied any intention of theft — in spite of his best wishes, urgent business had prevented his sending back the horse at the time agreed; but he was ready, and always had intended to pay for the extra time he had kept it.

The mayor exhorted him to reserve his explanations and defence for the justice of peace of the next town, whither he would be conveyed as soon as the carabineers should pass that way on their round. In the meantime, he ordered some national guards, then present out of uniform, to march off the accused to the town-hall, and to see that he did not make his escape. The case thus being disposed of, and the colonel removed, the mayor inquired who that seminarist was, pointing to Vincenzo. A dozen voices answered in a breath that the seminarist was the companion, and probably the accomplice of the thief. Vincenzo came forward boldly, and repelled the charge of complicity with the natural indignation of offended innocence. He briefly related the circumstances under which he had met, and been induced to accompany, the accused, and wound up by stating his own name and address, as well as those of his patron and godfather.

"A worthy gentleman, with whom I am well acquainted," said the mayor, "and who deserves better than to have godsons scouring about the country with horse-stealers. I will write immediately to the Signor Avvocato, that he may send for you, if he feels so disposed; but until that happens, you are my prisoner, sir," concluded the mayor with a half smile.

Vincenzo understood this announcement as a jest, and was confirmed in that belief by being invited half an hour later to sit down and partake of the mayor's dinner. There was a third person present at the meal, Ambrogio, the mayor's eldest son, a spirited youth of eighteen, who insisted on Vincenzo's relating all his adventures, and spoke of the innovations of the day and of the war with an enthusiasm which more than once drew down upon him a severe rebuke from his father.

The dinner over, the mayor took Vincenzo to an upper room, or rather a loft, in which there was a bed, and said to him, half in joke, half in earnest, "This is your prison for the time being, young man. As the Signor Avvocato will hold me responsible for your safe return to him, I had better take precautions against your giving me the slip."

Having thus delivered his sentence, the mayor locked the door on the outside, and put the key in his pocket. The joke was rather too true to be pleasant; but, as there was no remedy, Vincenzo had to be resigned. With no book to read, and no more interesting objects to look upon than the dead wall of the adjoining house, or a number of ropes of onions and strings of garlic, pendant from the rafters of his loft, the poor prisoner had ample leisure for speculating on his own concerns.

So here was an end of all travelling and soldiering for him, and a beginning to a new series of humiliations. He shuddered at the thought of having to go back on compulsion, with an escort as though he were a criminal, with the stigma attached to him of having consorted with a quack and impostor, probably a thief! Ah! what a contrast to his dream of presenting himself at Rumelli a proved soldier, the cross of honour on his breast, the pride and envy of all who knew him. What a misfortune to have stumbled upon a rogue, instead of a real officer able and willing to assist him. As things had turned out, how could he expect any one ever to believe that he had seriously wished and intended to join the army? Not even Miss Rose. Well, whatever mortifications the future might have in store for him, on this he was determined — to have done for ever with seminary, theology, and priesthood. No, though he had to work like a peasant, he would a thousand times rather do so, than live in case by a profession for the duties of which he felt himself unfitted. One could be a good Christian, and work out one's salvation without being either a priest or a monk; otherwise, what was to become of that immense majority who were neither?

Vincenzo had the presentiment of a coming struggle against his resolution, and he girded up his loins to meet it. Just as the sip of some cool beverage increases one's thirst, so did the little taste Vincenzo had had of the world add to his longing for more of it, and make him desire to wander through it without tether. The last few eventful days had marked the turning point in his life; they had steeled his hitherto vague aspirations after freedom into an indomitable purpose of conquering it. Many an apparently soft and pliable nature needs but the pressure of some extraordinary circumstances to harden at once, just as water needs but a strong degree of cold to consolidate into ice.

Towards five o'clock in the afternoon, Vincenzo's *tête-à-tête* with himself was interrupted for a few instants by a visit from his *pro tempore* gaoler, who brought him a large slice of bread and some cherries; and again about eight o'clock in the evening, when the mayor bid him come downstairs to supper. During the repast, Vincenzo was rather put out of countenance by the frequent kicks which his *vis-à-vis*, the mayor's son, inflicted on his legs, a proceeding from which the sympathising, nay, friendly expression of the kicker's face, took away all character of hostility; he could only construe them as a warning, the object of which was for the moment a mystery; or perhaps they might mean a promise of succour. As nine o'clock struck, Vincenzo was reconducted to his loft, and there left with a cordial good night, but no candle. He sat up hour after hour in the dark, with a vague expectation of something happening, until, having heard eleven strike, and silence reigning supreme indoors and out of doors, he came to the conclusion that the kicks meant nothing beyond an assurance of sympathy, conveyed in the only shape of which circumstances allowed, and then he decided that the wisest thing he could do was to go to bed and to sleep.

CHAPTER XII.

A New Start.

WHETHER hours or minutes had elapsed he knew not, when he was awakened by the grating of a key in the lock of his door. He sat up in his bed, and by the light from the window (the night was clear and starry) he saw the door open gently, and a noiseless form steal towards his bed.

"I am awake," whispered Vincenzo; "who are you?"

"All right; I am Ambrogio," answered the mayor's son in the same cautious tone. "I dare say you expected me; didn't you?"

"Truth to say, I had lost all hope of anybody coming; I sat up till past eleven."

"Father has been uncommonly long in going sound asleep," explained Ambrogio, "and I dared not venture into his room to get the key of your door until I heard him snore. He is safe now till five in the morning; I know his way. Well, I have come to ask of you if you have still a mind to go and have a crack at those Tedeschi."

"I should think so," said Vincenzo, "if I only knew how to manage it; but where to enlist, that's one difficulty, and the second, that I haven't a penny."

"I have money enough for two," said Ambrogio, "and I know the country well. We'll make straight for the camp."

"But your father — think how angry he will be," objected Vincenzo.

"Of course he will," returned the other; "but he will forget and forgive for all that. My father, between ourselves, is all for the Statuto and the war, though before me he pretends to turn up his nose at one and the other. The fact is, he prefers me to either, and, as he well knows how I long to volunteer, he does all he can, poor man, to throw cold water upon my zeal. Well, shall we be off?"

"Ah! he will lay all the blame of your going on my shoulders," again objected Vincenzo, "and so will my godfather, the Signor Avoccato; they'll both of them accuse me of enticing you away."

"But how could you, shut up in the loft, and with no way of seeing me, be accused of enticing me away? No one in his right senses could do so; on the contrary, my having got hold of the key will prove, as plain as two and two make four, that I was the one to entice you; don't you see that? And then, haven't I a tongue in my head to clear you, if necessary?"

"As to that, I have no doubt but you would," said Vincenzo, whose scruples melted away rather from the effect of the winning warmth of his new friend's manner, than from the stringency of his arguments. "You are a brave fellow, and I will go to the end of the world with you. I shall be up and dressed in a minute."

"Stop," said Ambrogio; "would it not be safer for both of us that you should leave your seminarist's dress behind? It would be a sure mark, if we are pursued, by which to track and identify us; and, if I know anything of my father, pursued we shall be." Vincenzo asked nothing better than to part with what he considered as the outward badge of his thraldom, and which was, moreover, in a very deplorable condition. The two youths accordingly proceeded with all possible caution; Vincenzo carrying his shoes (Ambrogio had come up barefooted) down to the latter's bed-room, where Vincenzo, with great relish, dressed himself in a suit of fustian, rather the worse for the wear, which big Ambrogio had outgrown, and which suited the slim figure of the seminarist tolerably well. The three-cornered hat was replaced by a round straw one; and, despite the old adage which declares that the frock does not make the monk, Vincenzo felt quite another being in his novel attire. Ambrogio put a change or two of linen, and some provisions, in a knapsack, and then they stole quietly out of the house.

The night was beautifully clear, the air fresh and pleasant, and the road less dusty than Vincenzo had anticipated from his late experience. So they went on at a brisk pace, exchanging confidences, and laying out plans for the future. Ambrogio, being the elder, the bigger, the more adventurous, and the better acquainted with things in general, of the two, naturally and without opposition took the lead of the expedition. Indeed, his knowledge of the road to the camp, of its position, of the different corps of Piedmontese assembled there, and of contemporaneous politics, was quite amazing in one who had scarcely received any education, and had always been engaged in the usual labours of a peasant.

He explained to Vincenzo that all the information he possessed, about the interesting topics of the day, he had gathered from the Official Gazette of Turin, which his father, as mayor, received *ex officio*, and which Ambrogio never failed to read and study by stealth. He had a positive passion for reading; and a student living in the neighbourhood during the vacations had lent him the novels of D'Azeglio, Manzoni, Guerrazzi, and other authors of the liberal party, all of which Ambrogio had devoured with intense pleasure. His political tenets had been instilled into him in his early childhood by the schoolmaster of his village, now dead, an ex-soldier, ex-monk, and a thorough republican, who had served under Murat in the short and unfortunate campaign of 1815, and whose passion to the last was political speculation.

Vincenzo learned also from his comrade, that his four days' wandering with the *soi-disant* colonel had not brought him farther from Ibella than one good day's journey. "If you trust to me," summed up Ambrogio, "that is, march when I say march, and stop when I say stop, I reckon upon our reaching Novara by dusk this evening, and fresh enough to get on a stage towards Lombardy. From Novara, you know, to the Ticino is but, as one may say, a leap — and beyond the Ticino is Lombardy itself."

"Very well; but," insinuated Vincenzo, who liked to conduct matters methodically, "since we have to pass through Novara, had we not better, while we are there, go to the proper authorities, and be regularly enlisted?"

"Catch me at that!" cried Ambrogio. "Novara is unsafe ground for us to linger on, my dear fellow; that's just the place where father will look for me first. And what's the use of enlisting? why, only to be sent to some depôt to drill, and drill, and drill, till, perhaps, all the fun is over."

"But," observed Vincenzo, "without being drilled we cannot make good soldiers."

"There is no drill so good as actual fighting," said the mayor's son sententiously. "I know that the companies commanded by Major Griffini and Captain Longoni, now actually at the camp, are made up of youths, most of them students who have had no drill at all, and they do very well; so why shouldn't we? We'll volunteer into one or other company, eh; what do you say, Vincenzo?"

Vincenzo had little faith in volunteers, because he had heard the Signor Avvocato repeatedly express a poor opinion of their discipline and usefulness — all men past fifty are incredulous about volunteers — and he would have preferred, therefore, to enlist into a regular regiment; at the same time he was not insensible to the advantage of entering the lists without going through a tedious, and perhaps long apprenticeship, during which the war might come to an end; and then farewell all hope of distinction. Vincenzo was at that happy age, when the justice of a cause seems the best guarantee for its success; and, the Italian cause being justice itself, in his eyes, he felt not the least doubt of its ultimate, nay, speedy triumph. He accordingly started no new objection, contenting himself with observing that, so as he had his heart's desire of meeting the Austrians in a fair stand-up fight, he cared little whether he did so as a volunteer or a soldier of the line.

The morning was passing beautiful. The sun had risen in all its glory; the country far and near seemed to quiver with pleasure under the salutation of its early rays; from farm to farm cock answered cock; phlegmatic cows, lifting up their heads, lowed forth their satisfaction; calves capered cheerily over the dewy pastures; larks sang themselves drunk in the newly born light — it was ecstasy to walk amid this revival of nature. But, as the sun rose higher and higher above the horizon, so did our pedestrians' elasticity of spirits and steps lower in proportion. About seven o'clock the inconvenience of heat and dust began to make itself felt rather severely — another hour, and they had entered the outskirts of that zone of territory, where the cultivation of rice begins. A wide-spread carpet of the tenderest green, intersected by canals, bordered by pollards and poplars, and here and there agreeably relieved by substantial farmhouses, and rich oases of mulberry and other fruit trees — such was the general aspect of the country. The smiling rice-grounds bear nothing on the face of them to warn the passengers of the foul emanations which rise from their water-steeped foundations weltering in the broiling sun — quite the contrary; they look as placid and innocent as the finest expanse of delicate English turf. But the pale fever-stricken creatures, whose lot it is to labour in these nurseries of disease, know better. Vincenzo was born in a region like this; had lived in it till the age of nine years; and he now gazed upon the familiar prospect with the twofold melancholy which attaches itself to the scenes of one's childhood and of one's first great sorrow of life. It was in a rice plantation near Vercelli that his mother had died, and that his father had been infected with the germs of the malady which had also carried him to an untimely grave.

Ambrogio too had recollections of his own, and very disagreeable ones, connected with rice-grounds — that is, recollections of ague, which had kept him low for ever so long; and, as he thought of it, he fell to inveighing against himself for having forgotten to put a bottle of wine in his knapsack. "What an ass I was not to have thought of it! A couple of glasses of Monferrato would have carried us on triumphantly to Cascina Grande, there to have our siesta; whereas we shall have to stop at the first house on our way — for rest we must, and, heated as we are, we cannot lie down in the open air without, I may say for me at least, the certainty of catching the fever. I have had it twice already, and I have no wish to recommence. The heat is so extraordinary also for the end of May."

"I wonder if it is as bad on the banks of the Mincio?" gasped Vincenzo.

"No doubt of it, if not far worse," answered Ambrogio; "and, when Peschiera is taken, then comes Mantua, and the swamps there are famous for their unwholesomeness."

"Poor soldiers, how they must suffer, and what lots of them will die," said Vincenzo, feelingly.

"No doubt of that either," returned the other; but, at the sound of wheels in their rear, all Ambrogio's sympathy for the sufferings of the army vanished. He exclaimed, "Hallo! a gig behind us in the road, comrade; we must ignominiously squat down behind this friendly bank; this is the most critical moment of our journey. If my dad gives chase, as I warrant he will, depend on it that he is at our heels now."

Squatting down in the fields below the road, or skulking behind trees at every new alarm, their weary march at last brought them to a haven of refuge — a wretched tumble-down cottage. As they entered it without much ceremony, an old forlorn-looking woman, with a babe in her arms, and two little urchins at her heels, attracted by the sound of steps, came from a back-room and inquired their business. Their business, said Ambrogio, was to purchase a bottle of wine, and beg the permission to rest their weary limbs. Rest, said the woman, they were welcome to, and a cup of coffee, and a dish of *polenta*, if they could wait till it was cooked; but wine she had none — that was an article of luxury she had not seen for many a long day. Her husband had been laid up with the fever, and unable to work for the last four months, and they were as poor as could be.

While saying this, and to the great amazement of the two youths, who had taken it for granted that she was the grandmother of the children, she put the baby to her breast — the only available means of effectually hushing the screams in which it had never ceased to indulge since the entrance of the strangers. Each of the exhausted wayfarers accepted gratefully and swallowed the cup of coffee proffered to them. Coffee is rather an article of necessity than of luxury in these pestilential districts, and is always to be found, even in the most miserable hovel. Half an hour later, provisions were *hinc inde* put in common, and a substantial meal improvised, consisting of the woman's *polenta*, and Ambrogio's bread and sausage.

"Do you know if the war is likely to come to an end soon?" asked the woman between one mouthful and another.

"I am afraid not," replied Ambrogio. "Peschiera is as good as taken; but then, there's Mantua, and after Mantua, Verona — two teeth hard to draw."

"People about here say that the men on the reserve are to be called into active service; pray, do you happen to know if it is true?" inquired the woman.

"Not true as yet," said Ambrogio, "but very likely to be so in a short time."

"Then, I say, it is a downright abomination," cried the woman, in a sudden burst of passion.

"Surely you are aware," put in Vincenzo, conciliatingly, "that it is according to the law of the service."

"Those who make such laws ought to be ashamed of themselves," said the woman vehemently.

"But my dear madam," urged the ex-seminarist, "the laws may seem hard — actually be hard, without ceasing to be just."

"Just! not a bit of justice in them," screamed the exasperated woman. "Is it just to wrench a father from his family, and leave wife and children all to starve?"

"A very pitiful case, and very hard to bear," persisted Vincenzo; "still, if the country requires the father's arm to defend it —"

"The country!" interrupted she, in anything but a respectful tone; "and what does the country do for me, that I should give it the life of my husband, the father of my children? The country indeed! An hospital to die in, suppose there's a corner vacant in it — that's what the country gives to me, and such as me."

Vincenzo was going to reply; but Ambrogio nudged him to hold his tongue, and said himself to the woman, "My good friend, what's the use of exciting yourself now? Very likely your husband may never be called on to quit you; very likely there may not be any occasion to call out the men on the reserve; but, if the worst comes to the worst, and your husband and other husbands should be required for active service, depend on it, the King and the Government, and the public, will not leave the bereaved wives destitute, but provide for them and their children in the absence of their natural support." The woman was a little soothed by this assurance — one which the event fully justified. But no liberal allowance to their families ever succeeded in reconciling to active service a whole class of soldiers, who had hitherto considered themselves, and had practically been, lawfully exempted from it, and whose heart besides was in their homes. Thus, the then actual Government was paying the penalty of the want of foresight of the Government which had preceded it, and which, in no prevision of war, had given permission to as many of the men on the reserve as had asked for it to marry.

Eight hours of weary walking, without a wink of sleep, had so exhausted the two lads, that they began to doze on their seats; seeing which the hostess led them to the sleeping-room of the family, the only one which contained a bed, and there she bade them lie down, and rest as long as they pleased. Begging her not to let them sleep over a couple of hours, they threw themselves, dressed as they were, on the bed, and in two seconds were fast asleep.

We beg the judicious reader, who may have felt scandalized by the unpatriotic language of this poor drudge in the plains of Novara, or otherwise shocked by the want of public spirit in the few characters hitherto sketched — we beg the reader, we say, to bear in mind that we are dealing with a country the seat for ages past of a far from always enlightened despotism, and where all that goes to make the education of a people, representative institutions, public instruction, free speech, free press, and so on, had had but a two months' growth at the time to which we refer. That sublime abstraction, "the country" — an abstraction, the comprehension of which, by the bye, presupposes a certain training, and consequent enlargement of the mind — was little likely to be understood and felt, little likely to carry weight with it against tangible and dear realities, in hard-toiling districts, within reach of no other authoritative voice than that of a parish-priest, oftener than not the humble servitor of the powers that were.

Where, then, was the strength of liberal Piedmont? In the prestige and example of royalty, in the devotion of the army, in the public spirit of the populations of the large cities, in the enthusiasm of the youths of the university, in the common sense and love of order of all classes.

CHAPTER XIII.

An Eventful Day.

It was nearly five o'clock in the afternoon when Ambrogio woke of his own accord and roused his still sleeping comrade. The woman pleaded in defence of not having kept to their instructions, and her promise, that they had looked so weary, and slept so soundly, that she had not had the heart to waken them. Nor did Ambrogio find courage to quarrel with the well-meaning soul, though the delay incident on her transgression interfered sadly with the plan he had traced out.

Ambrogio's intention was, as we know, so to manage both their time and their legs as to arrive at Novara about dusk, pass through the town, and push on straight to Madelli on the Ticino, and there to rest. Whereas, the three hours they had lost at the cottage left them no chance of reaching Novara before eleven at night, and that too after a tramp sufficiently long to put the further stage to Madelli quite out of the question. Nothing need hinder them, to be sure, from passing through the town at eleven at night as at dusk, and trusting to find shelter for the night at the first cottage they might come to. But to secure admittance at so unusual an hour was more than problematical; and, in case of denial, there would be no resource left but to discover the driest ditch for a bed, and the softest stone for a pillow — a resource anything but palatable to one so fearful of the marshy grounds as Ambrogio had every reason to be.

He, however, kept all these perplexing reflections to himself, and took leave of his hostess, as Vincenzo did, with those hearty thanks and good wishes that Italians never grudge to anybody. The heat was less oppressive than it had been during the last hours of their morning's walk; at least they felt it less, because of the refreshment and long rest they had enjoyed; but the dust was as bad as ever, nay much worse, when after a few miles they struck into the high road between Turin and Novara. An additional drawback also was the increased number of vehicles, and the consequent necessity for the runaways to stop and skulk more frequently, in order that those conveyances, going in the same direction as themselves, might pass. This being the direct line of communication between the capital and the camp, the great concourse there of carriages of all descriptions, of strings of horses and mules, of riders and pedestrians, was easily accounted for.

The majority of those on foot were soldiers; and Vincenzo remarked with pleasure, that scarcely a civilian passed a uniform, whether single or in groups, without giving a hearty cheer. Many of the inhabitants of the houses scattered along the road, waited, wine-bottle in hand, on their thresholds, for the soldiers; went up to them, and bid them stop and refresh themselves. The great majority of the military looked in high spirits, and sang in chorus as they marched along — it was only the few who jogged on heavily, or rested with a weary and dejected air by the roadside. The advent of a Government courier, whirling past in a chaise, or at full speed on horseback, never failed to excite universal enthusiasm; hurrahs, shouts, waving of caps, hats, shakoes, greeted the messenger, every one taking it for granted that he could be the bearer of none but good tidings.

Amid the diversion offered by the animation of the road, it was a comparatively light task for our young friends to walk steadily and briskly on; they enjoyed the change from loneliness to bustle and cordial salutations. They had prudence enough, however, not to yield to the friendly advances of any fellow-travellers, lest, at some moment, when the sound of wheels in their rear necessitated hiding, their movements should either be hampered or engender suspicion. Nevertheless, what with excitement, and growing familiarity with danger, much of their former vigilance wore off; and a deaf ear was more than once turned to ominous sounds, fortunately without any untoward result.

A second allowance of bread — they had had a first one on starting from the cottage in the rice-grounds — seeming now fairly earned by a three hours' trudge, they shared between them the last half of the last loaf; but, in spite of hunger, the process of swallowing was not easily accomplished, from the quantity of dust that had to be swallowed with the bread. The propitious sight of a dry pine-branch above the door of a house they were passing, suggested the advisability of moistening the bread and their throats; accordingly, they entered the wine-shop, and ordered a couple of glasses of Nebbiolo. A long row of deal tables, with benches to correspond, stretched from end to end of the lurid hole;

no table was occupied, save one — at which sat two young gentlemen, wearing on their heads sugar-loaf hats, with tricolour cockades, and on their chins all the stock of beard, scanty though it was, with which Mother Nature had gifted them. A thick layer of dust on their clothes and boots witnessed to the fact of their having journeyed far, and on foot.

The customary salutations were exchanged between them and the new comers. "No lack of dust, eh?" said the shorter of the couple with cockades to the couple *sans* cockades. "We look like so many statues of the Commendatore in *Don Giovanni*. If the question is not indiscreet, are you going much farther?"

"As far as —— Novara," replied cautious Ambrogio; "and now, may I put a similar question to you?"

"Oh! we are students from Turin going to join our comrades at the camp," answered the one who had already spoken.

"That is to say," here interposed the taller, who had hitherto kept silence, "we are going to place an enthusiasm and a spirit, which, well directed, would take us straight to Vienna, at the service of old martinets, procrastinators and blunderers, who will soon use it up to no purpose in marches, counter-marches, and the like — that is what we are going to do."

"Nonsense," remarked his companion; "remember the proverb that the better is the enemy of the good. Of what avail lamenting that which we have not? Let us instead make the best of what we have. Napoleons cannot be improvised for the occasion."

"Who asks for Napoleons?" rejoined the other, warmly; "there is no need of them. Only give me new men and a new system — that is what I want. For new things, new men; for revolutionary ends, revolutionary means. Take any lieutenant full of pluck and faith in Italy's future — place him at the head of the army — sound the tocsin — rouse, arm the land — set the popular passions in a blaze, and then — at the foe — that's the way to conquer! Instead of which, what are you doing? You entrust the army to leaders without zeal and capacity, who waste precious time and blood before strongholds best let alone; you distrust and discountenance our volunteers; you throw cold water on the enthusiasm of the masses; you dwindle a national war down to the pitiful proportions of a dynastic one. I say that is the road to certain ruin. I appeal to these gentlemen if it be not so," wound up the orator, with an interrogative gesture to the two young strangers.

Ambrogio answered, not without embarrassment, "I am but a poor ignorant peasant, whose opinion can carry no weight; but I would remind you that, up to this date, the army has done very well, and that looks as if it were tolerably well commanded; and, as to pluck, why, who has shown more of that than his Majesty the Commander-in-Chief? Nor do I agree with you as to the national enthusiasm, which you accuse the Government of stifling, and of which you would make your lever. Well, in the cities, the popular spirit may be great and unanimous — I don't say no; but in the country districts, such as the one where I live, for instance, you would discover but a precious small amount of enthusiasm for the war."

"Exactly," insisted the tall student, "because the Government does nothing to arouse it. Only scatter a number of chosen men throughout the country, establish a pulpit of patriotism in every hamlet, and then see how easily you will bring the agriculturists up to the boiling point."

"May be so," said Ambrogio, with a doubtful shake of the head, and rising to go; "Rome, you know, was not built in a day. But it is getting late, and we must be off; pleasant journey, gentlemen, and good luck; perhaps we may meet again before the campaign is over. Farewell till then."

The sun had set, and Vincenzo and Ambrogio walked silently for some time in the soft twilight; the hour was propitious for meditation, and apparently neither of them lacked matter for reflection. "Ambrogio," said Vincenzo at last, "do you think that that gentleman's denunciation of the way the war has been carried on has in it any reasonable foundation?"

"About as much," replied Ambrogio, "as my criticism of a Greek play, or yours on some point of navigation, might possess. His knowledge of war, I fancy, may rank with mine of Greek, or yours of seafaring matters. How, then, can he be a judge? Common sense points out that those who have made certain subjects the study of their lives must know more about them than those who have not, and common sense also tells us that the man who knows must be the one to be trusted."

"Common sense says so," echoed Vincenzo; "yet we have instances of the contrary. It is bewildering and disheartening to perceive such discrepancies of opinion among those who belong to the same party, and who ought to be of one mind. If we, of the liberal party, cannot agree among ourselves, how can we hope to succeed?"

"True," said Ambrogio; "still we must not exaggerate to ourselves the practical bearing of these differences of opinion. Often they do not affect the actions of those who entertain them, as we see in the case of this student, who, in spite of his professed distrust of old martinets and blunderers, not the less goes himself to the camp, and stakes his life for his country. I will tell you what will clear away all these different shades of way of thinking, and make all men of one mind — a signal victory."

"God grant it, then, and soon," cried Vincenzo.

"Amen!" pronounced Ambrogio.

Engrossed by such speculations as these, our travellers reached the outskirts of Novara. It was then a quarter past eleven. They had been taking notice for some time of a huge muffled sound, which every now and then broke upon the stillness of the night; they wondered what it might be, and compared it to the rushing of a distant torrent, or rather, perhaps, to the uproar of a great throng; but at this late hour Novara, a quiet town even in broad daylight, was not likely to be up and astir. As they drew nearer, they caught vibrations in the air rising distinctly above the confused rumble they had first heard, which no ear could mistake for aught but snatches of the human voice.

"A fire probably," said Ambrogio.

"Or a *fête*," suggested Vincenzo; "I can see something like illuminations in the distance." They hurried on, and presently came to a large house with lights in every window; then they saw a second and a third, and so on, more or less illuminated. Meanwhile the hum of voices and the tread of feet became distinctly audible; the tunes of the national songs that were being sung, even the very words of them, could be easily made out. Following in the track of these sounds, our two youths, quite out of breath, less from fatigue than from anxious anticipation of some great event, made their way into a large square, as light as if it were midday. This was evidently the focus of the rejoicing. Turning to the first person they met with, Vincenzo and Antonio eagerly asked what was the cause of this demonstration of joy. "Bless me! where do you come from?" said the man thus questioned, in the tone of one offended. "Why, Peschiera is taken; a great victory at Goito. Italy for ever!"

The two friends would have gladly echoed his words; but impossible — they had no voice left; they threw themselves instead into each other's arms, and sobbed like children. (*Italico more*, if you will, fair critic, and stern objector to the melting mood; but why not allow that it is *more humano?*)

"We have it, hurrah!" shouted Ambrogio, at last.

"Henceforth we shall be all of one mind," added Vincenzo, not less elated.

"It is so already — have you no eyes, no ears? don't you see the proofs of one common feeling of confidence and thankfulness pervading this great throng? Let us stop at that *caffè*, and have something to clear our throats; strange that good news should choke one worse than road dust, and make one's legs as weak as water." It was not easy among the tangle of men and chairs to discover two empty seats outside the *caffè* designed by Ambrogio for a halt. But, having at last succeeded, and procured something to eat and something to drink, our two volunteers in embryo recovered the full use of their tongues, and eagerly entered into conversation with their neighbours; and, on its being ascertained that they were new arrivals, and, therefore, fit recipients for the particulars of the great news, they were soon put in possession of all the official and unofficial information by a dozen of obliging informants speaking all at once.

And, even strip them of all the unavoidable exaggeration, the tidings were glorious tidings. Peschiera had surrendered after scarcely a fortnight's siege; 30,000 Austrians had been routed by 18,000 Piedmontese; these were the events of one and the same day, the 30th May, the most auspicious day of the campaign of 1848. Well might the hearts of the citizens of Italy dilate, well might their gladness overflow in songs, *vivas*, and fraternal embraces. People ran to and fro, shouted to each other, fell on each other's necks, capered like mad; at one spot a veteran soldier on his knees was thanking God that he had lived to see such a day, the by-standers cheering him lustily; farther on a group of artizans sucked in every syllable of the blessed despatch from the camp, read aloud and commented upon for their benefit by an officer of the national guard; acclamations of "Long live the army! long live the king!" hailed the appearance of the few stray uniforms scattered among the crowd, which opened before them. Bands of citizens of all classes — gentlemen, tradesmen, day labourers, soldiers, national guards — arm in arm, ten or twelve abreast, paraded round the square at military pace, singing national hymns in chorus. Nor was there wanting a good sprinkling of the fair sex, gentlewomen as well as women of the people, to enliven the scene, on which fell floods of light from the windows of the houses rising on the three sides of the square, all splendidly illuminated and studded with Italian flags, or with transparencies appropriate to the occasion. Ladies waved their handkerchiefs from balconies, or threw down bouquets, after which gentlemen in their zeal occasionally sent their hats. There is nothing like small places for the heartiness of such demonstrations — joy, like caloric, when diffused over a large area, cannot but lose a part of its intensity.

CHAPTER XIV.
Dangers of Excitement.

As repose, with solid and liquid restoratives, gradually lessened the fatigue consequent on their long journey, our young patriots began to grow weary and ashamed of being merely passive spectators of the joyous proceedings going on before them, and felt themselves called upon to lay their meed of noise and movement upon the altar of their country. A childish whim, you will say, and quite inconsistent with the commonest dictates of prudence, and with their preconceived plan; for, if there was one good reason for shunning Novara in its slumbers, and its every night's scanty supply of flickering street lamps, there were two at least for not parading through Novara awake, astir, and in a blaze of light. But excitement has thrown wiser men than either Vincenzo or Ambrogio off their guard.

Yielding to the enthusiasm of the moment, they left

their seats and joined the moving throng; they hurried hither and thither in vague expectation of a vague something, occasionally attracted by some peculiarly striking transparency, but finding nothing to do in the patriotic line beyond buying large tricolour cockades, which they stuck in their hats, or exchanging an occasional shout or *viva* with some of the passers-by. At last they bethought them of falling into the rear of one of the joyous troops of citizens marching round the square, singing in chorus. No sooner had they done so than reinforcements came in from right and left, so that Ambrogio and Vincenzo suddenly found themselves promoted from the tail to the centre of a column on a par, as to numbers, with any of those that preceded. This looked like better sport, and they rather enjoyed it.

Presently the chorus they had been singing came to an end, and the singers to a standstill; calls for this or that song ran along the ranks. Vincenzo burst forth with Pio Nono's hymn. "No, no, none of that," cried several voices. Ambrogio, like the chivalrous friend he was, took up the air with all his might and main. Two or three of those nearest to him joined in, and then the opposition waxed fast and furious. A volley of groans, and "We won't have it," nearly smothered the hymn; in spite of which Ambrogio and Vincenzo, with one or two supporters, persisted. Upon this a young man — apparently, from his station in the front, one of the leaders — forced his way to the centre, and asked in a voice of authority who had begun the hymn to Pio Nono.

"I," said Ambrogio.
"I," said Vincenzo, almost in the same breath.

"Then have the goodness to cease it," said the young man, "or else leave our party."

"Can't one sing what one pleases in a free country?" asked Ambrogio.

"You are at liberty to sing whatever you please," returned the young man civilly, but not if you remain among us. We have purposely excluded the hymn you seem to patronize, and your continuing to do so while in our ranks can only create a disturbance. We are glad to have you in our party if your views and ours suit; if not, we had better separate —"

A terrific tantarara from the big drum put an end to the controversy and to its object by breaking up the columns; every man in them ran helter-skelter in the direction of the noise.

Vincenzo's mortification was extreme, less at his own discomfiture than at the disparagement it involved of a name dear to his heart. To Ambrogio, better informed through his assiduous perusal of the Official Gazette, this phase of public feeling with regard to the Pope was no novelty; and he explained to his friend that Pio Nono's refusal to declare war to Austria, together with sundry other acts indicative of his growing lukewarmness in the cause of Italy, had considerably lessened the pontiff's popularity, and the vogue of the hymn named after him. This explanation was a heavy blow to Vincenzo; it seemed that every inch he climbed up the tree of knowledge was to cost him one of his dearest illusions.

The stroke of the big drum, which had dispersed the singing columns, had also been the signal for the crowd to rush and converge towards a point at one of the extremities of the square. Ambrogio and Vincenzo did as they saw others do, and learned in answer to their questions that the band of the national guard was about to give the intendente a grand serenade. In fact, the music had begun before our youths had joined the compact throng blocking up all access to the town-hall. Presently, in a pause from the music, some one from among the crowd made a lengthy speech, at the close of which the multitude cheered tremendously, and the company in the balcony of the town-hall waved their handkerchiefs and hats, and made a profusion of bows. More music, more cheers, followed by a dead silence as a gentleman in black took up a position in the centre of the balcony, bowed, and began to speak. Every word he said was received with applause; and, when he ceased, and once more bowed, the cheers became positively terrific. From the place they occupied in the rear of the mass our two adventurers could not hear a word of the speech, or see much more than the tip-top of the head of the hero of the serenade; but they were near enough to enjoy the band, to unite lustily in the hurraing, and to catch a share of the magnetic current of enthusiasm which pervaded the very air. The musicians began to put up their instruments, the gathering to break up and disperse — the *fête* was over. The lads turned round to make their way to some place of shelter for the rest of the night, when —

But, to account for what follows, we must return to Barnaby, whom we left, on the afternoon of the preceding Sunday, driving at a quick pace to Ibella. He arrived there at half-past five, and went straight to the intendenza, where he found the bureaux shut, and of course nobody except the porter, who informed him that the Signor Intendente was gone a little way into the country. The Signor Intendente did not come back till past eleven at night — too late naturally to see anybody on business; and Barnaby, whether he liked it or not, had to champ the bit of impatience till the morrow. It was ten o'clock next day, Monday, before he succeeded in obtaining his credentials for the intendente of Novara, and was able to start on his search after the fugitive. There is a fine stretch of road from Ibella to Novara, and Blackie had neither the mettle of Bucephalus nor the wings of Pegasus, but only indifferent legs, and spirit which needed to be recruited by reasonably frequent allowance of rest and food. Blackie, to speak to the point, did not enter Novara much before midnight. Barnaby had sense enough to leave the intendenza alone at that hour, and go in quest of rest and refreshment for man and beast.

The intendente, applied to next morning, Tuesday, evinced a laudable readiness to do honour to the recommendation of his colleague of Ibella, and, after taking down in writing an accurate description of the runaway seminarist, desired Barnaby to call again at four in the afternoon, to learn the result, if any, of the intendente's inquiries. Barnaby was punctual to the appointment, and then received the assurance that no colonel of the name of Roganti existed in the army, nor was there any depôt or corps of volunteers at Novara. The man in authority further expressed his conviction that the young seminarist had been made the dupe of some charlatan, or even worse, who had played on the lad's credulity. A report, in fact, of a youth in a seminarist's dress having been seen on the previous Sunday on the road to ———, in the company of a suspicious-looking character, had reached the intendenza that very morning. Acting upon this information, the intendente had already transmitted orders to the different stations of carabineers, to track out and detain the two individuals. Similar orders had been given in the town itself, and all necessary measures taken for their apprehension, in the improbable case of their arriving at Novara at liberty. There was nothing, therefore, for Barnaby to do but to be patient and wait, calling from time to time at the intendenza for news.

Barnaby made use of his hours of forced leisure to pen and forward to the Signor Avvocato a series of hieroglyphics purporting to be a summary of the preceding information. Early on Wednesday he was again at the intendenza, in the hope of some fresh tidings — there were none. Barnaby's power of forbearance was now stretched to the utmost, and he was brewing *in petto* a famous *quousque tandem*, to be served hot to the Signor Intendente on the first opportunity, when, towards one o'clock of the same day, a hasty summons for him came from the intendenza. He hurried thither, and was introduced to a stranger, who had brought fresh and startling intelligence indeed. This person was no other than Ambrogio's father, who had, on discovering the flight of the two birds, started at once for Novara, and, like the practical man that he was, applied forthwith at the intendenza for intelligence and aid.

From him Barnaby learned the arrest of Vincenzo's companion the horse-stealer, and Vincenzo's detention at his, the mayor's, house, and consequent escape in the disguise of a peasant, in company with the speaker's son. The mayor made so sure that the runaways would come to Novara that he earnestly solicited the adoption of still stronger precautions than had been already taken, to prevent all possibility of disappointment. Thereupon, a description of the two youths was sent to all the inns and lodging-houses of Novara, with strict injunctions to let the authorities instantly know of any such arrivals. Besides this, two police agents, in private clothes, were posted at the gate through which the lads were expected to enter, and others scattered through the town. One would suppose it an impossibility to escape from such a sharp look-out; nevertheless, all these wise precautions were within an ace of being frustrated by the great news of victory, which a few hours after burst upon the town like a bomb. Owing either to a slack surveillance at the gate, or to the large affluence of people streaming in from the environs, the two lads got into the town unobserved, and might possibly have preserved their *incog.* to the end, had they had prudence enough to remain at the *caffé*, mere spectators of the rejoicings, and at their termination have left Novara. Instead of which, as we know, they were ill-advised enough to exhibit themselves all over the square; which led, in the long run, to their being identified by a policeman, who was at the time thinking of anything but them.

The police, be it known, had orders to spare the lads the mortification of an arrest in public, save in the event of some absolute necessity. The policeman, therefore, contented himself with dogging their steps, until he stumbled on one of his comrades, to whom he whispered the discovery he had made, desiring him to carry the news to the intendenza. The intendenza despatched the bearer of the news to a *caffè*, at which it had been preconcerted the mayor and Barnaby should take up their quarters for the whole evening. The mayor and Barnaby at once set out with the messenger. The policeman, by dint of certain peculiar shouts, succeeded in putting himself in communication with, and shortly after in joining, his fellow agent, who was keeping watch on Vincenzo and Ambrogio. The youths, with eyes and neck strained towards the balcony of the town-hall — the intendente was then speechifying — were as good as blind to all that was going on round them.

The mayor and Barnaby had all the leisure and facility they could desire, to choose their position close to the two unsuspecting lads, a little in the rear; and they had stood there a good twenty minutes before Ambrogio and Vincenzo moved. They turned round at last, meaning to go back to the *caffè*, and found themselves face to face — Ambrogio with his father, Vincenzo with Barnaby.

"Pleasure enough for one day, I should think," said the mayor, drawing Ambrogio's arm within his own. "Now to bed, sir; to-morrow we'll have a reckoning."

"Glad to see thee out of thy black robe all the same," said Barnaby to Vincenzo, taking him by the arm; "but now let's follow the mayor's advice, and go to bed."

Without a word of remonstrance the two young friends, struck dumb by surprise, followed their unexpected guides to a neighbouring hotel; and, without a further word of explanation, the quatuor retired to rest — father and son in one double-bedded room, Barnaby and Vincenzo in another.

CHAPTER XV.

The Stray Lamb in the Fold again.

Few but friendly were the words which passed next morning between father and son. The father began by stating most peremptorily that, as for any proposal which had reference to volunteering, it might as well not be mentioned, as he did not mean to listen to any. We have already had occasion to make the remark that men above fifty were at that period unconquerably averse to the volunteer force. If Ambrogio felt a real desire to be a soldier, he had nothing to do but to wait his turn of the conscription, which would be within two years. Then, and then only, could Ambrogio's wish, if it lasted so long, be indulged; but he must be a soldier in earnest, knowing what he was about, and doing it according to rule.

Ambrogio readily agreed to the terms, and for three principal reasons: first, because he was unwilling to thwart his father, whom he sincerely respected and loved; secondly, that he considered himself fairly beaten, and therefore in honour bound to submit to the fair conditions offered; and thirdly, that he believed the victory of Goito and the surrender of Peschiera would bring the war of independence to a close. Nor was the conversation which took place between Vincenzo and Barnaby less satisfactory. Indeed, it mainly turned upon the way in which the news of Vincenzo's escapade had been received at the palace, and the consequent sort of humour he was likely to find there. Barnaby's unalterable optimism, restricted though it was to this one particular, did not belie itself. According to his version, the Signor Avvocato had been rather agreeably tickled than otherwise by his godson's spirited freak, and was ready to back him up well against the seminary; and in support of this assertion Barnaby quoted the few phrases he had retained of his master's letter to the principal, unwittingly deepening their colour. As for the signorina, ah, poor thing! her eyes were sadly swollen with crying, which was no sign of anger; only to have seen her when she first heard that Vincenzo had enlisted, only to have heard her begging her father to send after him, was sufficient to satisfy any one that all was safe in that quarter; Vincenzo might take Barnaby's word for that. Vincenzo did not, however, take it without some mental reservations and abatement; still there was a good portion of comfort left, even allowing for such subtractions. After a hasty breakfast taken together, the two couples got into their respective gigs, and separated for the nonce, to meet again by special agreement at the mayor's house, which lay in Barnaby's road. The mayor's roan horse being a much faster trotter than Barnaby's black mare, as had been ascertained by a careful comparison of notes, the respective owners had chosen rather to part company for a time than for the one to be a drag on the other. This arrangement also effectually saved the old fire-eater's *amour-propre*, for the roan had been already an hour in his stable when Blackie stopped at the mayor's door.

The mayor and his son were of course there to receive their guests; but a third person was with them, at sight of whom Barnaby's features screwed themselves up into a curious grimace, expressive of alarm and pugnaciousness. This third person was Giuseppe, the young man, if you remember, whose growing favour with the Signor Avvocato gave the greatest umbrage to Barnaby. Giuseppe, seeing the storm gathering on the wrinkled brow of his elder, hastened to explain how, on receipt of the mayor's letter informing the Signor Avvocato of his godson's arrival and detention at the mayor's house, he had been dispatched in Barnaby's absence to meet and bring home the fugitive. Giuseppe's explicit admission that he had been used as a *pis-aller* for Barnaby fell like oil on the rising waves of the old gardener's wrath. Nevertheless, he observed in a very curt manner, meant to set at rest all doubt as to his own superiority, that the lad was in his charge, and should remain so until once more safe in the palace. Giuseppe said nothing to the contrary; upon which Ugly and Good condescended to disarm. The dinner to which they presently sat down was copious, if not varied. The poultry yard had supplied it almost entirely; but the two condiments of cordiality and cheerfulness made up abundantly for want of variety. The conversation ran exclusively on the victories of Peschiera and Goito; and many were the bumpers drained to the health of the king and army, and to the speedy termination of the campaign. The remotest hamlets were by this time sharing in the general intoxication caused by the great news; and all along the route our travellers had been struck by the universal excitement, and by the unanimous and almost magical celerity with which triumphal arches of laurel were erected, in addition to preparations for illuminations even in the humblest dwellings. It was a lucky coincidence that the glorious tidings should have reached these rural districts on a *fête* day — in fact, on Ascension-day; a coincidence which went far to enhance, and, to a certain extent, to hallow their celebration. As mayor of the village, Ambrogio's father had been able to get up a demi-religious, demi-political demonstration, in the shape of a procession to take place after vespers; and in which would figure all the notables of the place and the clergy, accompanied by the municipal body and the national guard with its band of music, not to speak of illuminations and fireworks in the evening.

The mayor urged Barnaby to stay over the night, if not for his own pleasure, to let Vincenzo enjoy the sight in Ambrogio's company; but Barnaby was proof against all entreaty. Cross-grained people are not necessarily without feeling — very often quite the contrary, as in this individual instance. No bribe could have induced Barnaby to prolong the anxiety he was aware his master and the signorina must be suffering. Such a good reason shut the mayor's mouth — he could not even plead mercy to Blackie as an excuse for delay; that valuable animal had been so recruited by rest and food that she looked brisk enough for double the work she had before her.

The gig was already at the door, an affectionate farewell spoken *hinc inde*, the two lads pledging themselves to an eternal friendship, when the mayor exclaimed to Barnaby, "Wait a moment; we have forgotten this youngster's cassock, though, to judge from appearances, I do not think he will be in a hurry to put it on again."

"Pray don't trouble yourself," cried Vincenzo; "I

prefer leaving it behind. Ah! but I remember now, it does not belong to me."

"Never mind that," said Barnaby; "let it stay where it is; we'll pay its value if we are asked for it; I'll be bound its price won't ruin us."

"Nor are the clothes I have on mine," added Vincenzo, in sudden and great perplexity, "and I really ought to return them to their owner."

Here Ambrogio interrupted him with a hurried "Keep them as a recollection of me and our journey."

"Yes, yes, keep them," echoed Ambrogio's father; "my son has long outgrown them."

"Well, we'll keep them, and be thankful for them also," interposed Barnaby; "but on condition that you allow us to give you something in return."

"No such thing," cried both father and son, as they saw Barnaby, after fumbling in his pocket, draw forth a time-worn leather purse.

"Now listen to me," resumed Barnaby; "I am not going to offer to pay you for the clothes, but answer me a question. There is some poor person in the parish to whom you would probably have given them? Well, give instead this couple of five-franc pieces, and thus we sha'n't feel as if we had been robbing our neighbour."

"But —" began the mayor.

"No buts," interrupted Barnaby; "either give such person this little help, or we can't take Ambrogio's clothes;" and Barnaby, with an irate jerk forward of his whole body, looked as if about to alight.

"Have your own way then, you obstinate fellow," said the mayor good humouredly, accepting the money.

"That's right, and thank you. Good day;" and Barnaby drove off in triumph with his captive.

Vincenzo hailed this final divorce from his seminarist's robe as a great victory; it was a *fait accompli*, which, at least in his eyes, raised his chances of emancipation fifty per cent. Another cause of inward satisfaction was the unmistakeable admiration of which he had seen himself the object to a circle of urchins gathered round the gig, who had never ceased staring at the would-be volunteer during this last debate between Barnaby and the mayor — Vincenzo's first sip of popularity. The drive presented no incident worth relating, unless it be the meeting at a late hour with a band of merry youths belonging to Rumelli on their way home, who, on recognising the well-known grumbler, opened a battery of jokes against him, keeping up, till they lost sight of him, a brisk fire of "There goes Radetzky!" to the incredible exasperation of the old man, who swore he would make an example of them. Nothing came of the threat, however, save some useless slashes with the whip at the innocent bushes by the road side, responded to by derisive laughter and redoubled discharges of the obnoxious nickname.

As to what was said between the couple in the gig — and the conversation did not languish — it all related to the main question at issue — cassock or no cassock — and was summed up on Barnaby's part in this short formula, "If you ever put it on again I have done with you;" and in still fewer words from Vincenzo, "I'll die first."

No glimpse of light lingered in any of the windows of the palace when they reached it at midnight; so both groped their way up to their respective rooms in the attic, and tired as they were soon went to sleep. Vincenzo awoke early the next morning, and could not close his eyes again for thinking of the dream he had had. He had dreamed that the Signor Avvocato had received him with so much kindness, and had begged him in such a paternal manner to reconsider his resolution of renouncing the priesthood, had urged him so earnestly to resume his studies at the seminary, that Vincenzo had ended by giving a reluctant consent. "God grant he may not be such as I saw him in my dream," thought Vincenzo; "I would rather a thousand times he were angry and harsh than kind and gentle to me. I could not resist his kindness — that I am as sure of as that if I go back to the seminary it will be the death of me. Nothing, no, nothing in the world could ever reconcile me to a profession for which nature most certainly never intended me." During this soliloquy Vincenzo dressed himself, and then opened the window; it was a gusty rainy morning, the sky one uniform tint of grey. The lad inhaled with delight the cool air and the racy scent arising from the moistened earth. He stood there long, listening to the thrushes, and looking with the keen pleasure of one newly returned to a dear home, at the row of familiar dwarf acacias, which, with their rounded tops, had a considerable likeness to broomsticks surmounted by periwigs. Vincenzo had no idea of what hour it might be; the clock of the village, owing to the direction of the wind down the plain, could not be heard that morning at the palace. Barnaby had promised to come to him early; probably, as he had not made his appearance, it was not yet his usual hour for rising; at all events, Vincenzo scrupled to wake the old man. Had it not been raining so hard he would have gone down to the garden, with the certainty of meeting his godfather taking his usual early walk, and so have got over their first meeting. As it was, no chance now of accomplishing that out of doors; but when and where, then, should he see the Signor Avvocato? It stood to reason that it was Vincenzo's duty to seek the Signor Avvocato; yet he was shy of doing so until somebody should have informed the Signor Padrone of his return. At last, unable to go on arguing the matter with himself alone, Vincenzo made up his mind to go and wake Barnaby. He opened his own door gently, and stood on the threshold listening if there were any sounds of moving in the house. Suddenly a door below opened noisily, and he heard a heavy step coming up the stairs. Could it be the Signor Avvocato? Yes, not a doubt of it. Where could he be going? Could he be coming in search of the truant? Vincenzo closed his door with the utmost precaution, and with a beating heart returned to his station at the window. It was actually the Signor Avvocato, who in his impatience to ascertain whether the carriage he had heard drive to the door during the night had brought back the seminarist as well as Barnaby, had got up an hour earlier than his wont, and in his dressing gown was making his way to Vincenzo's room.

This was, indeed, a good sign. The Signor Avvocato had, as we know, a real attachment for his godson, which at any time would have inclined him to be indulgent; and the elation of his spirits, consequent on the glorious news received on the preceding day, putting for the moment principals' of seminaries and political misgivings into the background, left full play to the promptings of his kindly disposition. The Signor Avvocato, when happy himself, was not the man to give pain to others.

"Ah! here thou art at last," said the elderly gentleman, pushing open Vincenzo's door; "I hope thou hast had a pleasant journey—how the sun has browned thy face! I expect thou wilt soon give the world a large volume full of thy notes of travel."

"Oh, sir!" faltered Vincenzo, moved to tears, and kissing his godfather's hand, "how very good you are — not to upbraid me . . ."

"Ta, ta, ta!" interrupted the master of the palace; then added, with a proper assumption of severity, "I don't advise you to rely too much on my goodness; better try to deserve it, sir."

"And so I will, with all my strength," was Vincenzo's eager reply.

"Very well, we shall see. Deeds, not words, is my motto. What, may I ask, has become of your cassock?"

"It was in such a threadbare state, really going to pieces," answered the youth, evading a direct reply.

"In truth, it was far from good," said the gentleman; "however, it can be easily replaced if necessary."

"Then I may be pretty sure it never will be," observed Vincenzo.

"How so?" inquired the Signor Avvocato.

"Because you added the condition of its being necessary; and, indeed, sir, I can foresee no case in which my resuming the cassock could be considered a matter of necessity."

"Fine talking. After all, what do you know about it, Mr. Arguer? the decision does not rest with you. You must do as you are desired."

"I am safe, then," rejoined Vincenzo, quickly, "for you, sir, will never require of me what you know to be out of my power."

"Methinks your travels have sharpened your wits," observed the Signor Avvocato, with a shade of complacency. "No wonder, however, considering the distinguished leader under whose auspices you commenced them. So, your colonel Roganti, was but a sorry knave, after all. Tell me about him and his tricks."

Vincenzo did so, to the infinite amusement of his listener, who chuckled amazingly at the notion of his godson's going about offering hymns and scapularies for sale, and gratefully receiving alms in aid of the State. While Vincenzo was still narrating his adventures, Barnaby came into the room, and, to show his satisfaction at the evident good understanding between his master and his *protégé*, went through a series of grins and winks that might have made a monkey jealous.

The Signor Avvocato, in the best of humours, at last returned to his own bed-chamber to finish dressing, while Vincenzo, in obedience to his orders, went down to the kitchen in quest of a breakfast, thankful and happy to have fallen so luckily on his feet.

As, with some malice prepense, he loitered after his meal in the dining-room, a large hall on the ground-floor, which adjoined the kitchen, Miss Rose, in a great hurry and excitement, came thither in search of him. On seeing him, she stopped for a second, as if puzzled or alarmed by the change in his appearance, then ran forward and shook hands with him, saying, "Oh, Vincenzo! I scarcely knew you at first; you look like another person!" Something there was in these words which gave Vincenzo a sudden pang. He said, sorrowfully, "Whatever alteration there may be in me outwardly, pray believe that my heart has not changed, signora."

"I am sure it has not," said Rose, with some warmth, "nor has mine, I assure you. I am very, very glad to see you back again; only I must tell you, that you looked much better in your seminarist's dress. It is really true, then, that you do not mean to take orders? What a pity!"

"Why a pity?" said Vincenzo; "on the contrary, it ought to be a matter of thanksgiving for you, as well as for me, that I have discovered in time my want of vocation for the Church. Is it not ten thousand times better to be a good layman than a bad priest?"

"Well, I don't know — I suppose so," said Rose, far from convinced. "We'll ask Don Natale. Ah! now you must explain the last part of your letter to me. I could not make it out."

"You remind me," said Vincenzo, drawing forth the purse, and taking it out of the paper in which it had been carefully wrapped, "that I have a restitution to make. Here is your purse."

"Why do you give it me back? Won't you keep it?"

"Keep it!" exclaimed Vincenzo; "only too gladly, if you tell me I may do so. As it was, having failed in the pledge I gave you, that I would force Del Palmetto to give it up, I did not feel entitled to keep it."

"I confess I don't see where you have failed," replied Rose; "however, as your conscience is so tender,

I make you a present of it anew. And now, please to explain this mysterious phrase;" and the young lady took from her apron-pocket Vincenzo's letter.

A flush of pleasure diffused itself over Vincenzo's pale cheeks. The fact that she had carried his letter about her, and the inference he drew from it, passed, as it were, a sponge over the little disagreeables that had clouded their meeting.

"This is the sentence that puzzled me and papa too," said Rose, pointing to it with her finger.

"You showed my letter, then, to the Signor Avvocato?" asked Vincenzo, blushing again.

"Of course I did;" and Rose read aloud the enigmatical passage: — *Should I never see you again, I feel sure that your kind heart will not disapprove of the way I shall have disposed of it.* "meaning the purse, you know," said the girl, interrupting herself; then continuing with emphasis, *that is, should the knowledge ever reach you.* "Now, what does all that mean?"

"It means this," said Vincenzo, giving her the little memorandum he had made upon the paper enveloping the purse, and which ran thus:—"May 27, 1848. — Should I fall in battle, I, the undersigned, beg, as a last favour of those who may find my body, to bury with it the inclosed purse. — Vincenzo Candia."

Rose changed colour and said, slowly and gravely, "I understand now. And so," resumed she, after a pause, looking up at him, "you deliberately intended to expose your life, without heeding for one moment the anxiety you would cause papa and me."

"How do you know I did not think of that?"

"If you had," retorted Rose, "you would not have had the heart to inflict such pain."

"But," said Vincenzo, "if every one were to shrink from being a soldier, because of inflicting pain and anxiety on friends, who would there be to defend our country?"

"I am not speaking of regular soldiers, who are paid for fighting; there will always be plenty of them; but of those who volunteer as you did," said Rose. "Besides, this is not a war for defending our country, it is one of attack; Father Terenziano says so."

Father Terenziano, a Capuchin, renowned far and wide for sanctity, was Miss Rose's confessor.

"I beg your pardon," said the youth, warmly; "this is a war of defence and not of attack. We do not attack Austria on her own soil, do we? We defend our own land, our own countrymen, from her unjust sway. Suppose a band of brigands were to come and take possession by force of this palace, wouldn't you and your father be justified in trying to throw them out of the windows, and, if you could not manage it yourselves, in calling in your neighbours to help you to recover possession of your own property? This is just what the Lombards have done: they have driven the foreign invader out of their towns and villages, and have called on us, their neighbours and brethren, to lend a hand in driving them beyond the mountains; and we are striving to do so at this very moment. Austrians are our born foes; they have been the plague of Italy for ages."

"I know nothing as to what Austrians have been to Italy," said Rose, in a tone of pique; "but this I know, they are Christians like ourselves. Father Terenziano says so, and Pio Nono said the same when they wanted to force him to declare war against Austria."

"I don't deny their being Christians, but how that gives them a right impiously to enslave and trample under foot other Christians, I am at a loss to understand," rejoined Vincenzo.

"Oh! for goodness sake let us have done with politics," exclaimed Rose. "How I do loathe the very name!" and so saying she skipped out of the room.

Rose had but repeated, parrot-like, the two great arguments in vogue at that time, and by which the yet covert enemies of the new order of things sought to prejudice the popular mind against the war. The war was one of aggression, of ambition; and the Austrians, were they not Christians? Such were the mighty discoveries, which, issuing from vestries and still holier places, made their way to the cottage and the workshop, nay, to far less humble abodes, and influenced persons who ought to have known better.

Such education as Rose had had the benefit of, if we may dignify by that name the string of idle nursery tales and miraculous legends with which her young head was crammed, and the routine of external practices of devotion from which the spirit that vivifies was absent — such education, we say, as had fallen to Rose's lot, had prepared her to be a fit recipient for, and a ready believer in any platitude, so long as it came from the quarter in which lay her earliest predilections. When yet a mere baby, Rose had been inoculated by her mother, a pious but narrow-minded woman, with a lively taste for the pomps and pageantries of the Roman Catholic Church; she had been taught to look on its ministers, and indeed on everybody and thing belonging to it, with a species of idolatry. Rose had thus from her earliest years learned to identify religion with priests and processions — her religion had in it more of the senses than of the spirit. To pray to God, she needed a church, and incense, and a priest. A forest, the sea, or an expanse of sky, would never have inspired her with a religious feeling. She had been sent to school to a convent of nuns of the *Sacro Cuore;* and there she had imbibed her first notions of right and wrong, received those strong impressions which bias the whole of after life. Even up to the present moment she still continued, when at Ibella, to frequent the sisters, to receive such instruction as they could or would impart. With what result we see. Rose, at fourteen, was deeply imbued with the opinions and views, the likings and dislikings, of the religious circle in which she moved; that is, with views, opinions, and prejudices diametrically opposed to those of her father and the times she was living in. The late political change in Piedmont was bringing this dissidence between father and daughter into strong relief.

The father, whose tongue was no longer tied by considerations of worldly prudence, tried to interfere and alter the obnoxious bent of her mind. It was too late. A condign punishment for his apathy and for years of time-serving complaisance! The parental authority which he had for so long allowed to remain a dead letter, was forfeited; it had passed into the hands of the nuns, the confessor, the priest. Not that Rose did not love her father; she did, and very tenderly; only she did not defer to his judgment. The Signor Avvocato gave up the struggle as hopeless, and consoled himself with saying, "After all, what does it matter whether she be a liberal or a little *codina;* she is only a woman, and women are zeros in politics." A dictum which proves that, with all his liberalism, the Signor Avvocato was not "a man of his century."

Rose was sulky with Vincenzo all the rest of the forenoon, and would probably have remained in the same pleasant mood the whole day, had he not made the first advances, and sought her society. The childlike part of her disposition soon got the upper hand of her temper, and they were again as good friends as ever. The rain ceased, the sun shone out, and so they strolled about the grounds, and no mention, not even an allusion, passed the lips of either as to what had occurred between them in the morning.

CHAPTER XVI.

Tenacem Propositi.

NEXT day, after breakfast, Vincenzo went to pay Don Natale a visit. He had a double object in doing so — to discharge a duty towards a superior and an old and tried friend, and also to show his deference to the recommendation given to him by Miss Rose the previous day. Don Natale listened to the lad's *mea culpa* and consequent outpourings with his usual indulgence and kindness, prescribed the daily recital of certain orisons to the Virgin, together with the daily perusal of the Gospels, and assured Vincenzo that if, in spite of prayer and holy studies, his alleged repugnance for the calling to which he had been destined continued unabated, he, Don Natale, for one, would not only discountenance anything like moral compulsion, but do his best to smooth the lad's path towards the attainment of what he stated to be his present wish.

Vincenzo, with a lightened heart, hastened to Miss Rose, and repeated to her, *verbatim*, the conversation he had had with her old favourite. Rose said it was well, thanked Vincenzo for having acted upon her advice, and expressed her confidence in the efficacy of the means counselled by Don Natale. After this she spoke no more on the vexed question; nor was it alluded to by the Signor Avvocato, whose behaviour made good the promise held out by his kind reception of the truant.

The month of June was full of occupation and excitement for Rose. Three great holy-days — Whitsunday, the Holy Trinity, and Corpus Christi — all occurred within the space of less than a fortnight; and on each of these solemnities Rose had many and important offices to perform, and a degree of activity to display corresponding to their number and importance. There was the adorning of the high altar, and the decking of the Image of our Lady to see to — duties which had devolved on Rose for half of her young life; seemingly easy tasks to the uninitiated, but not to Rose, who knew better what an amount of time and nice discrimination was necessary to apportion to each occasion, according to its hierarchic rank, its appropriate degree of splendour, and no more; its right number of tapers, and not one beyond — and so on. For instance, it is evident, is it not, that the same array, the same necklace, which befitted our Lady on

Whitsunday, could not, without a glaring anachronism, be suitable for Corpus Christi, or *vice versâ*.

Then, there was the new banner of the Sisterhood of the young Guardians of the Holy Heart, sent for the occasion by the nuns of Ibella to the Prioress of the Sisterhood, no other than Miss Rose, to be garlanded with natural and artificial flowers — there was the new anthem to be learned by heart by herself, and taught to the other sisters, and rehearsed *sine fine* — and last, not least, there were to be got ready for the procession twelve white robes with twelve blue sashes, twelve white veils, and as many wreaths of orange-flowers. All these and other preparations, the detail of which we omit, required a good deal of time, and of both physical and mental exertion — for many were the knotty points which had to be cut or untied in the course of the arrangements. Vincenzo, who was not deficient in knowledge of questions connected with religious festivals, proved now a most useful auxiliary to Rose, who generally admitted him to the cabinet councils wherein such difficulties were debated.

Thus slipped blandly away the first fortnight of July. About that time it began to be whispered about that Vicenza had been retaken by the Austrians, and over the day-dreams of the Signor Avvocato there came a change. Vincenzo noticed with a qualm the knitted brows and absorbed look of his godfather, as he started for Ibella in quest of official information. It was, alas! too true that Vicenza had been recaptured. The Austrians had received reinforcements, and had assumed a threatening attitude. Flying rumours from the camp exaggerated the too well founded truth; told of the lamentable mismanagement of the commissariat, and painted our soldiers starving with plenty of food within their reach.

There was, in the sad intelligence, taken by itself, more than sufficient to revive all the former alarms of the Signor Avvocato; and even the dose of comfort administered by the intendente, a clever and energetic man, failed to allay their poignancy. "My dear friend," said the scared mayor of Rumelli in answer to the intendente's remonstrances against desponding, "you forget that I have a private standing account to settle with the principal of the seminary, and which, under present circumstances, is not likely to be closed to my advantage. I would as soon have a pack of bloodhounds at my heels as that iron-faced Torquemada, with the bishop and chapter and all their confounded tail backing him. They'll set the whole parish against me; they will — you'll see they will."

"I advised you once already," said the intendente, "to make up your quarrel with the principal; and I tell you again, do so now while you are in time."

"Make it up, make it up," grumbled the Signor Avvocato; "it is easier said than done. How do I know he, for one, would make it up?"

"Trust the matter to me, will you?" said the functionary. "I am to see the bishop one of these days, on business; will you empower me to sign a treaty of peace on the following terms — withdrawal of your obnoxious letter to the principal, complete amnesty, and unconditional reintegration of your *protégé* to the seminary? Will that do?"

"Perfectly, as far as I am concerned," said the Signor Avvocato; "but the boy ... there's the rub, for the stupid fellow will not go back to the establishment on any terms."

"If that be the case ..." said the intendente, concluding the sentence with a shrug of the shoulders, and a projection of the lower lip, which intimated as clearly as any words, "then there's nothing to be done."

The Avvocato, who wanted to lash himself into a rage, went on: "And, after all I have done for him, this is the return he makes me — yes, against the express will of his father, that opinionated scapegrace sets up his own whims. Everybody, it seems, must have his own way except me. With not a penny in the world, I should like to know how he means to live? Much as any thing like compulsion is repugnant to my feelings, I am not sure if ... if I ought not in this case ... to use for his good ... some of the parental authority confided to me by his father."

The speaker's eager glance vainly endeavoured to screw out of the, for the time being, immoveable features of his listener a cue to the solution of the doubt he had expressed. The intendente was far too conscientious and really liberal a man to give, by word or sign, the least support to the immolation of a poor orphan boy.

"You say nothing?" at last exclaimed the Signor Avvocato.

"My good friend, if I am to speak on this subject, it would not be to advise you to use the authority of which you are the depository, in order to compel a reluctant consent to what goes against the lad's feelings. Reason with him; admonish, persuade as much as you will; but no compulsion. On my side, I will sound the bishop, and ascertain from him on what terms the lad might be received back, should he be disposed to return; all this, of course, as from myself, and without any commission from you. So that, in case you fail to influence your *protégé*, you preserve all your liberty of action." The Signor Avvocato agreed willingly enough to this arrangement, it remaining understood between the two friends that not a word should be said to Vincenzo about the seminary, until after the intendente's interview with his grace.

Vincenzo had had a presentiment from the first that the loss of Vicenza would recoil upon him, and the embarrassment he detected in the looks and manner of the Signor Avvocato towards him after his visit to Ibella confirmed this presentiment. The boy could have wagered his head that the subject of his re-entering the seminary had been mooted between his godfather and the intendente; so his heart thumped like a steam-engine when the Signor Avvocato rose from table, after having expatiated all through the meal on the folly of a little state waging war with a big one, and heartily complimented a certain set of unspecified gentlemen upon their cleverness in bestowing upon Piedmont the honour and the benefit of an Austrian occupation. It was generally on rising from his dinner, and withdrawing for his siesta, that the Signor Avvocato was wont to issue summonses to his study, and there deliver lectures or reprimands to such as required them. No summons came, however, and Vincenzo was thankful even for a respite; his heart told him it was only a respite — still it was a gaining of time, in which to gather courage and steel his resolution.

A week or more — ten days passed without bringing any outward or inner change; but he felt the sword of Damocles hanging over him. A messenger from the intendenza, with a letter for the Signor Avvocato, cut the thread to which it was suspended, and down it fell, on the eleventh day. The letter ran thus: "I was not able to see the personage of whom we spoke at our last meeting before yesterday. I hasten now to communicate the result of my overtures. A golden bridge is ready for you and your *protégé* — a visit to the principal from both of you, an expression of regret for what has passed, and everything will be forgotten. Should the lad be equally well disposed as those of whom I write, you had better avoid all delay. The sooner the better. Adieu." Acting upon this recommendation, and also upon the impulse natural to feeble natures, to get out of a state of suspense, the Signor Avvocato sent instantly to summon Vincenzo to his presence.

Vincenzo came as pale as ashes, trembling from head to foot, but proof against anything, save an appeal to his heart. Lucky for him that his godfather had not the secret of this weak point in his armour, and thrust his lance instead against the well-tempered steel.

"Well, now," said the Signor Avvocato, speaking, contrary to his wont, with great volubility, and frowning with all his might; "well, now, you have had time, I hope, to make your reflections, sir?"

"Sir, I suppose you allude to my intention of relinquishing the career for which I was brought up?" was the subdued answer.

"Of course; what else could I mean?" replied the

elderly gentleman, impatiently; "and, pray, what is the decision you have come to?"

"Pray, sir, bear with me for a little, and listen to what I have to say with patience," answered Vincenzo, joining his hands imploringly. "God is my witness, how unspeakably bitter is this trial; God is my witness, I would rather meet death a thousand times . . ." Vincenzo's eyes were fast filling with tears.

"Fine phrases and tears are not what I want — as I once warned you, 'Deeds not words,' is my motto. Speak plainly — will you return to the seminary or not?"

The harsh words and the scornful tone in which they were uttered sent back the tears, and arrested, in the very nick of time, the dangerous current of sensibility which was carrying away the lad. He resumed, composedly, "I begged of you to bear with me, and listen to me for a while, with your usual indulgence . . ."

"Will you return to the seminary — yes or no? answer my question," urged the Signor Avvocato.

"You are a great and highly-respected gentleman, and I the son of a poor peasant, a mere cypher in the world; and yet we shall be judged one day, and stand in need of indulgence at the same tribunal . . ."

"I ask for a straightforward answer, and not for a sermon," interrupted the Signor Avvocato, who was desirous of checking the softness which he felt beginning to gain ground upon him at this appeal.

"In the name of all that is holy — in the name of the dead you loved — in the name of your daughter," burst forth Vincenzo, falling on his knees, and beating his head against the ground, "do hear me, do hear me, for a moment." The Signor Avvocato rose, paced up and down the room, and said, sitting down again, "Get up, and say what you have to say. I am listening."

Vincenzo got up, wiped the tears from his eyes, and spoke as follows: "You are my benefactor, you are like a father to me; you are the being whom, after God, I most reverence and love; whom I would least of all offend or disappoint. Judge, then, what must be the violence of the feelings by which I am actuated, and which prompt me to resist your will, and encounter your displeasure. There is no sacrifice I would not make to you in return for your kindness; no sacrifice, save this one, which is, in truth, beyond my strength — one which involves not only the misery of all my life, but puts in jeopardy my eternal salvation; for, how am I to meet responsibilities, and discharge duties, from which I shrink? Indeed, indeed, it is not my fault that I feel thus; if what has been to this day but a want of vocation has grown of late into an invincible aversion. It is not of my seeking; it came all of itself. I strove against it, I did indeed; I have prayed to God, humbly and fervently, to help me in my need, to enlighten my blindness, to reconcile me to a lot which I know was your wish. God has judged fit not to grant my prayer — is not that a clear sign that it is not His will that I should enter the sanctuary?"

Vincenzo's simple eloquence, and the passionate earnestness of all his being, as he pleaded his cause, worked their way to the heart of the Signor Avvocato, which was not of stone, as we know; and, had it not been for that ill-omened letter, the chances are that he would have struck his colours unconditionally, and sent seminary and all the rest to a certain place unnameable to ears polite. As it was, he shrank from tying his own hands so as to prevent any future resumption of the offensive, and manœuvred to leave the question open by saying —

"Now that I have listened to you, you in your turn listen to me. It is not my intention to force your inclinations; but I warn you plainly and distinctly of this — henceforth you will have no one but yourself to depend upon for getting a living. What it has suited me to do for you up to the present period, in the view of your taking orders and living honourably by your calling, it does not suit me any longer to do, now that the hopes I cherished for you are frustrated by your obstinacy. Forewarned is forearmed; take time to consider of what I say, and —"

"No, thank you," cried Vincenzo, hastening to burn his ships. "I cannot accept time to consider that which I have already made up my mind to do. I earnestly wish that there should be entire plain dealing between us."

"Very well," said the Signor Avvocato, piqued to the quick; "shift for yourself, then."

"I shall work for my daily bread," said Vincenzo.

"Soon said," retorted the Signor Avvocato. "What is there that you can do?"

"What my father did before me," was the repartee. "I have two hands as he had, and I can manage a hoe."

"Welcome to do so. You will find it heavier than a breviary. I wish you all success. Farewell."

Vincenzo stooped to kiss his godfather's plump

hand, and left the room. Need we say that the Signor Avvocato did not mean a single word of the threat to leave his godson to his unaided exertions?

Vincenzo did not make his appearance at dinner. The cook explained confidentially to Miss Rose, that Vincenzo had come into the kitchen for a morsel of bread, which he had taken away with him, and had told her not to put a knife and fork for him any more at table. The Signor Avvocato took no notice of his godson's absence, except to say, when asked by his daughter whether he had sent Vincenzo on any errand, that he had given him no orders, and had none to give him. Vincenzo was his own master.

"But where can he have gone?" insisted Rose.

"Who can tell? Perhaps to join his colonel," said her father. "Can't you eat your dinner without him?"

Rose had no choice but to do so, and a poor affair she made of it. As soon as dinner was over, she filled her pockets with cake, and went out in quest of her missing friend. He was at none of their usual haunts. Barnaby, whom she met and questioned, had not seen him, and her heart began to misgive her that he had again left the palace. When Barnaby was made aware of Vincenzo's absence at dinner, he roundly declared that he should not wonder if the lad had drowned himself in one of the fishponds. If he had not done it to-day, well, he would do it to-morrow, and somebody would be served right. The old gardener had been made the confidant of Vincenzo's late doubts and fears, and at sight of a messenger from the Intendenza, had anticipated a cataclysm.

He joined Miss Rose in her search, and at last, in

a far-away field, they found the lost sheep. He was
with five or six labourers, knee-deep in the earth,
without a coat, his shirt-sleeves rolled up, using a hoe
with all his might. "What are you doing?" exclaimed
Rose. "Why did you not come to dinner?"

"I am serving my apprenticeship to the calling of
my father, that of a field labourer," replied the lad,
good-humouredly; "and labourers do not sit down to
table with gentlefolks."

"That is all downright nonsense," said Rose; "you
will never be able to dig properly; you are not strong
enough; it will kill you."

"See yourself if I can't manage a hoe as well as
my neighbours," said Vincenzo, letting fall a vigorous
succession of strokes; "it is not such hard work as
it seems; I feel I have the power in me; practice is
all I want."

Here Barnaby made a dash at Vincenzo, hugged
him, kissed him, and roared, "Bravo, my lad, I honour
and respect thee; I am proud of thee. Stick to thy
father's employment; it is an honourable one; far more
so than mumbling nonsense in Latin, and fattening on
other people's sweat."

Mingled were the Signor Avvocato's feelings when
Rose brought him word of Vincenzo's new occupation
— a combination of regret at having driven him to
such, of shame at the construction people would put
on it with reference to himself, and of sincere admiration of the lad's pluck. All of this, of course, he
kept to himself, only choosing to say carelessly, "Very
well, let him — the boy has been so lazy of late that
a little bodily exertion will do him good; it won't last
long; you know the saying about a fire of straw."

"Still," insisted Rose, "it looks so very odd, so unbecoming, that your godson, one who but yesterday wore a priest's gown, should be digging the ground and herding with labourers, without your interfering."

"Bless me! to hear you, one would imagine the lad had come out of Jupiter's thigh. Is it your pleasure that I should go and bring him back under a baldachin?"

Day succeeded day, and the fire continued to burn, for all that it was of straw. Vincenzo, by break of day, was at the appointed place with his fellow-labourers, and dug away lustily and cheerfully, with only such intervals of rest as want of habit entailed on him, and during which he would relate tales to the others, or explain the why and wherefore of the war and its ultimate aim. His diet was that of his comrades, and nothing would induce him to accept of the dainties Rose daily brought him, unless he might distribute them among the men. At the end of a week he had grown the colour of a blackberry, and as thin as a grasshopper; but he was hale and healthy, and in excellent spirits — a commodity, this last, which daily grew less and less among the inmates of the palace. Rose was out of sorts, particularly with her father; and so was Barnaby, who had cut his master entirely. As to the poor master himself, troubled at home and troubled abroad, he knew no longer what to wish. His situation with regard to his godson every day acquired more similarity with that of the boor, who had surprised the wizard's magic word for setting the bucket in motion, but knew not that whereby to stop it.

The fact of Vincenzo having become a day labourer

was the talk of the whole village. The marquis had, with polite irony, complimented his neighbour on his new acquisition. Don Natale had called on purpose to ascertain the truth, and had remonstrated with the Signor Avvocato; people came openly or by stealth to have a peep at Vincenzo with his hoe. Some of the ridicule, and much of the odium arising from the exhibition, could not but be reflected back upon the Signor Avvocato. It was urgent to put a stop to such a state of affairs.

One day — it was the eleventh since Vincenzo had taken to field labour — the Signor Avvocato went to the spot where his godson was working, and said, "It is high time that this farce should finish. Put down that hoe; I forbid you henceforth to touch it."

Vincenzo instantly obeyed. In the afternoon, about dinner-time, Vincenzo waited for his godfather in the hall of the palace. "Is it your pleasure, sir, that I should dine at your table?"

"I do not see the necessity," answered the Signor Avvocato, curtly; "you can take your meals with Barnaby."

Barnaby, in virtue of an old privilege, did not eat with the other servants, but alone. Old Ugly-and-good had never been prevailed upon by his first master and friend, Signor Pietro, to dine with the family.

CHAPTER XVII

What shall he be?

WHEN we said of the Signor Avvocato, that he was not only troubled at home, but abroad, we alluded to the painful pre-occupations with which the disastrous turn of the war oppressed his mind. The battle of Custoza, fatal to our arms, had forced the Piedmontese to retreat, a movement which ended shortly after in their total evacuation of Lombardy. Milan was once more in the clutches of Radetzky; an armistice had been signed between the belligerents, both of whom had accepted the mediation of England and France. Such was the deplorable end of the campaign of 1848. All this Iliad of woe had been consummated within the short compass of Vincenzo's term of apprenticeship as a labourer — less than a fortnight.

Bad and fraught with danger as the crisis was, the panic of alarmists of the Signor Avvocato's hue made it still more so. There was no sort of evil they did not prognosticate. Deprived of their scarecrow of an Austrian occupation, which the armistice distinctly put out of the question, they dressed up another, the inevitable abolition of the Statuto, and the restoration of the old state of things — that is, despotism, with its natural retinue of Jesuits and *Codini*, and consequent crusade against the Liberals. Nor were there wanting those who assumed, and *mordicus* contended, of course, backed by plenty of proofs, that the Statuto and the war had been a comedy played in concert with Austria, to bring to light the Liberals, and get rid of them at one blow. I would not chronicle here such absurdities, if I had not heard them with my ears *passim* — not in hamlets, but in large towns; not from illiterate folks in fustian, but from gentlemen in black coats, who knew how to read, write, and cast accounts.

Truth to say, even from quarters less prone to groundless fears than the Signor Avvocato and Co., arose indications of uneasiness touching the maintenance of the newly-born public liberties. These came from those who had watched the growing tide of discontent pervading the ranks of our soldiers, at the far from friendly reception given them by some of the elated population of Lombardy; at the taunts launched at them of coming to reap the fruit of a victory not their own (as if, with the quadrilateral in the hands of the foe, there remained nothing to be done); and at the systematic hostility of a considerable part of the press, never wearied of denouncing the king and the generals as incapable, and worse. Those, we say, who knew all this, and knew also what a ready engine for reaction an army embittered by ill success and injustice is apt to be, wore anything but cheerful countenances.

Nor were the feelings of the sovereign, as far as they might be prejudged, likely to differ much from those of his army. If man had ever had provocation, that man was Charles Albert. Of all those who figured in the campaign of 1848, not one had been more misconstrued, reviled, cursed, bespattered with contumely and insult, than Charles Albert. But a few days before the armistice, the palace he inhabited at Milan had been fired upon, and violently broken into by the mob. All the blood in his veins must have been turned to gall. And this man had only to nod his head to have all opposition silenced. It seemed almost impossible that he should not give the signal; the very certainty of success was an inducement. Diplomacy urged him, old and tried friends implored him with tears to put the Statuto aside, at least for a while.. Plausible reasons were not wanting to give weight to the advice. It was the only means of keeping his hold on the army; it was the only means of recomposing the unsettled minds of his people; it was for the good of the country at large, a temporary remedy, no opposition to be apprehended, no blood to be shed — a *coup d'état à l'eau de rose*.

It is to the eternal honour of Charles Albert that he did not will it — that he willed the contrary. He had sworn to the Statuto, and he would hold to it for better for worse. His first care was to issue a manifesto to re-assure the kingdom on this head. It spoke encouragement in dignified words. The sovereign exhorted his people not to sink under unmerited misfortune, but to stand by and show themselves worthy of those liberties which he had willingly intrusted to them, and which it was his own unalterable resolve to uphold and maintain. This manifesto, so firm and frank, went far to allay, if not entirely to uproot, the misgivings which had stolen into part of the Liberal camp. Even the chronic alarmists were surprised into hoping that the disasters of the army would exercise, after all, no fatal influence on the organic institutions of the country. Every day that passed carried away some particles of the remaining distrust, and brought with it a corresponding revival of confidence.

At the end of some time, even Rose's father felt in a magnanimous mood, and charged Rose to announce to Vincenzo, that his term of banishment from the family dinner was over. Vincenzo received this mark of returning favour with due deference, and resumed his accustomed place at his godfather's table in a modest and manly manner. This act of graciousness on her father's part, as it seemed to Rose — of tardy reparation, according to Barnaby's notion — did much towards restoring a good understanding between father and daughter, and master and servant. Rose entirely recovered her conversational powers and her merry laugh; and Barnaby, on his side, condescended no longer to ignore the existence of his master, as he had done ever since the famous day of Vincenzo's volunteering as a field labourer. The Signor Avvocato's intercourse with the lad was at first meagre and reserved, but it improved gradually, until at the end of a fortnight it was on the old footing.

Vincenzo no longer strolled about the grounds all day as of yore, but put some method in his life, a little to the annoyance of his fair playmate: regularly before and after mid-day he would sit down to his books and read or write for hours. Nor was it unusual for the Signor Avvocato to stop at his godson's desk, and take up his translation from Tacitus — a favourite author with the student — and nod approvingly at it, or suggest some improvement, which was thankfully received.

One day, towards sunset, Rose and Vincenzo were sitting in the green arbour, so often mentioned — the latter expatiating enthusiastically on the glories of the western sky, and trying, but with little success, to transfuse into his young companion a portion of that keen poetic sensibility to nature which he himself so largely possessed. Rose, who had been looking abstracted for the last ten minutes, as if lost in a reverie, said, as he ceased speaking, "Vincenzo, have you indeed made up your mind — quite determined to abandon the career for which you were destined from childhood?"

"Indeed I have," said Vincenzo.

"Are you sure that, in so doing, you are not yielding to a temptation of the evil one, whose aim is your eternal perdition?"

"How can I know? I hope not," said Vincenzo.

"You hope not, but you are not sure," resumed Rose. "Had you, therefore, not better try, and make sure of what are God's designs for you?"

"So I would, if I could see any means of doing so."

"I will show you the means," continued Rose, warmly; "that is, not I, but Father Terenziano, my confessor — you know him, he is a saint, and has performed miracles. Well, I asked his opinion as to your call, and he says that you are under the influence of some malignant agency, which ought to be fought against."

"I prayed so earnestly to God to enlighten my mind," pleaded the youth.

"I told the holy father so," went on Rose, "and he replied that it is not enough to pray — the great point is to pray well, and one cannot do that but under proper direction. He is willing to vouchsafe you his guidance, if you will retire for a few days to his convent, and go through the spiritual exercises that are being practised there for some novices. If, after that, you are unchanged, then we may set our hearts at rest that your want of vocation is real, and not a delusion of Satan."

"But—" faltered Vincenzo, with a shudder at the recollection of the wellknown tomb-like silence of the cloister, of the darkened church, of the sepulchral voice, evoking images of death and terror.

"Do it to satisfy me," said Rose, anticipating a refusal; "just for my sake, won't you? Should your mind remain the same after the trial, I promise to help you with papa in all your further plans; I will indeed."

This promise of support had far less weight with Vincenzo than the wish to please her; that was, perhaps, at this moment, the paramount desire of his heart. There were very few things Vincenzo would not have done, or endeavoured to do, to please his young mistress. He accordingly declared his willingness to grant her request, subject, of course, to the Signor Avvocato's approval, which Rose in high glee took upon herself to obtain. The Signor Avvocato offered to what he styled his daughter's childish whim just opposition enough, just loudly enough spoken, to clear himself of all responsibility in the matter, and yet let her have her own way. And so it came to pass that, one fine morning, shortly after the tête-à-tête in the arbour, Vincenzo disappeared from the palace, to return five days later much depressed, bewildered, and worn out, but, as to the main point, unchanged.

Rose, now satisfied that it was not the will of God that he should enter the Church, bore the disappointment with Christian resignation, and immediately began to busy herself to redeem the pledge she had given to Vincenzo. What would he like best to do? Barnaby had told her that he must make choice of a profession, and go to the university — was there any profession for which he felt more inclination than for another? Vincenzo answered dutifully that it was not for him, but for his godfather, to make a choice for him. Rose said yes — it was with her father that the ultimate decision must rest; yet, as there were several equally eligible professions, to none of which her father was likely to object, Vincenzo might as well frankly avow the one he felt most inclined to adopt. Vincenzo, thus pressed, said at last that, if at liberty to make his own selection, he would choose the army.

The declaration startled Rose, nor did she conceal the painful surprise it caused her, nor her unequivocal aversion to the profession of arms. She affirmed that it was not one fit for a Christian, least of all for one who had been intended for the Church. Only think what it was — making the killing of one's fellow-creatures into a science. She felt that she could never bear to look at him again if he were a soldier. Vincenzo was at no loss for arguments whereby to vindicate the honour of a soldier's vocation, but he preferred giving up the point without further discussion. His prepossession for a military life was not so strong as to make him run the risk of never being looked at again by sweet Miss Rose. And then — the thought was uncharitable, but such thoughts will steal, like thieves, into one's mind — and then Rose's sweeping condemnation of soldiers had this drop of honey in it, that it included of necessity young Del Palmetto. Del Palmetto was, so to say, Vincenzo's born rival in Miss Rose's affections, and that young nobleman's considerable outlay of amiability of late seemed to point to an issue which, natural as it was, and quite in the regular course of things between young people of fortune and station, and near neighbours, Vincenzo could not contemplate without discomfort.

The only career for which the lad had any predilection being once excluded, there was no reason why his proposal of leaving his fate in his godfather's hands should not be agreed to; and upon this understanding Rose prepared to open negotiations with her father. Her first attempts met with anything but encouragement. A man is not checkmated, let his disposition be ever so amiable, without his feeling a little sore towards the giver of the check. It was not his business, said the Signor Avvocato, to find employment for those who spurned his good offices. He spoke of employment, because, as to any of the liberal professions, there could be no question of such for Vincenzo — he was far too backward in his education, and without much natural talent.

"What he does not know he can learn," said Rose; "and, as for cleverness, you said yourself that he wrote a far better letter than you had thought him capable of doing."

"A letter — a letter — what does a mere letter prove as to ability, even taking it for granted that he concocted it himself? Any one may have a moment of inspiration. And then he is ignorant of mathematics, my dear; and, without mathematics, how can he ever get Master of Arts tacked to his name — the *sine quâ non*, those two letters M. A. for the study of law or medicine? I mention medicine for form's sake, as it ranks as a liberal profession; but what man who might go to the bar would be such a goose as to prefer medicine?"

"Are mathematics, then, so dreadfully difficult to learn?" asked Rose.

"Very — indeed, it is not every head that is capable of the study of mathematics."

"Who can tell but that Vincenzo may have just the head for that sort of thing?"

"Even supposing it to be so, it would be too late for him to begin — the greatest aptitude is lost for want of early training. By the time I was fifteen years of age I had my Euclid at my fingers' ends."

"Can't he be a merchant then?"

"Ah! yes, to be sure, a merchant — you are a clever little woman when you like. And the capital on which he is to trade, will you provide him with that?"

"Not I, but you, papa; everybody says you are rich."

"And if I am, is that any reason why I should fling my money at the head of the first fellow who wants it?"

"But Vincenzo, papa, is quite different; he is your godson, and you promised his father to take care of his orphan son."

"Have I been untrue to my promise?" asked the Signor Avvocato.

"Oh no, dear papa, you have been always very good to Vincenzo, and he is the first always to say so. Next to God, I do believe, he loves and reveres you. You used to be fond of him too."

"Well, well," interrupted the father, touched, and endeavouring to dissemble his emotion under a certain brusquerie; "what is the good of all this bothering of yours? Have I cast him off, or turned him out of the

house, or said I would do nothing for him, or given
any one the right to suppose I would not? Methinks
he is not so ill off as it is; he lives under my roof,
dines at my table, has all he wants, I believe; where
is the necessity for such a hurry? I can't see it —
surely I may be allowed a little time to look about
me — something available for him may turn up; if
not, well, I shall keep my eyes open; but give me
time. I have some friends still, thank God, some little
interest; but let's hear no more about liberal professions."

CHAPTER XVIII.

Barnaby pitches into it, and settles the Question.

THE substance of the above conversation — re-
ported, as was natural, by Rose to Vincenzo and Barnaby, assembled in council — made on both a lively,
but quite opposite impression. It so clearly evidenced
the formal renunciation by the Signor Avvocato of his
original scheme for his godson, that it was welcomed
by that young man as the best news he could possibly
receive. Now, then, he felt finally relieved from that
awful sword of Damocles, which had been hanging
over him for such a length of time. What mattered
it to Vincenzo whether he was to be a barrister, a
clerk to some merchant, or in some office, so that he
was the one or the other with his godfather's consent
and approbation? Barnaby, however, took quite a
different view of the matter. His master's exclusion
of any of the liberal professions for Vincenzo was, in
Barnaby's eye, nothing less than a denial of justice, at

which he naturally chafed. Talk to him of employment, indeed! He knew what employment meant — sweeping the floor of some counting-house with neither profit nor honour, and plenty of people to lord it over you. Nothing short of the law was worthy of a young fellow who knew Latin. Vincenzo must be an avvocato; if the Signor Avvocato grudged his being so, let him till the earth — better handle a hoe than a broom. That was how Barnaby reasoned. The chief gardener *ad honorem* had been a Jack of all trades before his meeting at Mexico with his old master and benefactor, the Signor Avvocato's father, and probably he had seen enough of the drudging of clerks to give him an enduring horror of that way of gaining a living. As to his high conceit of a lawyer's calling, it took its rise forty years back, when Signor Pietro, then on the eve of sending his son to study law at the university, used to descant to Barnaby on the glories of the bar, and pronounced the title of avvocato to be one of the highest and proudest.

The month of September was half gone, and still Vincenzo's fate was hanging in the balance. More than once had Rose, during the interval, returned to the charge, without eliciting from her father any more definite answer than when she had first mooted the subject. Did Vincenzo complain of the life he was leading? If not, then he could wait. Somehow or other he would provide for him. So far the Signor Avvocato pledged himself — was not that sufficient? must he also be dictated to as to the time and manner?

Was the good gentleman concealing any settled plan under this procrastination? Not at all. He was only yielding to a little pique, and to the natural indecision of his character. He was not sorry to keep Vincenzo and his aiders and abettors on a gentle rack, as a sort of retaliation for the defeat he had sustained at their hands; and then there was another and more humane reason for this dilly-dallying. Though in his heart of hearts greatly inclined to give Vincenzo the chance of being called to the bar, the Signor Avvocato still hesitated to send him to Turin for that purpose, lest the lad should be plucked at his first examination, and ignominiously sent back, to his own and his godfather and patron's great mortification.

Barnaby, in the meantime, who was not in the confidence of his master's secret inclination, and who, moreover, with a logic all his own, saw in the system of dilatoriness pursued in regard to Vincenzo a perverse determination to refuse him what was his due, and consign him to the dust of some office or other — Barnaby, we say, had reached that pitch of exasperation which no longer finds a safety-valve in negative tokens of indignation, but must needs assert itself in action. One day, accordingly, as his master was passing him in the garden, Barnaby put on his ugliest face and said, "If you please, sir, I shall soon want that little money of mine, which is in your keeping." (Ever since the death of Signor Pietro, the Signor Avvocato had been the depository of the old man's savings.)

The tone of the demand, trenchant, almost threatening, accounted for the cold laconic answer it met. "Very well; do you want the whole of it?"

"Yes, every farthing of it, at your earliest convenience."

"It is all in my desk; you can have it whenever you like."

"Thank you, sir."

"It is a pretty round sum," observed the master; "may I know to what use you destine it?"

"Welcome to the knowledge," replied Barnaby, with the savage joy of an Iroquois scalping an enemy. "I destine it to make a man of a good lad, shamelessly abandoned by those whose duty it was to uphold him."

"Abandoned! duty!" exclaimed the gentleman in unfeigned surprise.

"Yes, abandoned; what do you call burying a Christian for life in an office, but abandoning him?"

"Who means to bury anybody? You seem to have lost your senses, Barnaby."

"Would to God I had," retorted the infatuated old man. "I should then, at least, be spared the shame of seeing you disgrace yourself."

"You ought rather to be ashamed of imputing to others the bad dreams of your fancy," exclaimed the master, nettled.

"What do you mean to do for the lad? answer me that," cried Barnaby, his arms akimbo.

"What I consider best for him," was the cool rejoinder.

"Will you send him to Turin to study law; yes or no?"

"I tell you again, I shall do that which I think best for him," repeated the master.

"Ah, then, you won't do it; you confess you won't!" shouted the exasperated servant. "Well and good; he shall be an avvocato for all that."

"I wish you and him joy of it," said the Signor

Avvocato, turning away; "the sooner you come for your money the better."

"And I give you warning I am going also," called Barnaby after his master; "I give you warning I am going also."

"With all my heart," answered Rose's father. For once our easy-going gentleman's blood was up. Not that he attached more importance than it deserved to the outpouring of Barnaby's irate dotage; it was Vincenzo's black ingratitude which stung him to the quick. After all that he had done! after all that he intended to do! such was the return he was to meet. He had not expected it from that quarter; well — let it be so — the lesson, though rather late in the day, would serve him for the rest of his life. Never too late to mend. For the first time in his life, this kind-souled man felt intensely misanthropic — all this on the assumption, and, it must be allowed, a very natural one, that Vincenzo was art and part in Barnaby's project. For, how suppose that a man in his right senses would push things so far, without first making sure of the acquiescence of the person most interested?

Barnaby's bravado to his master had occurred between seven and eight in the morning. The Signor Avvocato returned home for his coffee, swallowed it hastily, withdrew to his study, and immediately began examining his account-book, to ascertain how many years' wages he owed to Barnaby. He then added the amount to Barnaby's savings, put the whole sum, most of it in bank-notes, into a canvas bag, and drew up a minute and explanatory statement of capital and interest, debit and credit — as minute and explanatory, as if, instead of his and his father's confidential servant and friend, it concerned the most punctilious and hairsplitting of his tenants. This was all done furiously and before the least dawn of a reaction of feeling, as was unmistakably indicated by the sharp "Come in!" which he gave in answer to a rap at his door.

It was Vincenzo, who craved admittance, and who appeared looking much disturbed.

"Are you come to fetch the money?" asked the Signor Avvocato, in the bitterest tone he could command.

"Oh, sir, how could you ever believe this of me?" said Vincenzo, at first almost with reproach in his voice, which ended in a pleading. "Oh, for God's sake, sir, don't think me worse than I am; never, till now, had I the most distant surmise of Barnaby's extravagant scheme in my behalf; I swear to God I had not. I no sooner heard of it, only a minute ago, than I hurried to you, sir, to disclaim all knowledge of it — all idea of taking advantage of it — to protest to you my entire acquiescence and contentment in whatever you may decide for me. Ask Miss Rose, if I have not always said so; the most promising offer would have no temptation for me, if it did not come from you. I will not be indebted to any one but you; from you I will accept of anything with thankfulness. Do believe it, sir, for it is the truth; it is indeed."

The Signor Avvocato felt it to be so, felt relieved and happy in that belief, and all the sluices of his heart opened and flowed over at once. He drew Vincenzo to his bosom, and said with much emotion, "I do believe you; you are a good brave boy, and I bless you for it; it was wrong of me to doubt you even for a moment — yes, it was, and I will make amends for my fault. Perhaps I have not dealt with you according to your deserts...."

"Oh, sir!" interrupted Vincenzo, with half a sob.

"But my confidence," went on the Signor Avvocato, "is yours from this moment. You have no idea, my boy, of all the good you have done me — I was waxing distrustful, suspicious — I felt as if I could dislike my fellow-creatures. Of all the misfortunes of this world, dislike of one's fellow-creatures is the greatest — you have cured me of that, thank you; you have been a consolation to me in this instance, and so you will be to the last, I am sure. I don't tell you to dry your tears" (Vincenzo's were flowing fast the while) "because I know that their source is sweet."

After a pause, the Signor Avvocato continued, "And now that we are good friends again, better friends than we have ever been, let us talk of the future. What do you really wish to do, Vincenzo?"

"Anything that may please you, sir."

"Then, suppose we realize Barnaby's plan, and make you an Avvocato? Law leads to everything, you see. What do you say?"

"If it is your pleasure, sir, it will be mine."

"Very well; but, to be accepted as a student of law, you will have to go through an examination, of which geometry forms part. Are you disposed to work hard so as to conquer geometry?"

"If hard work will do it," said Vincenzo, resolutely, "I don't think I shall fail."

"If so, there is no time to lose. The university re-opens in two months; if you set to it in right earnest, two months, with the assistance of a good teacher, will be enough for such geometry as is required for your first examination. Time is precious, as you perceive; go to Ibella after dinner, buy yourself a hat, and order a suit of black. Whatever other additions your wardrobe may require can be easily procured at Turin. Persuade the tailor to fix as early a day as possible for letting you have your clothes, and on that same day I will go with you to Ibella, and secure you a place in the diligence for Turin. There's a family from Rumelli there, poor but kind and honest people, who used to take lodgers and boarders. I will give you a letter to them; if they have no room themselves for you, they will find one somewhere else. But no word of all this to any one. If Rose and Barnaby question you as to what has passed between us, say you are under orders from me to be silent."

"I must take leave of Don Natale," observed Vincenzo.

"With him you are safe," was the answer; "only caution him as to my wish. There, now you can go."

"Thank you, sir, from the bottom of my heart," said Vincenzo, covering his godfather's hand with kisses; "it shall be the study of my life to behave so as never to give you cause to rue your fatherly kindness to me."

"I am sure of it," said the Signor Avvocato.

"Will you allow me, sir, to ask a last favour?"

"Let me hear it."

"Barnaby was mistaken, but he meant kindly by me; do, pray, sir, forgive him."

"Set your heart at rest on that score, my boy. Barnaby for many a year has been like a constitutional king with me — irresponsible for his sayings and doings. His only punishment shall be the not knowing, for a little time, that his plan for you is being carried out by me."

Four days later, immediately after dinner, the smartest of the Signor Avvocato's gigs came to the door. Rose and Barnaby, indeed the whole household, assembled by special command, were standing by it. "Now then," said the Signor Avvocato, drawing forth his watch as Vincenzo, unusually pale, joined the group, "five minutes granted for leave-taking — Vincenzo is starting for Turin — no questions allowed;" in spite of which warning, the announcement, received at first by a general oh! of surprise, was instantly followed by a cross fire of questions, remonstrances, wailings, and what not.

"One minute gone; look sharp!" cried the Signor Avvocato, jumping into the gig, watch in one hand, whip in the other. Action and look bespoke determination to adhere to his programme; so everybody made the best of the remaining time, and hand-shakings and kisses followed in quick succession. "If you want anything, mind and write to me," whispered Rose to Vincenzo, who received a similar recommendation from Barnaby.

"Now then," cried the Signor Avvocato, clacking his whip. Vincenzo got free at last, and jumped in. Adieu — good-bye — a good journey — and the wheels were already grinding on the smooth, well-kept drive. Down rushed mistress, maids, and men, to the Belvedere, there to shout once more adieu — good-bye — a good journey — as the gig passed below it. Vincenzo waved his hat — poor soul, his voice had got drowned in his tears. The Signor Avvocato, in extraordinary elation at having for once taken his own way without consulting anybody, used his whip lustily.

CHAPTER XIX.

Turinese Silhouettes.

There was no railroad from Ibella to Turin in the year 1848 — the only line that existed at that time in the subalpine kingdom was one which, with sundry gaps here and there, connected Turin and Genoa. So for many an hour had Vincenzo to jog along in a stiflingly close and far from capacious cage, before he arrived at his destination. He reached it at last, and went straight to the address given him by his godfather. Fortunately, the family from Rumelli, who took in boarders and lodgers, had an unoccupied room, or rather a light closet, with just space enough in it for a bed, a small table, and two chairs — and with just light and air enough to allow of seeing and breathing — but it was very cheap, and that decided Vincenzo to take it. He had determined with himself to cost his godfather as little as possible. He made his arrangements at once; he was to have his lodging and board for a trifle more than two sovereigns a month.

Turin was not in 1848 what it is in 1862; but even then it was inferior in nothing to any second-rate capital in Europe — neither in grandeur, comfort, activity, nor population. What with refugees from Lombardy and other Italian provinces, and what with foreigners, Turin counted that autumn from thirty to forty thousand inhabitants more than at the beginning of the year. Vincenzo who had no other point of comparison to go by than Ibella or Novara, felt positively crushed by the magnitude and splendour of the city, and the immensity of its population. His first impression was naturally one of bewilderment and discouragement, and more than once did a rush of impetuous and fond regret seize his heart at the thought of that quiet haven he had left, and which absence still more embellished. But he bravely shook off this mood, nor lacked arguments wherewith to spur himself on to manly exertion. He had his godfather's good opinion to justify — his kindness and affection to deserve — Miss Rose's good graces to improve — fortune's high favour to show himself equal to. Such were the cordials which helped him to overcome his momentary faintheartedness.

Vincenzo's most urgent need, as we know, was to find a teacher of mathematics. Without an acquaintance in Turin, he had no alternative but to consult his landlord, Signor Francesco, and this he did on the very afternoon of his arrival. Signor Francesco knew that there were plenty of teachers of mathematics, and every other branch of science; only at that instant he could not bring to mind the name of any one of them. His memory had sorely failed him since his misfortune, but he could and would inquire. Ah! by-the-bye, he would ask Signor Onofrio. Signor Onofrio was sure to know; he knew everything. "Pray, who is Signor Onofrio?" asked Vincenzo. Signor Onofrio was a refugee of 1821, who had just returned from exile — a member of parliament, a statesman, philosopher, a literary and scientific man of the very first calibre — worth his weight in gold, or rather in diamonds. If he had not a seat in the Cabinet, it was not from want of proposals. He might be prime minister any day or hour. Signor Onofrio was one of Signor Francesco's lodgers and boarders, and Vincenzo would meet him at dinner that very day at six.

Such was the character given of Signor Onofrio by Signor Francesco, in his way also a remarkable individual, remarkable for his tendencies to superlativeness and querulousness. The first he applied to everybody and everything, the second exclusively to "his misfortune." He took it for granted that his "misfortune" was as notorious as the Siege of Troy, or the earthquake of Lisbon, and allusions to it studded his speeches even when addressed to utter strangers. The fact is that, previous to living himself and his family in incredible holes to make room for lodgers, Signor Francesco had begun life as a bookseller in a very small way, and want of capital and industry had soon sent his little concern to the dogs. This consummation had been shortly preceded — not in the least influenced, mark — by a summons to the police, and the administration of a severe reprimand for the clandestine sale of a certain pamphlet against the Jesuits. This happened in the good olden time when Jesuits and police were hand and glove. Signor Francesco, denying the charge, was shown a copy of the obnoxious book, and told the exact day and hour at which it had come out of his shop. Upon no stronger foundation than the circumstances just related, and the supposition, false or true, that the buyer and informer against him was a Jesuit in disguise, did Signor Francesco lay at the door of the Jesuits the ruin of his business, and give himself out as a victim of the company of Jesus — an assumption which, by dint of repeating, he ended by believing himself. Accordingly, he had never ceased, since the promulgation of the Statuto, to petition king, parliament, and every individual minister and deputy, for redress and damages. His panegyric of Signor Onofrio, and the assiduous court he paid him, were in reality with the aim of ingratiating himself with the minister *in posse*, and securing an indemnity through his patronage.

The Jesuits at that time were the scapegoats for all sins, the Alpha and Omega of all evil, the cloak under which to conceal all meannesses and asking of alms. No official dismissed for dishonesty or incapacity but was their victim; no humbug asking for Government employment but had suffered persecution from them on account of his Liberalism; no petitions — and God knows that there were bushels of them, for petitioning was the social evil of this epoch — no petitions, but Jesuits some way or other figured in them. Never had the proverb that "only the rich find lenders" received a more extreme application.

When asked by Signor Francesco whether he could recommend a good teacher of mathematics, Signor Onofrio, without turning his face from his plate, inquired for whom; and, on being told that it was for his new fellow lodger, he looked up at Vincenzo with that particular corrugation of the brows and shutting of the eyelids which denotes at once shortsightedness and a habit of concentrating attention on any given point. "Is it for cramming?" he asked.

"I beg your pardon," stammered Vincenzo, not understanding the question.

"I mean," explained Signor Onofrio, "do you wish to study mathematics in earnest, or only just enough to allow of your passing some examination?"

"To pass an examination is certainly my motive

for learning mathematics," said Vincenzo, "but that does not exclude my having the wish thoroughly to master them, supposing I have head enough to do so. I should not like to learn as a mere parrot."

"Rationally thought and spoken," said Signor Onofrio, evidently pleased; "I think I know of a man who will suit you. We'll go to him to-morrow morning at seven. Come and remind me, will you?"

On the morrow, at seven, Vincenzo, after a little hesitation, rapped at Signor Onofrio's door — their rooms were contiguous. The door was immediately opened by Signor Onofrio himself, in a very much worn-out dressing-gown. The glimpse Vincenzo had of the room did not speak much in favour of the tenant's habits of order — everything, books, papers, clothes, lay pell mell, as if they had fallen at random from the ceiling. Signor Onofrio was neither tall nor short, neither fat nor thin, neither handsome nor plain — a very commonplace sort of man for the superficial observer, though his friends gave him credit for a commanding figure and a very fine head. Probably his was one of those mobile faces which, like some pictures, must be looked at near, and in a particular light, to produce their effect and be duly appreciated. Certain it is, that his profile was full of character and distinction, and bore a striking similarity to that of Tatius, King of the Sabines, which must be familiar to all students of figure-drawing. His dark chestnut hair had preserved all its original hue and thickness, and fell in three distinct graceful wavelets, separated by high receding interstices, upon his large forehead and temples.

Such personal advantages, however, as he possessed, he seemed to ignore; certainly he neglected them to a fault; witness his dishevelled hair, his week's unshorn beard, his whole attire made and worn at random, and rather shabby than not. Let us add in extenuation that Signor Onofrio was poor. In the course of a whole life spent in gathering treasures of knowledge and experience throughout the world, he had never once tried to improve his material condition, or lay by anything for old age; on the contrary, he had spurned all occasions of doing so which had presented themselves, content with earning his daily bread by teaching languages and mathematics. Still, poor teacher as he was in Paris, London, or New York, he had won high esteem and respect for himself and his country, and counted staunch and numerous friends everywhere.

"Sit down, my young friend," said Signor Onofrio, making an armful of the medley of articles that incumbered a chair, and throwing them in a bundle on the bed, "sit down and let us have some talk. I mentioned last evening that I had a teacher in view for you — I meant myself — I have taught mathematics for seven-and-twenty years, and I think I know them well. Besides, if I teach you at all, I shall do it *con amore*, it being in my nature to do nothing by halves. In saying this I mean to imply that with me for a master, if you have any talent, you will improve steadily and rapidly. Wait a moment. But — there is a but you see — but only on three conditions will I undertake your tuition: the first, that your lessons shall take place between six and eight in the morning, for I have other engagements which leave me no other available time; the second, that you apply yourself in earnest to master mathematics thoroughly; the third, that you will devote, exclusive of the lessons, six hours daily to this one pursuit. Now, do you agree to my conditions?"

"With all my heart, and with grateful thanks!" cried Vincenzo, enraptured.

"Very well; then we will begin to-morrow. I have got plenty of books, compasses, slates for the purpose, so you needn't buy anything. And now, that we may feel quite at ease with one another, tell me something of yourself. Where do you come from? How old are you? What sort of education have you received? Are your parents alive? What relations or friends have you? Have you ever turned your thoughts to politics? Now, mind, if you have an objection to answer any one of my questions, let it alone as though unasked."

Vincenzo replied to all without reticence, and with the candour and warmth belonging to his age and nature.

"Very good," said Signor Onofrio; "I see we shall soon be friends — indeed, we are so already; but keep in mind our agreement, and good day for the present."

"But —" said Vincenzo, who had his *but* also, one very hard to put into words; "but you have not mentioned — the — return — I mean, compensation —"

"Ah! you are right," replied Signor Onofrio; "for your sake and mine it is best you should pay me. I'll write to your godfather, and settle the matter with him. Adieu."

Vincenzo, on his side, wrote immediately to the Signor Avvocato, to acquaint him with his safe arrival and whereabouts in Turin, and with his subsequent good fortune in meeting with Signor Onofrio, contenting himself for the nonce with sending, instead of a letter to Miss Rose, as his heart prompted, only his kind remembrances to her and Barnaby, and, indeed, every one in the palace. Until relieved from the prohibition to reveal the object of his stay in Turin — a prohibition which would cease, as he guessed, in a couple of months, that is, after the passing of his examination — Vincenzo thought it safer not to write to Miss Rose, in order to avoid even a shadow of risk of betraying, by implication, the secret trusted to him. After all, it was superfluous care, Rose and Barnaby having perfectly guessed, the moment Turin was spoken of as Vincenzo's destination, the object for which he was sent thither.

The lessons in mathematics began on the morrow, and continued daily without intermission, save on Sundays, to the mutual satisfaction of master and pupil. Signor Onofrio's room, in which they were given, looked into a spacious court, and from the very first day Vincenzo noticed bursts of sound coming from the windows opposite, as if from some one declaiming while in motion. One morning he caught sight of the mysterious orator, who, absorbed in some train of thought, had come to a stand-still at one of the windows, continuing, however, his harangue aloud. The bust was all that was visible, and that was square-built — the head round and massive — the eyes shaded by gold spectacles. Vincenzo drew Signor Onofrio's attention to this gentleman, observing, "I suppose an actor studying his part."

"An actor in truth, but not in the limited sense you mean," answered Signor Onofrio — "an actor in the grand drama of the world, and who may, for what we know, play one of the principal parts in it. At least, he is full of ambition to do so, and has the iron will that will accomplish what he desires. Ambition and will are the two great levers by which men achieve success. That is Count de Cavour, a newly-elected deputy. I hear him morning and evening addressing an imaginary audience, to qualify himself to address and master a real one; possibly he has, like Demosthenes, some defect of utterance to conquer. He used to practise thus even before he was in the House. It says much for him. He is evidently a man thoroughly in earnest, and who knows his own mind — a good example to follow."

Signor Francesco's boarding-house happened to adjoin the Palace of Count Cavour, situated, as every one now knows, in the street of the Arcivescovado, part of which, at this time of writing, is deservedly named after the great departed statesman. The trifling incident, just related, was not without some influence on Vincenzo's future — and that is the reason why it is here put down — inasmuch as it acted upon him as an encouragement not to allow himself to be rebuffed by difficulties, but to work steadily on, and imitate, in his minor career, the living example before him.

Master and pupil took to each other every day more and more, and before the lapse of a month they used often to go out together for a lounge in the solitary avenues on the banks of the Po; when Signor Onofrio, for ever lighting a cigar, which was for ever being extinguished, would repeat his demonstration of the morning, or sift to the bottom some point of the politics of the day; oftener, perhaps, descant on the grandeur of the Alps frowning down upon them from the north, or on the beauty of that delicious crown of hills, smiling on them from the contrary direction. Signor Onofrio was sober of words in company, and seldom spoke in Parliament; he would say that there, where every body was bit by the tarantula of long speeches, silence was the best way of serving one's country; but with only a few friends, or, better still, in a congenial *tête-à-tête*, he could be even talkative and humorous. Some of his political opinions and dicta Vincenzo remembers to this day with grateful acknowledgment of the great benefit he derived from them in after life.

Onofrio took anything but a sanguine view of the Italian movement in 1848; he likened it to a child inevitably doomed to stumble and fall in its first attempts to walk, but still learning something from every fall and failure; and those who wondered and wailed at the loss of the first campaign, to a mother silly enough to expect her baby to walk without learning to do so at its own cost. The objectors to C. Albert, on account of some of his precedents, he compared to pioneers, who, having a strong gate to burst open, quarrelled with the axe, which could alone do the deed, because of some spots of rust on it, and threw it away, to use their nails instead. The only clear and incalculable gain which had accrued to Italy out of the hurly-burly of 1848 was, in Signor Onofrio's eyes, the accession of the Italian Idea to the throne, by which he meant that the House of Savoy henceforwards stood openly and irrevocably pledged to the triumph of the Italian Idea.

The Liberal party in Piedmont — indeed, throughout Italy — was just then divided into two great sections — those who were for renewing the war, and washing away the stigma of the late defeat as soon as possible, and those who deprecated all aggressive measures for the present, leaving to time and circumstance to fix the moment for a new struggle. Signor Onofrio sided with these last, and openly advocated their policy in Parliament; which, by the way, made him very unpopular out of doors. But he little cared; and to his opponents, who taunted his politics with being wanting in generosity, he answered, "Be just before you are generous; war is not an affair of sentiment, but of calculation of probabilities; and probabilities, under the circumstances, are eighty per cent. against us" — an opinion which after events but too sadly confirmed. However, we must not anticipate.

To fit himself for the examination, which was to open to him the way to the temple of Themis, Vincenzo had other studies to follow, besides that of mathematics, of all of which, however, he had already a smattering; and in the pursuit of these he found a precious auxiliary in his elderly friend, who grudged him neither advice, direction, nor encouragement. Thus helped on by friendly hands, and his own steady will, our youth made great strides towards the attainment of his first honours.

In the accommodation, and especially the diet, at Signor Francesco's establishment, there was room for improvement. The deficiencies, such as they were, Vincenzo and Signor Onofrio did not, however, remark; and might have ignored for ever, but for the tolerably plain hints of a third boarder, a notary's clerk, only seen at meal-times, and who, not unreasonably, considered that salad and salad, and always salad, should not be the staple of every repast. Perhaps Signor Francesco thought light food better for the stomachs of perseveringly studious persons than substantial meat, which, in fact, was scarce at his table, and generally tough. But, in God's name, what dainties can one expect for forty shillings a month? Washing, it is true, was not included in that sum; but it was seldom that Vincenzo was put to any expense on that score, thanks to the motherly care of Signora Francesco, who managed so that he never knew what it was to want clean linen — and all for love. She had neither means nor time otherwise to show her good will to the lad, who came from so near her native place. Signora Francesco was the maid-of-all-work in the house — she made the beds, swept the rooms, cooked, washed, marketed, and waited at dinner — all this in incredibly dirty gowns and caps, and with three little ragamuffins for ever hanging on her skirts, whom she unceasingly implored to return to some mysterious hole in which they were hid at night.

Sunday was her only grand gala day of the week. Attired in a black silk gown and red velvet bonnet, with her eldest boy properly washed and decently clothed, forth sallied to mass Signora Francesco on the stroke of twelve, Signor Francesco remaining at home to watch over the safety of the other two little scions of the house. By two o'clock she returned home, and sat in state in her drawing-room, until her invariable Sunday guest for the last six years, Signor Tommaso, made his appearance. Signor Tommaso was perhaps the dimmest of all the nebulæ which had left the sky of Rumelli for that of Turin. He was head clerk to an official vendor of lottery tickets, and sat as his employer's *alter ego*, in a dingy shop, icy cold in winter, stifling hot in summer, perfectly idle during five of the working days of the week, and slaving like a negro on the sixth, to meet the demands of a throng of applicants, who naturally waited to the last moment to make their choice of numbers. His salary was, of course, in proportion to his amount of work in the five first days of the week, that is, of the scantiest, and his appearance corresponded to his salary. A leaner, shabbier little fellow of fifty or thereabouts, it would be difficult to conceive.

Then, a little after two o'clock of a Sunday, Signor Tommaso called at the establishment, in the street of the Arcivescovado, invariably bringing with him a penny bunch of violets, or of orange flowers, for the Signora, as well as the tidings of the last great lottery prize, and of the favourite numbers for the next drawing. On hearing them, Signora Francesco would observe with a deep sigh: "Oh! if you could bring me word of the three numbers sure of coming up."

"Ah! if I were a priest, I could," sighed Signor Tommaso, in answer, alluding to the common belief among the vulgar, and in which he shared, that at the moment of the elevation of the host the priest sees the numbers that will come up; "but I shouldn't, though, for to tell is a mortal sin."

Signora Francesco, after a little, expressed a hope that Signor Tommaso would do her and her husband the honour of taking pot luck with them, a hope immediately nipped in the bud by Signor Tommaso's plea of impossibility. Upon this Signor Tommaso took his leave, but looked in vain for his hat, which had disappeared. At this juncture Signor Francesco intervened, and said it was all nonsense; the lost hat should not be found till after dinner, &c. New protests from Signor Tommaso, who now, joining action to words, would squat on the floor to look under tables and chairs, and poke his nose into all sorts of cupboards, till, panting and hot, and still protesting, he sank on a seat, and surrendered at discretion. The dinner hour was four o'clock on Sundays, instead of six.

At the end of his first month at Turin, Vincenzo had a great surprise and a great joy. He received by the diligence *franco* a deal box, bearing his address in Miss Rose's well-remembered writing, and containing half a dozen fine shirts and as many handkerchiefs, neatly arranged, and strewn with lavender and bits of a sweet-smelling red stuff, which answered the same purpose as sachets of patchouli. He took up with reverence one article after the other, laid them out side by side on his bed for his own admiration, kissing as he did so the initials her dear fingers had formed. And not contented with that, he called Signor Onofrio and Signor and Signora Francesco to come and admire also, which they did unreservedly. Beautiful as, no doubt, the shirts and handkerchiefs were in themselves, they had a superlative merit in his eye; they were the work of that sweet Miss Rose, who was for Vincenzo the type of all that is beautiful, good, and worthy in womankind.

CHAPTER XX.

A Pilot in a Troubled Sea.

Prudence, or no prudence, Vincenzo wrote what was a hymn of thanks to Miss Rose, in which he awarded her the palm over Arachne — an expression which greatly puzzled the girl, who had never been taught mythology, and her father, who had forgotten it, and had to look in his cyclopædia for an elucidation. Of himself and his prospects Vincenzo said as little as he decently could — that he was well and happy, as happy as he could be separated from his kind benefactor and young mistress, and that he hoped to give them both some satisfaction before long. This letter he discreetly inclosed in one to the Signor Avvocato, as he had done on the occasion of his enlisting for the war. In that to his godfather, among other topics, he touched for the first time upon the subject of his wardrobe. This was of the simplest: consisting, in fact, of the black suit made at Ibella, and which, whether as to cut or material, was not much to boast of; of three shirts, and a couple or so of white handkerchiefs, hitherto only used when he went to pay his yearly visit to the palace for St. Urban's *fête*, and which, for the reasons we know, had remained there. Now, the arrival of the beautiful linen shirts had made him feel the desirableness of some articles of outward apparel more in unison with Miss Rose's gift; in other words, the fine shirts had been the occasion of developing for the first time in our young hero that wish so natural to his age, of looking his best. Moved, then, by this desire, Vincenzo submitted for his godfather's approval a very modest list of the clothes he should like to have, putting forward in favour of his request that one of the benefits resulting from the possession of these other garments would be to spare the black suit, and thus keep it in good condition for the examination.

Nor was it to the first tailor that came in his way that Vincenzo, on receiving the Signor Avvocato's permission, gave his orders, but to one recommended by his fellow-boarder, the notary's clerk, whose black surtout, with velvet collar, had greatly captivated his fancy. And, when the happy moment at last arrived to put on this new town-made attire, it was not without a decided feeling of self-complacency that Vincenzo saw his renovated self in the looking-glass, and enjoyed in anticipation Miss Rose's surprise at the metamorphosis in his appearance. At any rate, this little and very excusable fit of vanity did not slacken his ardour for study, nor at all interfere with his habits of retirement. It was in Miss Rose's eyes alone that Vincenzo wished to appear to advantage; for what the rest of the world might think of his person, he did not care a straw. Lucky that it was so; for never had Vincenzo needed the free and entire disposal of all his energies and time so much as at this moment. The opening of the university had, in fact, doubled his task. Let us explain how. For the accommodation of those students who had volunteered for the war, and who had, in consequence, been debarred from preparing for their examinations — and there were a good many in this predicament — a special provision of the Minister of Instruction not only prolonged to the end of the year the legal term for their going up for examination, but also empowered them to follow at the same time the lectures of the class above them, so that, if successful in passing, they should have lost no time by their patriotism. The benefit of this privilege was now, thanks to Signor Onofrio, extended to Vincenzo, who thus had to read for his degree, and also to attend the lectures incumbent on students of the first year of law. Hard work as ever was; and it was only an inflexible will that could have carried him victoriously through it, especially if we take into account the heated and noisy medium amid which it had to be accomplished.

Political passions ran high every where at this epoch, and nowhere so high as among the young bachelors of the university. The party of action, secretly favoured by the king, was evidently in the ascendant; the cry for a "Gioberti Cabinet" grew louder and louder from the youths of the capital. The students, believing war to be imminent, were already organizing themselves militarily; and many and tempting were the solicitations to which Vincenzo had to turn a deaf ear, and great the force of resistance he had to exert. But Signor Onofrio's earnest counsels on the one side, and, on the other, the lad's own desire not to disappoint his godfather's expectations, or show himself unworthy of that godfather's kindness, kept him steady in the path traced out for him.

Vincenzo's examination was fixed for a day in the beginning of December, and he and Signor Onofrio, about four in the afternoon of the day previous, were sauntering arm in arm down the Via San Francesco di Paola, towards the Via Po, in which the university is situated; when, as they neared the Hotel Feder, where

Gioberti had apartments, they descried a great multitude coming towards them, headed by men carrying tricolour flags, and shouting, "Long live Gioberti!"

"Here is a demonstration bent on destroying the prestige of one of the finest names that Italy can boast," exclaimed Signor Onofrio, drawing up close to the wall to let the procession pass.

"How so, when they are precisely acclaiming that name?" asked Vincenzo.

"The louder the acclamations of it now," replied Onofrio, "the greater will be the disappointment when its owner is seen at work. Rarely do minds addicted to lofty philosophical speculations possess that practical insight into men and things which makes the efficient statesman."

Signor Onofrio was too entirely of the practical school himself not to underrate Gioberti, on account of his Utopia of an Italy renovated through and by the Pope.

A tall long-bearded young man, with one of the finest and most melancholy faces imaginable, led the advancing column, tossing high the banner in his hand, and shouting with all his might. Signor Onofrio, by dint of frantic gesticulations and loud calls, succeeded at length in attracting the flag-bearer's attention, who, on recognising Signor Onofrio, forced his way to him.

"*Et tu quoque, Brute*," said Signor Onofrio to him; "as if thou didst not know the man thou art shouting for!"

"I know him and shout for him," was the handsome stranger's reply. "We want a name, and he has one. Diplomacy has left us no choice between an act of madness or an act of cowardice, and I, for my part prefer the first;" and so saying he roared again, "*Viva Gioberti!*"

"There's truth in what he states," sighed Signor Onofrio. "England and France, the mediating powers between us and Austria, with more of resemblance to the gods of Olympus than to Cato, side with the conquering cause, and abandon us to the tender mercies of our foes."

The street was now entirely blocked up by the demonstration, and the cries for Gioberti waxed louder and louder. Gioberti at last showed himself in the balcony of the hotel, and addressed the crowd. The thin thread of voice in which he did so was in striking contrast to the orator's tall large person and powerful blond head. His eloquence, fluent, classic in form, wanted strength and nerve.

"*Verba, verba, prætereaque nihil,*" was Signor Onofrio's definition of it. Such as it was, however, it had an immense success with his audience, who cheered him heartily, and afterwards dispersed peacefully at his bidding. This demonstration gave the death-blow to the existing Cabinet. Gioberti was summoned on the morrow by the king, and had the mission of forming a new ministry confided to him.

"What are you going to do now?" inquired Signor Onofrio of Vincenzo that same evening.

"To work till break of day," answered the student.

"No, no; that will never do," declared Signor Onofrio. "You have read far into the night for more than a week, and now you are worn out. A few hours' more work at this moment will add nothing to your knowledge, but rather prevent your being clear-headed to-morrow. You require some amusement strong enough to keep you from thinking of your examination. Have you ever been to the theatre?"

"Never."

"Then it's the very thing for you. We'll go."

They went to the Sutera Theatre, under the porticoes of Via Po, where, for the sum of fourpence, they secured comfortable places in the pit, and three hours and a half of music by one of the first masters, very tolerably executed. The opera was one of Paer's, the "Pianella perduta nella neve." A good opera buffa, for being long out of fashion, does not become less amusing and effective. Vincenzo laughed to his heart's content, and forgot both university and impending examination. This was exactly what Signor Onofrio had aimed at. Vincenzo slept like a top all night, and got up in a frame of body which made his mind equal to any ordeal. He passed most successfully, and he would not have exchanged his lot for that of the mightiest monarch when, at the end of the third day (the examination lasted three days), he could sit down to his desk and write:

"I have passed, and with praise. I do not lose a moment in communicating this news, which will, I am sure, afford you, my dear godfather and Miss Rose and Barnaby, indeed, all my well-wishers, as much pleasure to hear as it gives me to tell. I must candidly aknowledge, however, that the happy result is far less owing to any merit of my own, than to the luckiest of chances which turned all the questions just upon those subjects in which I was best prepared. Except, perhaps, mathematics, in which, thanks to Signor Onofrio, I felt quite at home, and afraid of no surprise. And, speaking of Signor Onofrio, I don't know if he has written to you as he said he would, as to the remuneration he was to receive for the lessons he gave me. Should he not have done so, pray be so good as to take the matter in hand yourself. Signor Onofrio is far from rich, or, I ought perhaps to say, he is poor; and if, as I surmise, he declines money, he might nevertheless accept of some return in another shape. Excuse me, dear and honoured sir, for presuming, as it were, to intrude advice upon you, who know so much better what is right than I do; I only mean to remind you of what may have slipped your memory, and thus I trust you will excuse the liberty. In all cases, I beseech you to take it for granted that I have no greater desire than to please you. And now I will conclude, by wishing that all happiness may attend you and yours, and begging you to believe me always

"Your dutiful and affectionate godson,

"VINCENZO.

"P.S. I think that the study of law suits me very well; at least, I have come across none of the difficulties which made philosophy so irksome to me at the seminary. All I read I understand pretty well."

This letter brought a very kind one from the Signor Avvocato, who gave, with no grudging spirit, the praise Vincenzo so well deserved for his success, and for the modesty with which he had met it. The Signor Avvocato wrote back: "I have communicated your letter to Don Natale, the Marquis, and the Intendente of Ibella; I read it aloud to all my household assembled expressly for that purpose, and I am commissioned by one and all to offer you their congratulations and affectionate remembrances. So you see that the end and aim of your residence in Turin is now made public, and you are relieved from the bond of secrecy which I exacted from you. I write by this same post to Signor Onofrio, to thank him for his great kindness to you, and to beg him to let me know the amount of my debt to him for your lessons. In case he should be unwilling to name the sum, I shall find means, nevertheless, in a round-about way, to give him no cause to regret the timely assistance he afforded you." The few lines at the bottom of the page, in Miss Rose's rather clumsy round-hand, sent a glow of pleasure through the innermost fibres of Vincenzo's heart. She wrote: "Barnaby sends you his love, and so do I; papa is so happy at your success, and very proud also, and, indeed, so is everybody. It seems a great while since you went away. I am longing for the holidays, to see you again. I always remember you in my morning and evening prayers. Do as much for me, for I hope you do say your prayers; don't you? Your affectionate "ROSE."

Vincenzo cut off Miss Rose's postscriptum, and treasured that scrap of paper — she had never written to him before — as he would have done the autograph of some saint in heaven. The boy swam in a sea of bliss. He had the goodwill of all those for whose goodwill he cared, and the testimony of his own conscience, that he had done all in his power to deserve that goodwill. To finish with all that has reference to Vincenzo's first examination, let us note that, a fortnight after, a cart from the country left at Signor Francesco's house, directed to Signor Onofrio, a hamper of game, a Parmesan cheese, as big as an ordinary card-table, and two casks of wine, the lesser of the two full of ten years' old Nebbiolo. Such was the upshot of the negotiation carried on lately by letter between the Signor Avvocato and Signor Onofrio.

Vincenzo's task, from the day of his having taken his degree, became comparatively light and easy, but the evenness of mind, indispensable to its steady continuance, was sadly interfered with by the pressure of external circumstances. Political affairs were fast hastening to a crisis, and great was the excitement throughout the country. The Gioberti Cabinet, now in power, had issued its programme, peaceful in form, bellicose in substance. According to it, the Government professed to be willing to treat of peace on honourable terms, but, rather than submit to such as were not so, it would resort to the dire arbitration of war. Now, the honourable terms alluded to by the Piedmontese Cabinet were those embodied in the Hummerleyer Memorandum, and which Austria, elated by her recent successes in Italy and elsewhere, was no longer disposed to grant. Austria was eager for war; but too wily to take upon herself, in the face of the mediating powers, the odium and responsibility of an aggression. She did her utmost, through a well-contrived system of temporization and provocation, to goad the Piedmontese into madness, and in that succeeded only too well. Piedmont took the first step, attacked her enemy, and was defeated at Novara. Would she have better served the cause she advocated, by bowing to necessity and passing under the *caudinæ furcæ?* A doubt may be permitted. A man may get a licking and have a fine to pay, and yet not be a loser after all, if he comes out of the contest with a good character for pluck. Why should what is true of a man not be so of a nation?

The situation was supremely critical. Conquered, divided against itself, thrown suddenly into the hands of a young and inexperienced chief, with the enemy encamped within its frontier, the second city of the kingdom in open insurrection, Piedmont seemed a doomed prey to anarchy or despotism. Now was the moment for all stout hearts and hands to join in a desperate effort, to keep the storm-tossed vessel from going to pieces on either of those rocks. To preserve order without endangering liberty was the problem those stout hearts had to solve; and, to their glory be it said, they *did* solve it.

Onofrio was among those who worked the hardest to find this solution. He had constantly refused office, when office was comparatively an affair of honour and emolument; he accepted it now that it was the post of danger and of unregarded thankless labour — the post dear to heroes, who disdain to be known as such. There are men, devoured by zeal for the public weal — men destined to die for its service.

Onofrio's was not the foremost, but the most laborious and responsible, place in one of the Secretaryships of State. Unfortunately for Vincenzo, what the country gained by this, he lost. It soon became a matter of physical impossibility for Signor Onofrio to continue a boarder in Signor Francesco's house. Not that the simplicity, nay, penury, of the establishment was, in his opinion, incompatible with his own new position. Though one of the principal functionaries of the Government, he was, to all intents and purposes, as simply and unostentatiously inclined, even as poor, as heretofore. But at Signor Francesco's there was an absolute want of space for the numerous visitors, whom it was part of Signor Onofrio's duties to receive in his official capacity. This it was that obliged him to shift his quarters to a more capacious abode, to the intense grief of his former pupil, and to the incredible distraction of Signor Francesco, who believed he had thus lost a golden opportunity of pressing for, and obtaining, the redress and damages he had been so long entitled to from the Jesuits.

The rest of that year continued tempestuous and pregnant with anxieties. Tranquillity out of doors, thanks to the moderation of the Government and to the common sense of the governed, was never put in jeopardy, it is true; but the minds of men remained heated and disturbed. The Chamber of Deputies, convened with the view of concluding with Austria a treaty of peace, become really indispensable, grew factious and unmanageable. This led to a dissolution and to a new appeal to the several constituencies, accompanied by an explanatory address from the throne to the electors. This last proceeding was accused of being unconstitutional, and so perhaps it was; not the less, however, did it save the country. The loyalty and the reason of the constituencies were not appealed to in vain, and the majority of the members returned felt the necessity of getting out of the Provisionary, and settling the vexed question of the Peace.

Vincenzo, thanks to Signor Onofrio, who sent him tickets for the gallery of the Lower House, did not miss one of the debates on this topic of vital interest. His judgment formed and ripened apace under the influence of the contemporary events developing themselves before him, and also by contact with that superior mind which it had been his good fortune to come across. Though more rarely than before, he still had the incalculable benefit of intercourse with Signor Onofrio — still gathered knowledge from the stores of his rich experience. Signor Onofrio's chief effort as regarded Vincenzo was to put him on his guard against indiscriminate enthusiasm. "Youth," would he say, "is too apt to be swayed by sound and colour. However high and generous a purpose in itself, if not practically attainable, it cannot form the legitimate scope of a political man's aspirations and exertions. Of what avail descanting on the convenience of flying, from the moment we are sensible it is a power out of our reach? Of what avail evoking a political Beau-Ideal, in the face of the sad reality which surrounds and crushes us? I say this in reference to ——'s high-flown speech against the conclusion of peace. I agree with him, that it would be more agreeable to sign a peace at Vienna than at Milan, with Milan still in the gripe of Austria — pleasanter far to impose, than to accept of conditions. A wonderful discovery indeed! But do a few sensation phrases about Rome and Papirius, the Lombard League and the Barbarians, change our position from the conquered into that of conquerors? Do they do away with any of the dire necessities laid upon us? They do not; and yet you heard, perhaps joined in, the frantic applause from the gallery which followed those empty tirades. I remarked there were many students present; the greater the pity. Leave to the unreflecting, the thoughtless, such vain demonstrations of feeling. Acknowledge and endure the inevitable. Endurance has its grandeur and its uses. It fosters the native energies of the soul, and tempers it for high deeds, just as a coating of winter snow warms and fertilises the ground."

CHAPTER XXI.
Sunshine and Clouds of the First Vacation.

At the expiration of the scholastic year, Vincenzo went to spend the vacation at the palace. This was the great reward he had looked forward to throughout the whole term, this was the Shibboleth he had whispered to himself in all his difficulties, this was the sign that had banished all his faintheartedness. And yet, golden as were the hues in which his imagination had revelled, the reality even surpassed his day dreams.

On alighting from the diligence, at Ibella, he found the Signor Avvocato, Rose, and Barnaby waiting for him at the coach office, and received from each and all of them as cordial a greeting as son or brother could have desired. The Signor Intendente himself presently joined them, and they all walked together to the intendenza, where the Signor Avvocato had left his carriage and horse. Vincenzo's progress through the streets was a positive triumph — strangers stopped and raised their hats, acquaintances shook hands eagerly, shopkeepers left their shops on gratulatory errands, or stared from their thresholds as if the bishop himself was passing. We need not explain that Vincenzo was known by sight to the immense majority of the Ibellians, and that the fame of his brilliant examination had become a household topic in the little town. His modest demeanour and good looks also did much in his favour. No one had hitherto surmised he had in him the making of a very handsome young man — not even Rose; and no wonder; a three-cornered hat and a cassock would have been an effectual disguise even for an Antinous. Now that he had grown three inches taller, and that his well-proportioned figure was set off by a well-fitting coat — now that an abundant crop of dark brown hair, and a thick down on the upper lip, gave to the long delicate oval of his face both colour and relief — Vincenzo no more resembled his former self of a year ago than the butterfly does the chrysalis from which it has burst forth.

In one word, his success was complete. Was it as spontaneous and genuine as it was well deserved? Had the pomp and circumstance of his reception nothing to do with it? Would it have been the same had Vincenzo, instead of parading the streets in state, as we may say, walked along them with no other escort than the porter carrying his trunk? We cannot answer these questions; but this we can say for certain, that it was not haphazard which had directed the intendente's walk towards the office where the diligence stopped, but a wish to humour a whim of his friend the Signor Avvocato. Nor was it blind god or goddess Chance that had enticed to their doors most of the shopkeepers of the Regent Street of Ibella, but most positive information received through Barnaby on that very morning, to the effect that Signor Vincenzo was returning from Turin loaded with honours, and would pass through that same Regent Street, on his way to the intendenza, about noon, in company with the Signor Avvocato, the Signorina Rosa, and the Signor Intendente.

After all, it was an amiable weakness in the Signor Avvocato to make a fuss about a godson who had done so much credit lately to his patronage, and to try and prepossess public opinion in the youth's favour, as the best way of answering the disparaging innuendos and false reports circulated by the black party of Vincenzo's failure in Turin, and consequent open rupture between him and his godfather. This black party was no longer the bugbear it once was to the Signor Avvocato; the year had been so fruitful in gloomy anticipations, in predictions of catastrophes, belied by the events, that the fidgetty gentleman had ended by taking heart, and had nearly persuaded himself that old times would return no more.

We pass over the hearty welcome given to the student by his acquaintances of Rumelli, old Don Natale at their head, and also that he received from the household of the palace. The very field labourers of the estate flocked to shake hands with him, merrily reminding him of those few days when he had made one of their number. A little dinner party at the palace, which took place on the morrow, a Sunday, put the climax to the cordial demonstrations of affection of which Vincenzo was the object. Friendly Don Natale, who was of course one of the guests, inspired, as usual, by what he called old people's milk, viz. long-bottled Barbera and Nebbiolo (two famous Piedmontese growths), made a fellow speech to his famous one of seven years ago, that, as this, addressed to the same hero, *mutatis mutandis*. Don Natale hailed Vincenzo now as a future luminary of the bar, just as formerly he had prophesied he would become a shining light to the Church.

Life glided on smoothly and happily for Vincenzo. The Signor Avvocato treated him in every way as one of the family, with, perhaps, a new shade of respect. As for Rose, she had from the first moment resumed all her former intimacy and childlike intercourse with her old playmate; only at her father's suggestion she ceased to speak to him in the familiar colloquial form of the second person of the singular, and adopted that of the second person of the plural. This substitution of the comparatively formal *you* for the intimate *thou* was a little sorrow to Vincenzo, who, though an innovator in politics, was a staunch Conservative in all that pertained to sentiment. However, he was too reasonable not to feel the propriety of the change; and then it was not Rose's own doing, but her father's — a reflection which took away much of the smart of the sting. Moreover, this loss was more than compensated for by a gain in another direction.

Vincenzo had not been without his apprehensions as to a repetition of the young lady's complaints and regrets about the profession he had renounced. Now, never once during their nearly endless colloquies did she so much as hint at the unpalatable topic. We say endless colloquies, because with the deduction of two, or at most three, hours, devoted daily by Vincenzo to his books and writing, he and Rose, whether in the house or out of it, were constantly together and generally alone. But, though this was all very pleasant, Vincenzo could not help noticing and taking umbrage, even from the beginning of his visit, at a novelty he discovered in the habits of life at the palace.

The Marquis and the Signor Avvocato drew better together; they visited each other frequently, and sought each other's society abroad. This improvement in the relations of the representatives of two opposite principles, besides foreboding ill for the political consistency of the Signor Avvocato, had the additional fault in Vincenzo's eyes of marking a decisive step towards the realization of a contingency, of which, for some time past, he could never think without his blood tingling; that is, of a marriage between young Federico and Rose. Vincenzo had long decided *in petto* that Rose ought not to be Federico's wife, without, however, even in thought laying claim to the prize himself. This improved neighbourly feeling between the two fathers had begun with the accession of the Gioberti Cabinet, and had been cemented by the declaration of war to Austria, which followed within three months afterwards. The Conservative-Liberal had felt as keenly as the Absolutist Marquis the foolhardiness and the dangers of such a step, and a common cry of indignation and alarm had expressed their common feeling; "We are at the mercy of a pack of maniacs — this is not governing, it is rather a mad steeplechase; the king is imposed upon, the ministers ought to be impeached."

They were so full of terror of democracy, or demagogy, as they preferred to call it, so preoccupied with the expediency of making head against the new foe, that, for a time, they lost sight of the distinctive shades of their respective creeds. Nor were these shades deep or numerous. In fact, setting aside an elective House of Commons (a senate named by the Crown he went so far as to adopt); setting aside, then, an elective House of Commons, to which the Marquis altogether objected, as essentially and necessarily a democratic institution, his political programme differed little or nothing from the one advocated at that period by his plebeian neighbour and friend, the Signor Avvocato, and which was as follows: — "The statuto amended in a conservative sense; the royal prerogative reinforced; a government strong enough to be independent of factions; a national, that is to say, a purely Piedmontese policy, with no taint in it of Italianism, knight-errantry, or unitary Utopias; above all, respect to religion and to its ministers."

This last clause had been mooted and carried by Don Natale, whose liberalism had been singularly cooled by the chill air blowing from Rome. Had not the Pope said, in his famous Encyclic of the 8th December, 1849, that the Revolution was inspired by Satan himself, and that it had for its object the utter destruction of the edifice of Christianity and the reconstruction upon its ruins of the social order of Paganism?

On the aforesaid broad basis, the wise heads of their generation in Rumelli were willing and ready to save the State. The Unwise — that is, the immense majority of those who cared but indifferently for the welfare of the kingdom, and a great deal for their own pockets — had a far more simple plan: "Enough of novelties; let those govern who could; but no new taxes, no loans, no additional burdens." Advice more easy to give than to act upon. How pay the bill of costs for the war, and an indemnity of sixty millions of francs to Austria, without adding further imposts?

To swim against this current of tenets, formed *ab irato* and antagonistic to his own, without either hurting ticklish self-love (and thus running the risk of injuring the cause he wished to uphold) or of being false to the right, or what he believed to be such, needed the utmost circumspection on Vincenzo's part. He had all the modesty befitting his age and station. Rarely, when in company, did he put forward his opinion in opposition to that of his superiors and elders, unless called upon to do so; which he often was by Don Natale, who delighted to hear the young student assert his own way of thinking fearlessly and unreservedly, yet with a tact, a measure, a discretion, and a good humour, which conciliated even his opponents. More than once had the Signor Avvocato been heard to say on some of these occasions, with a chuckle, "Any one may see thou wast born to be a barrister."

"A very flattering compliment for the cause I plead, since barristers profess to accept of none but just and lawful ones," observed the young fellow, playfully.

Anyhow, it was not on these desultory fencings over their dessert or coffee that Vincenzo reckoned for working his godfather's re-conversion; it was on the serious talk they had in the long *tête-à-tête* walks they took together now and then during the week, and regularly every Saturday afternoon, as on Saturdays Rose was too busy about the house-linen for amusement. It was then that Vincenzo brought all the weight and stringency of his young logic to bear on the doubts and vacillations of his political adversary. The Signor Avvocato liked argument for argument's sake, and was always the one to strike the first blow, which was always returned with interest.

"Prudence, as much as you please, my dear sir,"

would Vincenzo say. "I will willingly join you and cry Prudence from the house-tops, but no relinquishment of principles for all that. Principles are the moral centre of gravity for nations as well as individuals, and they cannot be renounced, except under the penalty of self-abdication. Have you ever abjured yours? No, to your honour be it remembered. You have stood by them, and have lived to see their triumph. Purely Piedmontese politics mean neither more nor less than the abandoning of the principle of Italian nationality. Now, what is Piedmont without that? A little insignificant State, impotent alike for good or evil, and doomed to fall between two stools. Whereas Piedmont, the depositary of the national idea, the representative and standard-bearer of a whole people — Piedmont, in course of time, becomes the *tête de pont* of twenty-four millions of Italians; and, circumstances aiding and abetting, can strike an effective blow for national unity."

"Dreams, dreams!" exclaimed the Signor Avvocato. "Italian unity is a physical and moral impossibility, my dear boy. Europe will never allow us to coalesce into a body; and, supposing that Europe willed it, or could not prevent it, our own internal divisions and jealousies would stand in the way. Fancy Florence or Milan ackowledging the supremacy of Turin — it is the height of absurdity."

"But Florence and Milan would not object to acknowledge the supremacy of Rome," urged Vincenzo. "No doubt, when Rome is the capital of the kingdom of Italy; but when will that be? Rome is the Pope's, the centre of catholicity. Try to get it, and see what will follow — religious war, schism, the world in flames, civilization at an end, universal chaos."

But enough of a controversy, the only object of relating which is, to make the wide distance between the ways of thinking of the rising and sinking generations of liberals stand out in high relief. Occasionally, Vincenzo succeeded in wringing some concessions from his godfather; which, however, were too surely retracted on the very next day. The Signor Avvocato was less accessible to the logic of arguments than to that of facts. So that Vincenzo's toil resembled that of the Danaides, in so far, at least, as liberal principles were concerned — though not as respected himself. Not one of these skirmishes but increased the godfather's estimate of his godson's talents and worth, and secured to the youth a sort of general influence.

Political discussions did not at all interfere with Vincenzo's enjoyment of his holidays and the merry days of the vintage. A fortnight before our hero's return to Turin, young Del Palmetto arrived at the castle, with the intention of spending his three months' leave of absence there. The cavalry sub-lieutenant had seen no active service in the field in 1848, but had amply paid his debt to his country and to the race from which he sprung in the short campaign of 1849. His name had figured, with honour, in the order of the day, given after the battle of Mortara, in which he had had two horses killed under him.

The eighteen months that had passed over Federico's head since we last saw him marching out of Ibella *en route* for Vigevano, had worked litte change, if any, either in his outer or inner man; though Vincenzo stoutly declared that he was wonderfully improved in looks and manners. But we know that Vincenzo could not be but a poor judge in this special case.

Del Palmetto had the good taste to drop the familiar *thou* he had used all his life to the ex-seminarist, and treated him altogether on a footing of equality, a behaviour which said more in favour of his good nature than of his enlarged judgment, since, at the same time, he made no secret of his less than moderate respect for the owners of "the gift of the gab," as he designated the body of advocates in general, or of his want of reverence for "their ladder of preferment," as he styled the statuto.

The young officer, as if it were a natural consequence of the better understanding between the Marquis and the Signor Avvocato, was very constantly at the palace, and for ever loitering in the grounds in search of the Signorina Rosa, to whom he had always something new to tell or to show. And this, to the great delight of the young girl, who liked being amused of all things; not quite so much to the pleasure of Vincenzo, who suddenly found his former duettos turned into trios. As to Barnaby, he looked on in burning indignation, and was heard to ask himself over and over again, whether the "old Notomy," as he termed the Marquis, had perchance bought back the estate, that his son made it his home. Barnaby, as the reader easily guesses, had taken the reconciliation between the two potent neighbours as a personal affront, and had again broken off all intercourse with his master. Barnaby was no leveller — no hater of the aristocracy — quite the contrary; being the good Piedmontese he was, and also a pupil of the late Signor Pietro, he was disposed to venerate all those born in an exalted social station. It was this particular Marquis he detested — cordially detested — for the many slights he had heaped upon the family Barnaby worshipped; and, even had he not decided long ago that Vincenzo and no other should marry Miss Rose, he would rather have seen her dead and buried than Marchioness del Palmetto.

Barnaby, like Vincenzo, was not without his misgiving that this growing intimacy between castle and palace might lead to the contemplation of a closer alliance, the realization of which the old ex-gardener was resolved to prevent, but the project of which would not the less add a new difficulty to those already in the way of his own private plan.

Vincenzo had but little joy in this last part of his holidays, and in spite of the guard of honour which accompanied him to Ibella, and of his godfather's kindly injunction to take a singing master as soon as he was again settled in Turin, he went away with a very full heart — full not only of regret, but of jealousy. Vincenzo was indebted to Barnaby's well-meant indiscretion for the discovery of his own feelings.

In his wish to cheer and encourage his troubled young *protégé*, the old blunderer had dropped in his ear this parting recommendation, "Thou needst not be jealous of Federico. She is no bread for his teeth, but for thine, if thou makest thyself a man."

These words raised the veil which up to this moment had hidden from Vincenzo the nature of his own sentiments. The knowledge filled the youth with confusion and awe. Yes, he was jealous; yes, he loved Rose, not only as his kind young mistress and benefactress, but as the woman he would wish to make his own for ever. Vincenzo turned giddy as he measured the distance which separated the son of the peasant, the dependent student, from the rich and accomplished heiress; and then said to himself, "If a strong love and a strong will can bridge over the gulph between us, I am the man to do so; if not, I shall still love, serve her, and watch over her from this side the chasm. So long as she is happy, I shall be happy also."

CHAPTER XXII.
Spokes in the Wheel.

It cost Vincenzo no effort, quite the contrary, to resume the course of his town avocations. Study had become a real passion with him, and his was the satisfaction given to few, of gratifying his own inclination, and furthering, at the same time, the object of his now defined ambition. The lectures on law did not engross his whole time, a considerable portion of which he devoted to other and self-set tasks. Intercourse with fellow-students, who had had the advantage of a more classical education, had made him aware from the first of sad deficiencies in his own. Little as he knew about the history and literature of ancient Greece and Rome, he knew still less about the history and literature of his own country. Not a line of Dante, Ariosto, or Alfieri had he ever read. Geography was to him a sealed book. He applied himself to fill up these gaps, and succeeded tolerably well in course of time. One of his first and most rapid acquisitions was the French language. The boarder who had come instead of Signor Onofrio happened to be a Savoyard, who wanted to learn Italian; an exchange of lessons was agreed upon between him and Vincenzo, which, aided by constant reading of French books by the latter, gave him, in an incredibly short time, a mastery over that language.

Excepting a daily good walk into the country, and two singing lessons in the week, in obedience to his godfather's express wish and command, few were the relaxations Vincenzo allowed himself from study — of an evening, the perusal of a newspaper at some *caffè*, a pit ticket at some cheap theatre, or going to hear a debate at the House of Deputies whenever there was one of any importance. This last was the treat he enjoyed most, and to which he did not grudge giving hour after hour, sensible as he was, from the amount of positive information and the enlargement of ideas he derived from such discussions, that he could have had no better employment for his time. Of the great benefit of the schooling he received there, Vincenzo had a striking proof that year.

Among other bills brought before Parliament in 1850, there was one for abolishing ecclesiastical jurisdiction and other clerical immunities, and rendering the clergy amenable in civil matters to common law. Vincenzo's *prima facie* impression was rather hostile than not to the measure. He had lived too long among priests, formed too high an estimate of the calling of a priest, not to resent personally, as it were, the curtailment of any of their prerogatives. But, when the subject was debated in the house (and not a sitting did he miss), when he heard the matter sifted from beginning to end, the inconveniences and abuses of the exceptional jurisdiction pointed out, and the considerations of morality, of justice, of dignity militating against it, victoriously enforced, then the scales fell from his eyes, and his only wonder was how such an unnatural state of things could have so long outlived the times and the circumstances to which it owed its existence.

The passing of this law consummated the divorce between Rome and Turin, between the clergy and the Government of Victor Emanuel. Rome protested; the clergy raised the cry of persecution. One fact will give the measure of the bitter feelings of these latter. Shortly after, one of the ministers who had introduced the measure, Rossi di Santa Rosa, fell dangerously ill, and asked for the last sacraments. By order of the Archbishop of Turin, the request was refused. He must either write a recantation of all that he had said or done in support of the obnoxious law, or die without the consolations of the Church! The high-souled Christian chose this last alternative. Orderly Turin waxed frantic at the news. The youths of the university were in a blaze in a twinkling, and for once Vincenzo forgot his books and his retiring habits to mix in the irritated groups, and join in the cry for vengeance on the Torquemada of the day. There was no outbreak after all, thanks to the foresight and decision of the Government, which, while making a display of force sufficient to keep down violence, cut at the root of the evil by removing the originator of the scandal — that is, by sending the Most Reverend Archbishop under a stong escort to the frontier.

A public subscription was set on foot to defray the expense of the erection of a column (the Column Siccardi now being raised in Piazza Savoja) commemorative of the passing of that law, each individual offering being limited to a few pence, in order to give the subscription a popular character. The names of those parishes (comuni) which should subscribe were to be inscribed on the column. Vincenzo, as may be conjectured, vowed to himself that it should be no fault of his if the name of Rumelli did not figure on the monument. But his first hint at the subject during his next holidays brought upon him from the Signor Avvocato a severe rebuff. What? subscribe to the Siccardi testimonial! was Vincenzo mad? not a soul in the parish but was against the law and the subscription. The fact is, that Rumelli, now under the mayoralty of the Marquis, had passed over in a body to the opposition.

Vincenzo strongly expressed his extreme surprise and mortification at his godfather's defection. What? a liberal of 1821, a man deeply versed in jurisprudence, a partisan of civil equality, to oppose a measure which consecrated that equality! The Signor Avvocato explained. He approved of the principle of the bill, but he contested the opportunity of its application. The moment was ill chosen, the public mind not sufficiently enlightened — everything that tended to diminish the prestige of the clergy was in reality a blow aimed at religion, and without the restraint of religion where would society go to? "See the fine result of your law," pursued the old alarmist, warming up; "protests from Rome, consciences troubled, a powerful class arrayed in battle against the state, the capital on the brink of insurrection, a pastor violently torn from his flock —"

"Say rather a wolf in sheep's clothing," cried Vincenzo, exasperated; "are you going to stand up for that —"

"I stand up for nobody," interrupted the Signor Avvocato, "least of all for intolerant fanatics. I was for toleration, for liberty of conscience and worship, sir, many years before you were born, sir. I only say that the scandal which has taken place would not have taken place, had the Government not given a pretext for it."

The immediate cause of the elderly gentleman's collapse on this, as on other questions, must be sought in the removal from Ibella to a higher post of the intendente, whose energy had hitherto kept up the flagging courage of the master of the palace. The change was the more unfortunate, as the new intendente was a sort of neutral being, neither bird nor fish, seeming solely bent on conciliating all opinions — that is, humouring everybody's bias; and the bias of our friend, the ex-mayor of Rumelli, we know too well by this time.

There can be no need, after this, to enter into any explanations of the sentiments of the present mayor, the Marquis, in reference to the law and the testimonial. Siccardi, the originator, promoter, and supporter of the measure, he likened to Arius, to Julian the Apostate, and the proposed column to the Tower of Babel. Even mild-tempered, jolly Don Natale could at times speak in the bitter tones of hatred of the great abomination; and on one or two occasions went so far out of his character as seriously to warn Vincenzo against canvassing for the subscription, under penalty of incurring the censures of Rome. Vincenzo had abandoned all idea of canvassing or propaganda, in so far as Rumelli was concerned, the moment the prop and stay on which he had relied, we mean his godfather, had failed him. That did not, however, deter him from defending the Government and their general policy whenever he heard them unjustly attacked; but even all the discretion and amenity of manners which accompanied his pleading of their cause did not always save him from the ill humour of the Signor Avvocato, when Rose would interfere, and act as peacemaker.

Vincenzo knew not what to make of Rose's studied neutrality when in company, or of her absolute reserve on the vexed point when alone with him; on the other hand, he dared not provoke an explanation, for fear of drawing forth from one so devoted heart and soul to the clergy, some profession of faith lamentably at variance with his own. As it was, he felt full of gratitude to her for her unwearied efforts at conciliation, and, when those failed, at reconciliation. One day, after a rather warm encounter between her father and Vincenzo at dinner, she said to the latter, "Had you not better drop politics altogether, since papa and you cannot agree?"

"I wish I could," said Vincenzo; "but you know that the Signor Avvocato likes an argument of all things, and if he begins how can I with propriety avoid answering?"

"True," said Rose. "Well, then, could you not humour his ideas a little?"

"If those ideas are what I believe contrary to truth, how can I humour them short of downright insincerity?" rejoined Vincenzo.

She reflected a little; then said, "Are you sure of being on the side of truth?"

"I am sure," replied Vincenzo, "that I am on the side of what I conscientiously believe to be the truth."

Rosa looked for an instant as if she were going to say something vehement, but she checked herself, and said, "Truth is God's alone; let us pray to Him for enlightenment."

"Amen!" agreed Vincenzo.

To Don Natale was due all the credit of Rose's guarded behaviour. He had been for the last eight months — in fact, ever since Father Terenziano's death — Rose's confessor and spiritual director, and as such had used his influence with her in a truly Christian spirit. Don Natale was not a zealot. He might, in the heat of controversy, or under the smart of a fancied injustice to his order, use strong language, and even storm when fairly roused; but in the discharge of his sacred duties he was far too conscientious, too deeply imbued with the maxims of the Gospel, not to discountenance anything like intolerance and fanaticism, especially in a young girl with more zeal than judgment.

Vincenzo's only ally was Barnaby — an ally far more compromising and dangerous than ten enemies. Nothing could satisfy him short of halters and gibbets. Arguing with his usual logic, Barnaby declared that, since common law was not good enough for the blacks, there was nothing left but to put them out of the law. There was no hope of peace for the state unless they adopted his panacea of the scaffold and the hangman; and, as the Government did not show any intention of applying his remedy, they were a set of asses, and, as Vincenzo demurred to this conclusion, he was an ass himself.

Altogether, this vacation was rather a disappointment to Vincenzo; and he saw the close of it arrive with far less regret than he had ever felt before on similar occasions. The next year ran its course quickly and smoothly in a quiet monotony. Not so the one following, the fourth he had spent in Turin. The year 1852 was marked by two occurrences, both of them calculated rather to cloud than brighten his prospects. The first was the death, after a short illness, of the Marquis. This very natural event, considering that the deceased was nearly eighty, and no great friend of the youth, did not affect him much. What did trouble him a good deal was the particular nature of certain speculations which sprung from the demise of the old nobleman. Vincenzo had to go by special invitation to attend his funeral; and what should he find at Ibella, where the Signor Avvocato and Rose were now settled for the winter (it was in the month of January) — what then should he find at Ibella, and at Rumelli, where the funeral took place, but a strong belief already established to the effect that with the old Marquis had disappeared the only obstacle to a matrimonial alliance between the two first families of Rumelli? It is not difficult to guess how agreeable to the feelings of the youthful lover must have been this public verdict, which awarded the great prize for which he was straining every nerve to his born rival.

By the bye, we must not forget to say that the journey between Turin and Ibella was by this time much easier and shorter than when Vincenzo had set out four years previously; it was, in fact, reduced to a few hours by railroad. Piedmont had not been idle in the interim, and a network of iron lines was now spreading over the face of the whole country.

Now for the second untoward circumstance, or rather complication of circumstances, which made this year an unlucky one to Vincenzo. We must premise that Signor Onofrio had been prevailed upon, a few months back, to accept a temporary mission to the island of Sardinia — a mission connected with the reorganization of the universities there. It was hoped by his friends, both in and out of power, that change of scene with movement might prove beneficial to his health, sorely tried of late by hard sedentary work and assiduous attendance in Parliament. When Vincenzo, on his return from the funeral, went to inquire after Signor Onofrio, he found him just arrived, and far worse than when he had set out. A few days more, and the deputy was down with fever. The distemper, which had been lurking so long in the system, broke forth with great intensity. Vincenzo offered his services, which were gratefully accepted. A friend in need is a friend indeed. Signor Onofrio's friends, and he had many, were most of them active politicians or men of business, who had everything to give save time. Vincenzo therefore found no competitor in his way; and little by little established himself permanently by the sick bed, transporting thither his books and papers. But of reading or writing there was soon no question. Signor Onofrio's illness was long and dangerous; and, Vincenzo having frequently to sit up all night, it followed as a matter of course that he must rest during the day, and consequently miss his lectures and forego his studies.

The worst was yet to come. Scarcely had Signor Onofrio entered the stage of convalescence when Vincenzo was seized by the same fever from which his late charge was just rallying. Thus the parts were reversed; and he who had been nursed had to nurse — a task which, though still weak, the convalescent performed with all the care and zeal of one whose naturally kind feelings were further quickened by the too late acquired consciousness of being the cause of this trial to his young friend. Signor Onofrio had never thought of asking his physician, and reproached himself bitterly for the omission, whether his complaint was catching, and only learned that it was so to a high degree on Vincenzo's being taken ill of the same. Once aware of this, Signor Onofrio felt it incumbent upon him to inform the Signor Avvocato without delay of his godson's malady; which he represented, at the patient's most urgent entreaty, in the least alarming colours — laying much stress on the infectious character of the fever, and adding Vincenzo's earnest request that no one should stir on his account. The youth was haunted by visions of the Signor Avvocato and Rose coming to Turin, catching the fever, and dying.

The Signor Avvocato's first impulse, to his honour be it said, on hearing of his godson's illness, was to go to him — an impulse which the perusal of the next paragraph, dwelling on the malignant nature of the fever, instantly put to flight. Age and growing obesity had not added to his courage; and, much as he liked his godson, he liked his own whole skin better. Still, to receive such tidings as he had received, and impart them to others as he must infallibly do, and to do nothing, or have nothing done, seemed harsh and unnatural. Yet, how could he decently send anybody on an errand from which he himself drew back?

Barnaby extricated him from this dilemma. Barnaby, with that fine discrimination and moderation of views which distinguished him, saw matter in the intelligence for coming to three conclusions — the first, that Vincenzo was dying, if not dead; the second, that his master was a monster not to be already on the road; and the third, that he himself must be off to Turin. This last was the only one that he thought fit to communicate to the Signor Padrone, and that in an indirect form, by inquiring if he had any message for Turin.

"I don't advise you to go," said the Signor Avvocato; "Vincenzo's illness has nothing alarming in it — and then it is catching, and —"

Too wroth to argue the point, Barnaby reiterated his question in a very peremptory tone: "Have you any message for Turin?"

"Besides," continued the Signor Padrone, "it is Vincenzo's express wish, and it ought to be attended to, that none of us should go to him." With a shrug of the shoulders expressive of infinite disgust, Barnaby withdrew. The master had to run after the servant to catch him before he reached the station (the family was still at Ibella) and, *since he would go*, give him directions. These were in the kindest and most generous sense. Vincenzo was to have the advice of the best physicians, and every comfort that could be had for money; Barnaby received *carte blanche* in that respect. Vincenzo was to be told not to fret about the loss of a term; he was to think of nothing but getting well again, and coming to the palace for change of air as soon as possible. The godfather felt a desire to make amends to the godson, and willingly paid in money that which he held back from giving in kind.

At dusk of the same day Barnaby fell, like an aerolite, upon Signor Onofrio, who, it being carnival time, took him at first for one of the masqueraders. The new comer's antiquated accoutrement, incoherent language, and style of ugliness, so grotesque as to seem scarcely natural, made the mistake quite plausible. Barnaby asserted his identity by walking straight into the sick room, much to the patient's amazement and alarm, lest the old man should catch the fever, and carry it to Miss Rose. Indeed, Vincenzo was growing so evidently worse under the lash of this fear, that even opinionated Barnaby saw the expediency of delivering his messages (he had one from Miss Rose also) and of withdrawing, after a parley with Signor Onofrio, to seek shelter elsewhere. His visit on the morrow met with no better success than that of the previous evening. So, seeing that he could be of no service, but rather the contrary, and satisfied from personal observation, and the physician's assurances, that Vincenzo was out of danger, Barnaby felt that the wisest thing for him to do was to return to Ibella — which he did, loaded with Vincenzo's best thanks and blessings for father and daughter, plus this sybilline message to be delivered, particularly to the latter, "that he had put it on."

What had he put on? Probably the contents of

a little sealed packet, that Rose had sent him by Barnaby, and which, on being opened, displayed to Vincenzo's view a very familiar object — a scapulary to be worn round the neck, and bearing impressed upon the silk of which it was made a flaming heart transpierced with arrows. Rose had written inside the paper, in which this had been wrapped, "Infallible against all fevers; pray, put it on." Vincenzo was touched by this childlike mark of interest; and, much as some years of schooling in a large town had worn out his faith in the efficacy of such spiritual remedies, he hung the scapulary round his neck, and wore it to its last shred. It was enough that it came from her to do him good. Sweet superstitions of love! who would, even if he could, do away with any of them?

Vincenzo's complaint, after a time, assumed an intermittent character; it left him long intervals of tranquillity, but, when least expected, reappeared. After he had shaken it off for good and all, he was too exhausted and worn out to think of resuming lectures and study for a long time. Towards the middle of April, Signor Onofrio accompanied him to Ibella, and there consigned him to the Signor Avvocato, who took him to the palace. His friend's illness and his own entailed upon Vincenzo the loss of a whole scholastic year.

Unusually long and happy were these holidays to the convalescent; father and daughter vied with each other who should spoil him most. And, though the reigning Marquis called daily at the palace, and the new intendente came thither once or twice a week, and other young men from Ibella appeared on Sundays, and each and all looked sweet indeed upon the blooming heiress, Vincenzo had no pretext for jealousy. All Rose's little preferences were for him; his was the company that Rose liked best, his the only arm she would accept or seek; Vincenzo alone was admitted to the privilege of sharing the fatigues and joys of the rearing of her silkworms. What did this mean? Was her sisterly attachment changing into womanly love? Not yet. Rose at eighteen, with the form of a woman, had all the unconsciousness of a child. She liked Vincenzo more, but not differently — she liked him for all the good she had done him — in truth, for saving his life, as she confidently believed she had, by sending him the blessed scapulary of the Holy Heart.

CHAPTER XXIII.
Banished from Eden.

AN obvious effect of the kindness which had been interchanged between Signor Onofrio and Vincenzo during their respective illnesses, was a fresh growth of friendship and intimacy, which made each more desirous of the company of the other — a desire, however, not so easily realized, considering the unintermitting occupations of both, which left them but little leisure for visits. Onofrio had more than once urged Vincenzo, since the latter's return to Turin, to come and live with him; a very tempting proposal to the student, which he had, however, bravely withstood, out of good will, or, we might say, compassion to Signor Francesco and Co., whose circumstances were just then at the lowest ebb.

But, when Signor Francesco's establishment went

to the dogs — which it did in the beginning of that year 1853, owing, of course, to the unjust denial of the indemnity he was entitled to from the Jesuits — well, when the concern was finally given up, Vincenzo willingly accepted of his friend's hospitality, and went to live with him on the same pecuniary terms on which he had lived at the boarding-house. Signor Onofrio's apartment consisted of four clean and airy rooms on the fourth storey, having a fine prospect of the Po, and the smiling hills that look over the river from the south. The elderly gentleman allowed himself the luxury of an old female servant, who cooked and arranged the rooms, spending the rest of her time in sorting and combining numbers for the lottery.

Vincenzo had not been quite two months with Signor Onofrio, when he received a letter which set his head working like a windmill. It was from the Signor Avvocato, and said briefly: —

"If not absolutely impossible, pray start on the receipt of this, and come to me. I have something particular to say; I require advice and help. I shall not detain thee longer than four-and-twenty hours. If you leave Turin immediately on getting my letter, you will arrive at Ibella by the five o'clock train, p.m. Giuseppe shall be waiting at the station with the chaise.

"Thy affectionate Godfather.

"P.S. — No one is ill."

Vincenzo left word for Signor Onofrio where he had gone, and put himself immediately *en route*. It was the first time he was thus summoned from his studies. The business which called for this innovation must be important and pressing indeed. What could it be? A proposal of marriage for Miss Rose from Del Palmetto? But if so, even admitting that his advice was wished for, which was going almost beyond the limits of probability, what help could he be expected to give, what help could he give in such a matter? No, it could not be that. Some difference with the Marquis perhaps? Most unlikely. Del Palmetto was far too solicitous to please father and daughter to admit of that conjecture. Some quarrel with Barnaby? ah, that must be it. With that absurd head of his, no telling what scrape the old man might not have floundered into himself, dragging his master after him — and to get out of this scrape something had to be done or undone, towards the doing or undoing of which Vincenzo's assistance was in some manner needed — probably by using his influence with the obstinate old fellow to do or undo. But no; neither could that be. Rose's ascendancy over Barnaby was far more potent than that of Vincenzo; and what was the use of sending for him when she was on the spot?

The revolving of these and other hypotheses, no sooner accepted than rejected, served at least to beguile the way. Giuseppe was at the station with the chaise, and drove off at a smart pace. Vincenzo was too discreet to ask the driver any questions beyond the usual ones as to the health of the family, and Giuseppe was too prudent and little talkative by his nature to volunteer any information or guesses of his own, supposing he had any, on private matters. The day was on the wane when Vincenzo alighted at the gate of the palace. There was some one crouching on the terrace wall opposite. Taking it for granted that it was Barnaby, Vincenzo was going to call to him, though unable to identify him at that distance, when he heard his own name pronounced from above. "Is that you, Vincenzo?" The young man rushed up stairs like lightning, and met his godfather on the landing.

"How do you do?" said the Signor Avvocato, as Vincenzo kissed his hand, as he had been used to do from childhood; "very kind of you to set off directly; I knew you would; come in, my boy," and he led the way to his *sanctum sanctorum*, his musical retreat. "We shall be more private here; sit down — not there, take the easy chair; you must be tired — no? so much the better. I wish I could say as much for myself; and yet I have scarcely set foot out of doors these two days; walking up stairs puts me so much out of breath. I am breaking, my boy, I am."

This assumption was not new in the Signor Avvocato's mouth, any more than Vincenzo's mode of meeting it with a sonorous laugh of incredulity.

"If all breaking constitutions were like yours, physicians and apothecaries would have to seek a new trade. Come, come, my dear sir, you feel a little nervous and weak; who does not occasionally? If I am not mistaken, you have had of late some cause of uneasiness."

"You may say so," cried the elderly gentleman, with an emphatic burst of self-commiseration, "and from the very quarter upon which I had relied for support and consolation. But I am very selfish; — you must be hungry, I am sure."

Vincenzo protested he was not.

"Have a crust of bread and a glass of wine in the meantime till supper is ready."

Vincenzo again protested he was not hungry, and preferred waiting for supper. He was on thorns to know what had gone wrong at the palace.

"Well, then," resumed the Signor Avvocato, "I may as well tell you the doleful story at once. Here it is in two words;" and, dropping his bulky form at ease into the capacious arm-chair, he went on in a more business-like tone, "You know, as indeed everybody knows — *lippis et tonsoribus* — that for some time past, especially ever since his father's death, young Del Palmetto has been paying — how shall I say? — a good deal of attention to my daughter." (Vincenzo's heart started off at full gallop.) "Nor has it, I dare say, escaped your penetration, that for the last year I have rather encouraged than not, the young man's suit. Yes, the match met all my views and wishes. Federico has all the qualities for making a good son-in-law to me, and an excellent husband to Rose — he has an agreeable exterior, an unimpeachable character, an easy temper, and a most honourable position in the world. I am too much of a philosopher, besides being the son of a self-made man, to lay more stress than it deserves upon a title — still a title spoils nothing. Then he has known her from her cradle, so to say — he has been brought up with her, is familiar with her ways of thinking. He is not rich, to be sure, but that is not his fault — and then, what do I care for a fortune? Rose will have enough for two, thank God. Well, then, to come to the point. Federico, like the honourable man he is, proposed to Rose at the expiration of his mourning; and what did the silly minx do? — refused him flat."

Had not the zone of shadow projected by the screen

round the lamp, extended a friendly protection to Vincenzo's face, even Rose's pre-occupied father might have drawn some inferences from its sudden ashy paleness when Del Palmetto's proposal was mentioned, and the rush of blood that turned it scarlet on the hearing of Rose's refusal.

"Refused him flat!" repeated the old gentleman with increasing animation; "and for what? on grounds too nonsensical for any rational being to listen to with patience; first, because he is an officer in the army — as if the profession of arms was not, next to the bar, the most honourable — and secondly, that he had boxed her ears when she was a child. *Risum teneatis.*"

"Miss Rose's prejudice against the army," said Vincenzo, in order to say something, "is one of old standing. I remember, as far back as 1848, speaking to her of the career of a soldier as one suitable for me, and the positive horror with which she dissuaded me from any such project. This prejudice, as far as I can judge, is connected with, and has its root, I may say, in her religious views — a special reason for dealing with it carefully and gently."

"Then, I am not the man for that work," quoth Rose's father; "I have lost all patience with the girl. She is so opinionated — has a quiet impermeability to reason quite her own, which provokes me beyond measure. You will soon find it out, when you come to argue the point with her — yes, you must do so for my sake," the speaker hastened to add in answer to a possible objection conveyed by a wave of Vincenzo's hand. "It is a service I have a right to demand from your gratitude, but which I shall be glad to owe to your friendship. For this, and this alone, have I summoned you from Turin. You are my anchor of hope in this affair. Rose has for you the affection and deference of a younger sister. You possess both gentleness of manner and stringency of logic — your very disinterestedness in the matter will add strength to your arguments. In one word, I entrust Del Palmetto's cause and mine to you. Win Rose's consent to this match, and you will have laid me under obligations for life."

Vincenzo's contention of thoughts and feelings during this earnest appeal challenges description. To undertake the mission, and perform it, whatever it might cost him, was a piece of heroic folly, quite unwarranted by the circumstances — to undertake it, and, while acting up to the letter, fall short of the spirit, was, for one so upright, a moral impossibility. To decline it, and give no special plea for so doing, was to lay himself open to the charge of ingratitude in the present, and to that of equivocation in the future. There remained for him, as the young man conceived, only one honest, though dangerous course, whereby to reconcile his duty to his godfather with the claims of truth — that was to explain his refusal by laying bare his heart. Accordingly, he met the sentence with which the Signor Avvocato had ended — "win Rose's consent to this match, and you will have laid me under obligations for life!" — with a passionate, "I cannot — I will not — it is impossible."

"What do you mean? why impossible?" asked the other sternly.

"Because," faltered Vincenzo, — "I would a thousand times rather incur your anger than play false with you — because," he wound up firmly, "I love your daughter."

The Signor Avvocato was struck dumb by this announcement. All other feelings for the nonce were swallowed up by one of immense surprise. Had Vincenzo, instead of the handsome, rather abundantly whiskered young fellow of two-and-twenty that he was, had he been a girl, the notion of his loving beautiful Rose could not have taken her father more unawares.

"You love my daughter, sir!" at last gasped the amazed sire, dropping the familiar *thou* for the more formal *you*.

Vincenzo bowed his head humbly.

"You are an aspiring youth, by Jove; more aspiring than wise. And so, you have availed yourself of the intimacy I allowed you in my fatherly blindness, to make love to my daughter for God knows how many years!"

"You wrong me without cause," said Vincenzo steadily, yet respectfully. "I owned to you that I loved your daughter, not that I had made love to her — the word 'Love' has never passed my lips to her since I knew what love was. Ask her; she will tell you."

"Thank you — it only needs that I should set on foot a public inquiry as to what you have done or not done. I believe you. I will do you the justice to say you have always behaved honourably — played fair with me. I will be above board with you, and tell you in so many words that I have other views for my daughter. I am sorry that you love her, but you shall not have her. You have had your way with me so long, and in every thing, that no aim, it seems, is too high for your hopes."

"My hopes?" repeated Vincenzo dejectedly. "Have I expressed any, sir? Do you know if I ever entertained any? Bear in mind, sir, if you please, that the avowal I have made was not of my own choice. It has been forced from me by an entanglement of perfectly unforeseen circumstances. After what you have told me, could I, with the feelings I have, keep back the truth without duplicity? Put yourself for an instant in my place, sir, and say, would you have acted otherwise?"

"Eh, dear me!" said the Signor Avvocato, fretfully, as he rose from his chair; "you stick to it just as if the admission of its necessity was a cure for every evil. When you have demonstrated mathematically that, by falling in a certain manner, I could not but break my leg, will that remove the smart or the injury? Disappointment upon disappointment in the present, discomfort upon discomfort in the future, that is the consolatory vista your disclosure has opened before me. Discomfort of all kinds for me and for you — because, to begin with, you surely don't expect, things being as they are, I can allow my house to be your home, as I have done up to this day."

"On that, as on all other points, I shall abide by your orders, sir." The words were rather gasped than spoken, and so mournfully, so forlornly, that the Signor Avvocato had a glimmering of the immense sacrifice they implied, and accordingly said, much softened, "I don't give you orders. I am not angry. I only suggest what seems to me best for all parties. It is especially for your sake — to spare your feelings — that I advise a separation, a temporary one of course, only until

— at the most, one vacation or two. We'll find some reason — some pretext, I mean — to account for your not coming here as usual. Nobody must suspect, you know —"

"God forbid!" said Vincenzo, energetically; "not for me, but —"

"Of course, of course, I catch your meaning," interrupted the godfather; "and this will be the only alteration in our intercourse; as to the rest, nothing is changed; I shall be for you to the last what I have been to this day. Pursue your studies steadily; make yourself a man. The hand which has supported you from a boy will not be withdrawn until you are in a fair way of acting and providing for yourself, and not even then."

Vincenzo's tears were flowing fast. The door burst open, and Barnaby announced supper in as sepulchral a voice as if he had been announcing Doomsday instead. "We are coming," said the master. Barnaby, stiff as a poker, stood rolling his goggle eyes. "We are coming," again said the Signor Padrone. Barnaby did not budge. "You may go," added the master of the house. Barnaby lingered another moment, then turned sharply round and banged the door after him. The Signor Avvocato, his right hand raised in the direction of the door, stood listening to the sound of the retreating steps, and, only when they could no longer be heard, said in a whisper, "For God's sake, not a word to Barnaby!" The accent and look betrayed a real terror.

"Not a word to any living soul!" replied Vincenzo. "Rely on me."

"When do you go back to Turin?" asked the Signor Avvocato.

"To-morrow. I shall be off by break of day."

Rose's greeting of Vincenzo was most cordial, though not unmixed with surprise. She hoped he had come to make some stay. Vincenzo said he much regretted that it was out of his power to do so. He had come on business, and on business he must return. He was not ill, was he; he looked so pale. Vincenzo said he was very well, only he had felt a little chilly on the road. March winds were rather biting. The poor young man strove manfully to look natural, nay, cheerful, a task in which he succeeded tolerably well, save when the thought intruded upon him that this was possibly the last time he should set eyes upon her for God knew how long. Then his face fell, and a knot in his throat made utterance impossible. Rose's father took no pains to conceal his intense preoccupation. He scarcely spoke during the meal, and as soon as it was over left the table. Vincenzo, pleading his chillness, did the same, and took leave of Miss Rose for the night. Godfather and godson exchanged a few parting words and good wishes for the night on the landing; then the former entered his apartment, and Vincenzo went up to the third storey, locked himself into his room, put out the candle, dropped into a chair, and fell into thought — if thought could be called the perpetual revolving of one fixed idea, "Separated for ever."

Anticipating a visit from Barnaby, which he would willingly avoid, Vincenzo had locked himself in, and extinguished the candle, in order to make believe that he was sleeping. Not long after, in fact, there was an attempt from the outside to lift the latch, followed by cautious taps at the door. Vincenzo did not stir — indeed, scarcely dared to breathe. The tapping was renewed with intermissions for nearly half an hour, then it entirely ceased, and Vincenzo, left to himself, jogged on once more on his mental treadmill.

Towards midnight the paroxysm of passion abated a little, and he could think — oh! with what fondness — think on the many happy hours he had spent in that happy Eden, from which he was now expelled; and along with that thought came a gush of passionate thankfulness towards him, to whom, after God, he owed all that blessed time, to whom, in fact, he owed all that he was; and then followed a qualm of remorse at his own late unfeelingness, and a yearning to go and make amends, and pray for pardon. Acting upon this irresistible impulse, the young man lighted his candle, opened the door softly, and stole down to his godfather's apartment. He must be still awake, for there was a light in the bed-room, visible from beneath the door. Vincenzo knocked gently. "Who is that?" called a voice from within.

"It is I," said Vincenzo, opening the door. The Signor Avvocato was sitting up in his bed, his arms crossed over his chest. "What do you want?" said he, somewhat sternly. For all answer Vincenzo threw himself on his knees by the side of the bed, and, burying his head in the coverlid, cried in a voice convulsed with sobs, "Your pity, your forgiveness, your blessing."

There was no resisting the passion of this appeal. The old gentleman put both his arms round the aching head, saying, "I do pity thee; I do forgive thee; do bless thee with all my heart."

"To think that I should give you pain," continued the young man, almost frantic with grief; "I who would willingly die for you, it is too hard, too hard, too hard;" and he swayed his head to and fro, without raising it from the bed. Then, suddenly lifting himself up, and staring at his godfather through his tears, "Do you believe me when I say that I would willingly die for you? Do you believe that I do love you with all my heart and soul?"

"I do, I do," answered his godfather, soothingly.

"Indeed, indeed, it has not been my fault; it has grown up with me like a part of my being."

"What, my dear boy?" asked the Signor Avvocato.

"This love, this love," cried the youth; "she was so kind, so gentle to me, and then she was your daughter; how could I do otherwise than love her?"

"Well, well," interrupted the old gentleman, with some embarrassment; "no more of that; better avoid the subject, both for your sake and mine. It is painful and exciting; I am agitated enough as it is. Calm yourself, my dear boy; go and try and sleep. I will do as much on my side; I feel far from well. Let us say no more, and part in the faith of our mutual attachment. Go; good night."

Vincenzo was struck by the worn out expression of the speaker's countenance, and more than that by his look of age. There was no mistaking the fact, the Signor Avvocato had grown quite an old man. The bloom of his once florid complexion was all gone, and there were wrinkles on each side of his mouth, round his eyes, on his forehead, everywhere. Vincenzo was scared by the discovery, and rose to obey. The old face and the young one were once more pressed together in a long and fond embrace, and Vincenzo departed.

He stole quietly to his garret, put the light on the

table, and found himself face to face with Barnaby, standing on the other side of it. "So thou art skulking, art thou?" said Barnaby, in his bitterest tones. This was Vincenzo's finishing stroke — the poor fellow, faint already with emotion, dropped into a chair with a groan.

"Why didst thou lock thyself in?" pursued the old man with the look of an inquisitor.

"Some water. I am fainting," faltered Vincenzo. Barnaby pounced on a jug full of water, and kneeling by the youth's side so as to support him, made him drink out of the jug, and bathed his temples. "Poor dear, how white he looks! No wonder; all right in a twinkling, poor dear!" the old man kept murmuring to himself, while with the right hand, now free from the jug, he fondly parted the hair glued to Vincenzo's brow by a cold sweat.

"Thank you. I feel much better, thank you," said Vincenzo, reviving.

"Another sip of water," suggested Barnaby in the sweetest of voices, "it will do you good."

"I am now quite well," said Vincenzo, swallowing some more water; "thank you, my good friend, I don't know what has been the matter with me."

"I do," said Barnaby, emphatically.

"Do you?" said Vincenzo, perplexed.

"Yes, I do;" and the old man added in a suppressed shout, "I know everything."

Vincenzo started to his feet in a new terror, grasped Barnaby by the arm, and cried, "If you do, promise that no living soul" —

"Del Palmetto shall not have her,". interrupted Barnaby.

"Promise" —

"*You* shall; that's what I promise."

"Promise," urged Vincenzo.

"She loves you."

Vincenzo wrung his hands. Barnaby, thus set at liberty, jumped to the door, repeated, "She loves you," and vanished into the dark corridor. Vincenzo reached it with the light just in time to hear the click of the lock inside Barnaby's room, and, well knowing the old man's obstinacy, and afraid of being overheard by the Signor Avvocato, who might misinterpret a mysterious-looking communication with Barnaby at that hour, gave up a hopeless and dangerous chase.

Vincenzo spent the rest of the night in a state of agitation, bordering on delirium; stole out of the house at dawn, walked to Ibella, took the earliest train for Turin; and when, by eleven in the morning, he found himself seated in his own room, opposite to the hills overhanging the Po, he wondered whether he had been the sport of a bad dream.

CHAPTER XXIV.

Onofrio to the Rescue.

"WELL, what news from the country?" asked Signor Onofrio of Vincenzo when they met for dinner. "Far from good, I see by your face. Anybody ill, anybody dead?"

"Thank God, nobody ill — nobody dead. Except some hopes fondly and stupidly cherished by me," said Vincenzo.

"There are no hopes so positively dead, as not to

be capable of reviving at your age," said Signor Onofrio. "Come, come, let me feel the pulse of these said hopes, that I may judge if there is not a spark of life in them yet!"

Vicenzo's load of misery was just then so heavy, that he could not resist the temptation of sharing it with a friend; and for the first time in his life, the sweet name of Rose passed his lips in connexion with his secret. Signor Onofrio listened sympathetically to the simple tale — then said, "Is money a *sine qua non* with your godfather in this matter?"

"Not in the least," replied Vincenzo; "he whom he has chosen for his daughter is far from rich — nay, comparatively poor."

"Does the Signor Avvocato hold to birth and rank?"

"No more than is reasonable in the son of a self-made man sprung from the popular classes. His father began his career as a mason."

"If so," resumed Signor Onofrio, "we need not bury our hopes yet; the case is far from desperate. But before going further, I want a frank reply to a preliminary question; — it is almost ridiculous to put it to a young man in love; still I have so high an opinion of your judgment and straightforwardness, that I do ask it. My query is this, Can you answer for this young lady not becoming a clog to a political man?"

"I don't quite catch your meaning," said Vincenzo.

"I will make it plain to you," said Onofrio. "You know the sort of poor education given to our young women, even up to this day, especially to those belonging to small provincial towns. Take the most enlightened, the most independent, the most liberal-minded of them all, and, nevertheless, in any mixed matter, such for instance as that of the ecclesiastical jurisdiction, she will blindly follow the direction of a priest — that is to say, of a man who receives his inspiration from Rome. Now Rome is hostile to us, and likely to become more so, the more this little kingdom asserts its civil independence, as it is determined to do. Now you can fully understand my meaning when I ask; Can you foresee no day when this young lady will be on one side, and you on the other of a question — when to do your duty will cost you a severe struggle? More than one of the public men of the day are in such a predicament."

Vincenzo unhesitatingly answered that he could foresee no such day. Miss Rose, he candidly acknowledged, was no exception to the rule laid down by Signor Onofrio. She was prone to defer too much to priestly opinion, or rather had been prone to do so, for, as she had grown older and her judgment ripened, this bias of her mind had sensibly diminished. According to Vincenzo, she possessed an amount of good sense, which only required to be properly directed, to bring forth excellent fruit, and a docility equal to her good sense, which gave ample security for her listening to reason. All this the young man affirmed and reaffirmed, in the fullest belief that he was saying neither more nor less than the truth. Vincenzo was not in love for nothing.

"Supposing this to be so," at last interrupted Signor Onofrio, "and that your godfather attaches no undue weight to birth and fortune, it will be easy to demonstrate to him that a son-in-law of greater promise than Vincenzo Candia it would be difficult for him to secure.

Yes — of greater promise — I speak in sober earnest; not for the world would I trifle with you," resumed Signor Onofrio, replying to the young man's deprecatory gesture — "of promise, in the noblest acceptation of the word. I mean as to social distinction, influence, and usefulness — for, as to the emoluments, you will never be enriched from such a source. We live in a country, God be praised, where a man may hold the first offices of state for years, and leave office as poor as when he entered on it. But now to explain; only premising that what I am going to tell you I have been revolving for some time in my mind, and waited only for a fitting opportunity to make it known to you. In a rising state like ours, there is a fair field open for every noble ambition. Our ministry encourage high aspirations — particularly among our youth — they lie in wait, so to say, for talent and energy, to enlist them for the public service. The aim of those in power is to form a staff of young men imbued with their own spirit — young men able and willing to carry out their plans. You shall be one of this chosen staff; you are qualified for it, first by your general intelligence, and still more so by that precious and rarest of gifts at your age, the steadiness and the moderation of your views, which will save you from being hurried away by an impulse, however generous it may be. I will introduce you to my friend and chief, the Minister. He will discover at a glance your special aptitude, and will put you in the right place. In five or six years — by the way, how old are you?"

"Twenty-two," answered Vincenzo.

"Well, by the time you are twenty-seven or twenty-eight, you will be fairly launched either in diplomacy or in the Administration; and at thirty, the legal age for being a deputy, the patronage of the Minister, with the interest of your godfather, will secure you a seat in Parliament. Once that accomplished, there is no height to which you may not aspire. Even — if you have the mettle of one in you — even to be Premier! With such prospects, am I right or wrong, in saying that the man must be difficult indeed, who would not be proud of such a son-in-law?"

"I fear," said Vincenzo, blushing, "that after all this is only a brilliant dream conjured up by your friendship for me."

"Only bring a strong will to bear upon it, and, in its main features, the dream will become a reality. To give it quickly somewhat of substance, I shall begin by presenting you to the Minister no later than to-morrow, if the thing be possible. We will see afterwards whether we cannot do something for your father-in-law that is to be. Do you know at what epoch it was that he received his cross of San Maurizio and Lazzaro?"

"He has never had it — has never had any decoration," said Vincenzo.

"What! not the cross of a Knight? Did you not tell me he was a liberal of 1821?"

"Yes."

"Has he not been once or twice Mayor?"

"Twice, since 1848."

"Is he not a man of high character, of considerable landed property, and, besides all that, popular in his district?"

"All true — he is quite the leading man in Rumelli."

"Then it must have been an oversight," said Signor Onofrio. "According to all precedent, his right to the cross is unquestionable; unless there be some special reason militating against him, he shall owe it to you. It shall be your wedding gift to the good gentleman. Now cheer up my young friend," concluded Signor Onofrio, taking his hat to go out; "and put this well into your head, that from this moment a new era begins for you. It is I who promise you this, and it is my invariable habit to do more than I promise."

Vincenzo's body and mind were out of joint to such a degree that the ten hours of unbroken sleep which he had that night were not too much to recompose his troubled spirit, and rest his wearied limbs. All was no longer gloom in his mental vista when he awoke — there was a brilliant salient point now in it.

Rose had refused Del Palmetto — refused him "flat," as her father expressed it. Could it be that he, Vincenzo, had something to do with her refusal of the young Marquis? Could it be that she loved him, the penniless student? Barnaby had declared it was so. Barnaby, it was true, was a confirmed blunderer, but he was a favourite of hers, and it was not utterly impossible that she might have made him, to some extent or in some way, her confidant. Oh! if she loved him, what would a few years of waiting be to her — she was so young — a few years, until this new path opening before him should have led him into the Land of Promise; and, did she love him, there he felt sure it would lead him.

This train of rosy speculations was put to flight by Signor Onofrio bringing, in hot haste, the announcement that the Minister would see Vincenzo that same evening.

"Be sure to be on the western side of the arcades in Piazza Po by seven o'clock," said the excellent friend, "and wait till we come. After I have presented you, I shall leave you to a *tête-à-tête*."

Vincenzo knew the personage in question very well by sight from having seen him in the Chamber of Deputies, and at Signor Onofrio's bedside during the illness of the latter.

The Minister had nothing about him of the Jupiter Tonans — far from it — he looked like everybody else; yet the mere thought of meeting him made our hero rather nervous — a sensation that increased as he took his way to the rendezvous. The man on whose impression of you may depend your whole future — and future and Miss Rose were one and the same thing for Vincenzo, — that man, were he a dwarf or a hunchback, cannot fail to inspire you with a certain awe. Vincenzo's heart beat fast when he descried under the arcades the two familiar figures walking arm-in-arm towards him, and saw himself beckoned by Signor Onofrio, who for all introduction said, "Here's my young friend. I recommend him to thee — good night."

"I am very glad to make your acquaintance, or rather to renew our acquaintance," said the Minister graciously. "I have seen you so often at Onofrio's that I cannot consider you a stranger. Onofrio has just been telling me what a Godsend you were to him while he was ill. You have not been well yourself I hear. I hope you are quite recovered."

"Perfectly, thank you," said Vincenzo.

"You could not have bestowed care upon a more worthy person," continued the Minister. "A valuable man, is that Onofrio, and tells me many fine things of you. We'll go in here for a little quiet talk," and, as he said this, Vincenzo's interlocutor stopped before a wide entrance, drew a key from his pocket, opened the door, went in; and, as soon as Vincenzo had followed, shut the door again.

"Don't stir till I have turned darkness into light," resumed the Minister, lighting a match, and with that, a *rat de cave*, or coil of wax taper. This done, he led the way up to a third storey, produced another key, opened another door, and, going through a small passage, introduced Vincenzo into the salon — a well-sized room — saying,

"Here we are at last; pray sit down — where the deuce can the candles be?" looking for them in vain on the mantelpiece. "Excuse me for leaving you in the dark for an instant. Do, pray, sit down, without ceremony," added the Minister, returning with two lighted candles, and seeing Vincenzo still on his legs.

Vincenzo in silent admiration of this wonderful simplicity obeyed. The furniture was of the most unwieldy and oldfashioned kind; as far as Vincenzo could judge, there was not an article there with any pretensions to be gay, or elegant, either as to form or colour. The armchairs, if the one on which he sat was to be taken as a specimen, were anything but soft and comfortable. The Minister took up a newspaper from the table, examined the date, made a roll of it, lighted it at one of the candles, and with it set fire to the faggot and logs of wood ready laid on the hearth, commenting upon the operation with the remark, that the evenings were very chilly. "Do you smoke?" he asked Vincenzo. "No." "Very wise of you — an uncommon virtue in a young man now-a-days. Do you mind others smoking in the same room with you?" "Not at all." "Then I will have a cigar;" and the Minister lit one, and then threw himself into a corner of a sofa, and puffed away for some time in silence. "You were brought up at a seminary, if I don't mistake?" at last issued from the cloud of smoke.

"At the seminary of Ibella, up to the age of seventeen," replied Vincenzo.

"Was it from your own wish, or from some other cause, that you studied for the priesthood?"

"It was solely because of my father's desire that I should be a priest."

"You felt none of what is called a vocation?"

"Decidedly none," said Vincenzo.

"And how did you manage to get out of the seminary?" asked the minister.

"It is a long story, and I fear little edifying," said Vincenzo, smiling.

"Never mind the length," returned the minister; "and, as for edification, there is nothing more conducive to that, alike for listener and narrator, than the history of past blunders."

Thus encouraged, Vincenzo complied. He described the intoxication produced in him by the mere names of the innovations of 1848, told of his admiration for the Seminarists of Milan and their barricades, and of his unconquerable antipathy for the calling to which he was destined, which had grown and developed with the growth and development of these new feelings. He recounted his failure in his examination, his godfather's anger, the episode of the purse, and, avoiding any mention of names, his ill-fated expedition to Ibella, his foolish escapade at the Caffé della Posta, his consequent determination to enlist, his meeting with Colonel Roganti, and his wanderings in company with that worthy.

Vincenzo did not tell his tale in one breath; but, whenever he stopped, fearing to tire out his listener's patience, the minister would urge him to go on, professing much interest in the narrative; and, that he was amused, his hearty bursts of laughter at Vincenzo's description of Colonel Roganti's manœuvre, and his own sale of scapularies and songs, testified beyond all doubt.

"And, after your leader's arrest, what became of you?"

Vincenzo, in answer to this question, gave a summary account of his flight with Ambrogio, of their journey to Novara, of their taking part in the festival, and being captured in the very moment of forgetfulness of such a danger, of his return to the palace, the further struggle he had there, his eleven days' apprenticeship to the hoe, and the relenting of his godfather, who had finally sent him to study law in Turin.

"You have shown throughout all this a rare degree of perseverance, that ladder to all success," said the minister; "and, pray, what practical lessons did your experience teach you?"

"To be on my guard against boasters and perpetual fault-finders," answered Vincenzo; "and yet to give even such credit for acting better than they speak."

"You are thinking of your colonel," said the minister, smiling.

"Well," returned Vincenzo, "even he had his good points; but I was alluding to the student who was so violent against the government, yet in spite of his declamation was hastening to peril life and limb in defence of the country guided by that very government."

"Your theory," observed the minister, somewhat epigrammatically, "has at least the advantage of being pleasant. When are you to be received as barrister-at-law?"

"About this time next year."

"Have you paid any particular attention to political economy?"

"Not more than to the other branches of my course of study."

"Then, for the future, do so, and to statistics also. Do you know anything of English?"

"Not a word."

"Well, then, I advise you to set about learning it. You can teach it to yourself; it is the least complex of any language. You could easily master it sufficiently to be able in a short time to read the English blue-books, a study of which will be of the greatest future utility to you. I should like also to be able to form some idea of your style and manner of setting forth a subject. When you next pay me a visit, bring me a few pages of your composing."

"On what subject?" asked Vincenzo.

"On any that you choose. Are you for absolute freedom as to education, or not?"

"In theory, for freedom; practically, for our own country, I think it best for some time yet, that public instruction should remain under the control of the government."

"Put down in writing your reasons for this way of thinking, and let me have it." The minister considered for a few minutes, then went on: "I need scarcely say that it is my intention to do honour to Onofrio's recommendation of you in the amplest manner in my power. I might give you a place under me forthwith; but to do so would be to interfere materially with your studies. I think it better, therefore, to postpone all active interference in your behalf until you have taken your degree of doctor of laws. The title itself, though there is not much in it, will smooth the road to many things. In the mean time I shall ascertain what are your talents, and see how best to utilize them for the service of the country. That I may be able to do this, you must come and see me often. Do not be over scrupulous or discreet; for I tell you plainly, if you do not remind me of yourself by calling, I am not sure that I shall not forget you. On Saturday evenings — I tell you this for your own private use — I generally make my escape from work at dusk. If you like to come and wait for me here, we can have a little quiet conversation. I may sometimes be prevented from returning home, and you may have had your walk for nothing; but you will not mind that, I dare say. Lastly, let me give you one piece of advice; do not tell any one that you are in the habit of seeing the Minister, or you will be deluged with applications, for introductions and recommendations which I shall not be able to attend to: on this point I rely on your absolute discretion."

Vincenzo professed his readiness to abide religiously

on this as on all other matters by the directions the minister was so good as to give him, and, with many expressions of gratitude, rose to take his leave. The minister went with him to the passage door, cut a bit from the coil of wax taper which had served to let them see their way up stairs, gave it lighted to Vincenzo, and with a last caution not to run down too fast so as to put the light out, wished him a good night.

We should not be giving Barnaby his due if, in the enumeration of the agencies at work in favour of Vincenzo, we did not assign a signal place to the old blunderer. It often happens in this world that a blunder serves some particular end better than the most skilfully calculated move. Vincenzo's mysterious flying visit, combined with his disturbed looks and her father's pre-occupation, had not been without arousing in Miss Rose a certain amount of curiosity — a curiosity which Barnaby had the means and the most resolute determination to satisfy; for, as you have already guessed, Ugly and Good had listened, with malice prepense, at the door of the Signor Avvocato's sancta sanctorum, and overheard the dialogue between godfather and godson. Barnaby so managed next morning as to be at work in the alley of nut trees, which was the shortest way to the summer-house, the infallible goal of Miss Rose's morning stroll.

Miss Rose came as usual, and as usual stopped for a little chat with Barnaby. In times of yore — that is, only two or three years ago — she would have taken the bull by the horns, and bluntly asked Barnaby, "Do you know why Vincenzo came last night and went away again in such a hurry?" As it was, being no longer an *enfant terrible*, but a grown-up young lady of nineteen, with the sense and reserve of that age, she said instead, "Did you see Vincenzo before he left?"

Barnaby, with the most comical would-be gloomy grimace at his command, said "he had not seen Vincenzo; he must have started before dawn."

"I merely wanted to know how he looked, in case you had seen him," observed Miss Rose. "I fear he has not yet recovered from his last illness. He was so pale and flurried last night."

"I don't wonder at that," replied Barnaby, with increasing gloom, "considering what he was told. Pale, indeed! It's a miracle he is still in this world, poor fellow!"

"You frighten me, Barnaby; what was he told?" asked Rose — "that is," she added, checking herself, "if I may know."

"Not only you may, but you must know," affirmed Barnaby. "The matter concerns you as well as Vincenzo. He is gone away to return no more; he is banished for ever from this place!"

"Banished!" repeated Rose, turning the colour of ashes. "It cannot be true; it is one of your mistakes, Barnaby."

"I tell you I heard the Signor Padrone say so to him in so many words. The poor lad's eyes rained tears."

"But what can he have done?" exclaimed Rose.

"Well, I can tell you that also," continued Barnaby. "The Signor Padrone wanted to persuade him to speak to you in favour of the young Marquis. Vincenzo said he wouldn't, he couldn't, it was impossible. The Signor Avvocato asked him why. 'Because,' says

Vincenzo, 'I won't play a double game with you — because I love your daughter myself.'"

Rose turned scarlet, and the heaving of her bosom bore witness to the intensity of her agitation. Barnaby availed himself of her silence to go on.

"'Sir,' says the Signor Avvocato, '*you* love my daughter — sir — and so you have taken advantage of the intimacy I allowed to make love to my daughter.'"

"Stop," said Rose; "how did you come at the knowledge of all this, Barnaby?"

"Never mind how," growled the old man.

"Ah! I guess only too well," resumed Rose. "It was wrong, very wrong, of you to surprise a secret which was never intended for your ears; and it is wrong, very wrong, of you to repeat it to me. Good day." And she walked away.

"Wrong! wrong! wrong!" cried Barnaby, looking ruefully after her. "When that poor lad has broken his heart, which he will do one of these fine days, we'll see then who is right and who is wrong."

Barnaby's indiscretion, though punished by a whole week's severance from his young signorina's pleasant chat and bright smiles, had not the less hit the mark. A girl of nineteen does not hear with impunity that a young man is pining away for love of her, that he sheds showers of tears, and is, moreover, likely to die of a broken heart for her sake — especially if the young man be a handsome, well-figured fellow, and a tried friend of old standing. More than once did blooming Miss Rose, in her secret thoughts, revert to and dwell upon Vincenzo's plight; and the more she dwelt upon it, the more she found it hard, hard, very hard.

CHAPTER XXV.

The Signor Avvocato in his Glory.

"By the bye," said the minister to Onofrio at the close of a long conversation on official matters, "he is a wonderful young fellow that protégé of yours. I told him scarcely two months ago he had better learn to read English, and already he translates it at sight. He had quite the best of it in an argument we had last night as to the meaning of the phrase 'with a vengeance;' he had indeed."

"He is clever, and works very hard," said Onofrio.

"I am sure he does, and then he is so clear-headed — it is a pleasure to watch his quickness in grasping a question, and his method of discussing it. You must read a few short articles on sundry matters he wrote at my request. Cavour has looked them over, and thinks highly of them. I shall be perplexed as to a choice when the time comes for employing him. He has many of the qualities which would make a capital diplomatist — but then he has no handle to his name. Perhaps the administrative career will suit him best. What do you say?"

"I say that the question seems to me a premature one; you will be able to solve it best when you see him fairly at work."

"That's true; but, whether in diplomacy, or in the administration, your protégé will make his way. Now don't spoil him by telling him of my golden opinions."

"It would do him no harm if I did," said Onofrio; "Vincenzo is *intus et in cute* a modest youth."

"Yes; and straightforward. What I like in him is his independent way with me; he never humours or flatters me — whenever we differ in opinion, he tells me so candidly, and frankly asserts his own views."

Onofrio judged that the time was now come to strike his second grand blow in Vincenzo's behalf; that is, to acquaint his godfather with the new perspective opening before his godson. Even a change of ministry would not affect it much, for, though out of power, the actual minister so friendly to Vincenzo would still command patronage enough to push on his protégé; and he, Onofrio himself, would not be without interest with the limited number of his colleagues in the House, likely to take office in another Cabinet.

"If I could but make sure," thought Signor Onofrio, "that this Signor Avvocato has a stomach strong enough to digest a sound piece of advice, I would willingly give it him to swallow — but *in dubiis abstine*. I cannot answer for a man, whom I have only seen for an hour once in my life, not being narrow-minded; and, if he be so, ten to one but that self-love and pique will prompt him to defeat the plan I have in view; and then, instead of forwarding, I injure Vincenzo's interests. I will run no such risk. After all, there is no reason why I should tell him that one of my motives for pushing on his godson is that he may marry his daughter." And Signor Onofrio wrote as follows: —

"MY DEAR SIR, — When on our first meeting at Ibella, about a year ago, you kindly expressed the wish of hearing from me now and then, I little thought that my first letter to you would be an interested one.

Yes, my dear sir, I come to ask of you what in forensic language is called a *sanatoria* — namely, to confirm and ratify a step which I have taken in regard to your godson Vincenzo, and which, though conducive to his benefit, as I am convinced it to be, I am not sure I was quite justified in taking without having consulted you beforehand. Perhaps the general terms of your recommendation of the young man to me, on the occasion I have referred to above, might plead my justification. However, let me hasten to add that nothing has been done which cannot be undone, if you so wish it. And now, without further preamble, I come to the gist of the matter. Vincenzo, as you well know, is a remarkably clever and gifted young fellow; as to me, what strikes me in him is less the brilliancy and the extent than the rare harmony of his faculties. A more happily balanced young head than his I never met in my life. The more I have seen of him, and had opportunities of appreciating his qualities, the stronger has the impression become of how well he is suited for official life. Nobody thinks more highly than I do of the profession of a barrister — but *ars longa* — briefs come in few and far between to candidates for them, while in a rising State like ours advancement is rapid in Government employments. The Ministry ask nothing better than to encourage youths of talent, of activity and principle. I have, as you know, the ear of the Minister, my friend as well as chief — that was another temptation — in short, one fine day I presénted and recommended Vincenzo to him; and you may judge of the progress he has made in the Minister's favour within scarcely a couple of months, from the abstract I here subjoin of a conversation (to remain *inter nos*) which I had lately with the minister. [Here followed an abridgment of the dialogue beginning this chapter.] You see now as clearly as I do Vincenzo's prospects. After taking his degree, he will enter on official duty; in five or six years he is sure to be a good way up the ladder of promotion — at thirty a deputy; once in Parliament, there is no saying to what eminence he may not attain. The career is tempting; what do you say? There will be no fortune to be made by it, it is true, but a treasure of honour gained for himself, his country, and his friends. Should the independence of a barrister's calling outweigh all these advantages in your mind, should you object to a political life for your godson, or should you see any reason for discountenancing this plan, you have only a word to say, and that word shall be adhered to.

"Vincenzo is well, and sends his affectionate duty. Accept, my dear sir, my heartiest wishes, and believe me,
"Your obedient servant,
"Onofrio."

A word now as to the present dispositions of him to whom this letter was destined. At the moment of its arrival, Miss Rose's *vis inertiæ* had won the day. Her father, nill-he-will-he, had abandoned virtually, if not formally, his favourite plan for her, and a passing thought of throwing the handle after the hatchet, that is, of giving his daughter to Vincenzo, and having done with all this tear and wear of spirits, had of late crossed his mind more than once. Why not, in fact? A thousand times rather to Vincenzo than to that sneaking intendente of Ibells, or to that fop, the son of the fiscal, who had no thought in his wooden head but of the cut of his clothes! Once Del Palmetto out of the question, it was a matter of relative indifference to Rose's father who should have his daughter.

But why did he so hold to Del Palmetto? The Piedmontese have of late been much likened, and not inappropriately, to the English — they have, in fact, some of the striking qualities of these latter — steadiness, perseverance, practical spirit, innate distaste of idle speculations, and last, not least, if that be a quality, the profoundest respect for the advantages of birth and title. The Signor Avvocato was not a Piedmontese for nothing, and the perspective of turning his daughter into a marchioness, and hearing her addressed as such, tickled his *amour propre* to an amazing degree. There was another, though secondary consideration, which militated in favour of the alliance with the young marquis, and that was the making of the two estates into one, and that one, *mutatis mutandis*, second to none in the kingdom.

But now that this fond dream was over, Vincenzo's aspirations after the great prize were no longer met by the *non possumus* of a few months back, but were beginning to force themselves upon the old gentleman's consideration. Signor Onofrio's letter was exactly calculated to make Vincenzo's chances rise twenty per cent. "Well may they call that godson of mine a wonderful lad," muttered to himself, according to his fashion, the Signor Avvocato, "and lucky as well as clever. If any one ever deserved it to be said of him that he was born with a silver spoon in his mouth, Vincenzo does; he bewitches every one he comes across. This Signor Onofrio, for instance, one of the busiest and most independent members of parliament — the right hand of the minister — goes out of his way, and turns suitor for the boy. The minister, in his turn, takes a fancy to the boy at first sight — not much doubt of his getting on, indeed — he has only to will it, and if he takes it into his head that he will have my daughter, have her he will. However, it is only fair to say he deserves his good fortune; he has not his equal, that I know of, for ability, mettle, and real goodness. And this other original, who asks me for a *sanatorial* if the request did not come from a grave legislator, I should take it for a joke. I have half a mind to go and thank this Signor Onofrio in person, and at the same time I could see Dr. Moreri."

Dr. Moreri was at that time the most celebrated physician in Turin. The Signor Avvocato had been advised, and had made up his mind to go and consult him these last two years, without ever finding the opportune moment. Growing obesity, and the slow but steady weakening of the whole left side of his body, were the Signor Avvocato's ailments. They had intensified the man's natural indolence and repugnance to exertion to a morbid degree; and the half project of a trip to Turin was no sooner shadowed forth than given up. The Signor Avvocato had never travelled on railroads, and did not consider them safe. A letter will do as well, thought he, and he wrote one; wrote it in his best hand, and most flowery style, to befit the occasion and the recipient. It began thus: — "How can you talk of *sanatoria*, my dear sir, when all the ancient honours of the capitol would not equal your deserts? Not though I had the eloquence of

Demosthenes and Cicero combined, could I thank you adequately for all that you have done" — and so on for two pages. Happily for the writer and his grandiloquent style, Vincenzo gave Signor Onofrio the epistle to read, which he had received from his godfather, and which proved, beyond all doubt, that, off his Pegasus, the Signor Avvocato could write naturally, simply, and feelingly. Nay, there were in this second letter touches of felicitous humour, as when he expressed a hope that his godson, when he became Secretary for the Home Department, would not visit too heavily a poor rustic mayor's peccadilloes.

The Signor Avvocato was too full of his subject not to let something of it ooze out in Rose's presence. Rose did not seem at all dazzled by Vincenzo's brilliant worldly prospects. Indeed, she took the whole matter very coolly, and all she said was, that she was glad of it.

Shortly after, Vincenzo applied for a *sanatoria* in his turn. He had taken the liberty, he wrote, acting on the advice of his experienced friend, Signor Onofrio, to send in a request for the bestowal of the Cross of SS. Maurice and Lazare on the Signor Avvocato. The application had not met, and could not meet, with any difficulty. It was only affording the Government the opportunity of repairing an unjust oversight. He was now happy to say, that his Majesty had signed the nomination the day before, and he rejoiced to be the first to salute his dear godfather as Cavaliere. Official information of the honour conferred on him would be sent by the Minister of the Interior to Rumelli in a day or two, unless the Signor Avvocato could bring himself to come to Turin for forty-eight hours, which would simplify all formalities. On the great pleasure such a visit would give to Signor Onofrio and the writer, the latter would not enlarge. The Signor Avvocato had for some time expressed the wish to consult one of the eminent physicians of the capital — would not that be another inducement for coming? In that hope Vincenzo remained, &c.

Let not the reader suppose for an instant that this crescendo of stirring tidings was the result of a preconcerted plot, artfully contrived with a view to gradually heating the Signor Avvocato to the proper degree of malleability for being moulded to a purpose. No such thing. Both Signor Onofrio and Vincenzo, as we know, pursued a certain object, but pursued it by legitimate means, and without the alloy of any, the least particle, of humbug. Signor Onofrio's letter to the Signor Avvocato had not been written one single day sooner or latter than it would have been, had the Signor Avvocato not had a daughter, nor did it contain any single statement that was not in perfect accordance with truth: it was, in fact, only the reproduction of Signor Onofrio's conversation with Vincenzo. On his side, Vincenzo had drawn up the memorial in his godfather's behalf, when his patron, the minister, had told him to do so, and had apprised his godfather of the Cross being conferred on him the moment he had heard the news from the minister. Likewise, Vincenzo's hint to his godfather about coming to town proceeded from no deeper laid scheme, than the natural wish of seeing and partaking the gratification of one to whom his heart clung tenderly and deeply.

So far said, we resume our narrative. For the nonce, the excitement produced by Vincenzo's intelligence proved stronger than habit, ailments, and distrust of railways. The Signor Avvocato found a remnant of his activity of better days. He started immediately for Ibella, took the first train for the capital, and, by the evening of the same day, was comfortably installed, not a little to his own amazement, in one of the hotels in Piazza Castello. Vincenzo, summoned by a note, was by his side in no time.

The Signor Avvocato's stay in town was short, but full and fraught with none but agreeable impressions. Turin was so much enlarged, so much altered for the better, since he had seen it last, that it was a real pleasure to drive through it. Then the Home Secretary, through whom he had received the decoration, welcomed him so courteously, complimented him with such tact, and used so flattering an emphasis in begging the favour of the Signor Cavaliere's company at dinner! He would have done just the same to any one, to whom he gave audience on a similar occasion; but the Signor Cavaliere took it all as a mark of personal distinction. His recollections of men in authority dated from an epoch when stiffness, self-importance, and haughtiness seemed the distinguishing attributes of power.

Still more gracious than his colleague of the Home Department, and equally hospitable to the new knight, was the minister, Vincenzo's patron, from whose official lips there fell into his guest's ear, after dinner, a confidential confirmation (not the less effective for its laconism, and the somewhat guarded tone in which it was delivered) of all the good he thought of, and the hopes he founded on young Vincenzo. Signor Onofrio took the new Cavaliere to the Chamber, found him a seat in the ambassadors' gallery, and pointed out to him all the remarkable men of the Assembly. The relations of the old gentleman's deceased wife, and the few old friends he visited, vied with each other as to who should show him most regard and cordiality. Doctor Moreri treated the indisposition, of which he complained, very lightly, and merely recommended daily exercise, and light diet, principally of vegetables. The very waiters at the hotel seemed bent on contributing their share to his happiness by never failing to call him Signor Cavaliere. Nothing pleases and flatters people accustomed to live in the country more, than the being paid a certain degree of attention by the dwellers in great cities.

In short, the Signor Avvocato left town enchanted with everything and everybody, and within an ace of throwing the handle after the hatchet, according to his favourite figure of speech — only the fear of committing himself by a promise, which Rose, after all, might not ratify, kept him from binding himself more explicitly than by what might be implied from his parting words to Vincenzo, "By the way, mind you come to the palace for the vacation." Vincenzo, for all answer, grasped the old gentleman's hand within both his own, and pressed it to his heart. The gates of Eden were open again. "But —," added the Signor Avvocato, placing his finger significantly across his lips —

"Were my secret to suffocate me," said Vincenzo, fervently, "it shall not pass my lips without your leave."

"And if I never give it?" asked the Signor Avvocato, slyly.

"Then it shall die with me."

"Yes, sixty years hence," wound up the godfather, laughing outright. In this happy mood, the Signor Avvocato set off on his journey home.

All Ibella by this time knew, from having read of both events in the *Gazette*, of his visit to the capital, and of his having been made a knight, and at least half of Ibella equally knew of the exact moment of his return, from having seen Giuseppe with the gig on his way to the station. This was a task *de jure* devolving on Barnaby, but Barnaby was in one of his most intense fits of ignorance of his master's existence, and not to have saved his own soul would he have so much as lifted his little finger in that master's service. This the Signor Avvocato well knew, though unable to fathom the cause, and had accordingly sent word to Rose to despatch Giuseppe to the station. Well, one of those who had seen the gig pass in front of the *Caffè della Posta*, while sipping his coffee, was the Commandant of the National Guard of Ibella, a great friend, as we are aware, of the Signor Avvocato. "Hurrah! here comes the new cavaliere," said he to the company, "let us go and do him honour who does honour to the country." All present adopted the motion by acclamation, with the exception of two or three very young men, who shrugged their shoulders and declared that they were not going to stir for a *Codino*. The Signor Avvocato's growing conservative tendencies since 1849, and more than that, his close alliance with that *Arcicodino*, the late Marquis, had greatly damaged the popularity of the owner of the palace with the youth of Ibella.

And so it came to pass that, on alighting on the platform, the Signor Avvocato met with a cluster of

friendly faces, and a barricade of friendly hands, eager
to press his, and bid him welcome back. Behold him
presently walking up the High-street, the centre of a
momentarily augmenting body guard, stopping to shake
hands at every step, and nodding his head right and
left to the tradesmen standing on the threshold of their
shops. Other friendly faces, and other friendly hands
are waiting for him at the *Caffé della Posta*, which
cannot and will not be disappointed. A halt there becomes indispensable. "Come in, come in welcome,
Signor Avvocato, welcome Signor Cavaliere." The new
knight enters the *Caffé*, his train follows him, salutations recommence — hallo, waiters, a dozen of wine,
if you please. For in this blessed world of ours there's
no possible rejoicing without drinking. Corks pop, "the
health of the Signor Cavaliere — long live the Signor Cavaliere." Glass clinks against glass, and the
health is drunk with hearty cheers, in which the two
or three dissentient youths join. Who could find it
in his heart to dim the satisfaction beaming in that
honest benevolent old countenance?

In the mean time the Rumellians had not been
idle; that is, in one sense they had, inasmuch as they
had been dancing attendance on the Signor Avvocato
for these three hours. All the population of Rumelli
was there, from the parish priest, D. Natale, and the
Mayor at the head of the Town Council, down to the
babies at the breast. When the Signor Avvocato
reached his own gate he had to get out of the gig,
which he did amid the deafening cheers of the crowd,
the "present arms" of the National Guard, and a flourish
from the local band, which struck up with better will
than success. After that, the Mayor in *esse* — a

rich miller retired from business — came forward and read the ex-Mayor an address; and then D. Natale stepped forth, and read the ex-Mayor another address, or rather began to read it, for at the end of the second line he took to stammering and blubbering, seeing which the personage addressed took to stammering and blubbering also, and, to save decorum as much as possible, cut short all further orations by passing one arm under D. Natale's and the other under the Mayor's, and thus supported and supporting, limped up the avenue. D. Natale, if the truth must be told, was more than half in his dotage, and with him all emotion resolved itself into tears. Rose presently appeared, and there were plaudits and acclamations again, when the crowd beheld the father and daughter in each other's arms.

The whole household, including the out-door servants, were assembled on the flight of steps leading into the palace, and came to kiss the Signor Padrone's hand, and to offer their congratulations. One familiar face alone was wanting among the number — Barnaby was conspicuous by his absence. Was he then indifferent to his master's good fortune? Far from it. Barnaby, hidden in a corner, was melting away in tears of pride and joy — Barnaby would fain have kissed the Signor *Padrone's* footprints, but Barnaby had fancied grievances against this adored *Padrone* of his, and could not, and would not give them up — no, rather die first.

By this time the conquering hero, well-nigh spent with fatigue and emotion, after ushering into the great hall D. Natale, the Mayor, the Town Council, and other notabilities, sank exhausted into a chair. The scene of the *Caffè-della-Posta* was re-acted, bottles appeared, corks were drawn, bumpers of wine handed round, and toasts drunk *secundum morem*. "Thank you," said the hospitable host, who felt past speechifying, "thank you from the bottom of my heart. I can say no more for the present; my strength is not equal to my goodwill; come and dine with me to-morrow, when I hope I shall be able to acknowledge your kind welcome more formally, if not more sincerely, — no, no, my dear friends, you needn't go — stay and make yourselves at home — only, excuse me for not entertaining you, as I ought to do." The company tarried yet a little, glasses went round once more, and then they all discreetly withdrew. The folks outside had, each and all, in the meantime, partaken of the traditional hospitality of the family. Miss Rose was an invaluable mistress of the house on such occasions.

"Well, and how is Vincenzo?" asked she, as she was lighting her father up to his bedroom.

"Vincenzo is as brisk as a bee," said papa, "and in a fair way of becoming somebody. I wish you had seen him, my dear, at the table of the Minister, so self-possessed, every inch a gentleman. No one would ever have imagined him to be the son of a peasant."

"What does that signify?" observed Miss Rose. "Grandpapa was a peasant, was he not, and haven't you the manners of a Prince?"

"You little flatterer!" said the Signor Avvocato, pleased; "but, my dear, the figure of a man counts for a good deal in all that has to do with manners; and allow me to say, though I say it who should not, that between my figure and that of Vincenzo, that is when I was young, there is some difference — a great difference."

"I allow it, papa — Vincenzo is handsome in his way though."

Papa looked searchingly at her; then said, "I see how it is; had I proposed him to you instead of that poor Del Palmetto, you would have given me quite another answer."

"Who knows?" said she, laughing; "but I am not in a hurry to marry."

"Do you mean to tell me you would have refused him?" urged her father.

"Him? Who?" asked Rose.

"I speak of Vincenzo, of course."

"How can one refuse that which is not offered?" said she, laughing again.

"Ah! you hypocrite — suppose, for supposing's sake, that I offer him to you?"

"What is the use of answering suppositions? Good night, papa;" and she tripped away.

CHAPTER XXVI.

An Interesting Definition Cut Short.

It must not be supposed from Rose's ambiguous answer to her father's covert inuendo, that she had not drawn her own conclusions from the short dialogue given in the last chapter; and these conclusions were, that her father would never have spoken to her as he had done, had he not altered his mind with respect to Vincenzo's suit — nay, even accepted him as his future son-in-law, subject of course to her consent. She was confirmed in this view of the case beyond all doubt, when she heard her father, as the weeks passed, repeatedly alluding to Vincenzo's expected visit during the vacation as a settled matter. Well — the consciousness of all this, added to newly-awakened feelings in her own bosom for her old playmate, gave to her reception of him, when he did come, a tinge of reserve and embarrassment which made it quite a different affair from what it had been up to this day. The alteration in her manner could not fail to react on the young lover, even had he not had other causes to make him look and feel embarrassed on his side: the chief among these causes being his certainty that she was in possession of his secret through Barnaby — the old fellow's evasion of any promise of secrecy, when Vincenzo had tried to extract one from him, too clearly implying a predetermination to use his own discretion, or rather indiscretion, as to telling or not telling.

Nor was this shadow, which had fallen upon them, confined to their first meeting: it resisted the action of time, and hung more or less over their subsequent intercourse. Now and then the one or the other would fall into old ways, use the once familiar intonations, talk on once familiar topics; but, then, this always occurred in the presence of a third person, never when alone — though, indeed, that they seldom were. Not that they positively avoided each other's company, only they did not seek to be *tête-à-tête* as of yore; and, when a chance rencontre threw them together, it was curious to observe how studiously one or the other, or both, tried to put between them somebody else — either tottering Don Natale, or Barnaby, or Giuseppe, or (at a later period, when there were several visitors staying in the palace) any of the guests. Since we have named Barnaby, let us mention that, from the moment of Vincenzo's arrival, he had magnanimously resumed communication with his master on the old footing. Even Rose's father, who was anything but a keen observer, could not help at last noticing this state of constraint between the two young people; and, much as he wished to set them at their ease, he still shrank from pronouncing the word which alone could do so. Had he, then, once more changed his intentions? Yes, and no. The Signor Avvocato still faithfully adhered to the engagement he had taken with himself to give his daughter to Vincenzo; at the same time there is no denying the fact, that all the ardour in the matter he had brought back with him from Turin had vanished. Two full months of reflection had given him time to measure the void which Rose's absence would leave in his home — surely it was a sacrifice for which there need be no hurry! She was so young — but just nineteen — and Vincenzo himself was hardly yet of the age at which young men marry! He should have her — in a year or so — when his bright prospects began to be realized! And so, from one thing to another, the good gentleman had ended by consigning the evil to that distant future *sine die* so dear to spirits irresolute.

Having once established himself comfortably in this passive position, Rose's father naturally dreaded nothing so much as shifting it for one where there might be something to do; hence his unwillingness to break the ice, at the risk of making a question, which he hoped he had set at rest for ever so long, one open to discussion. But, being as soft-hearted as he was incapable of decision — that is, wishing to mend the situation without renouncing the *status quo* — he hit upon a middle course, which only made matters worse. He took to giving little hints, which were meant to be encouraging, but which proved only the source of new perplexity to the parties concerned. For how could Rose, a bashful girl just awaking to love, or Vincenzo, discreet as we know him to be, and bound moreover by a solemn promise — how could they be expected to take advantage of such vague insinuations?

Luckily, the acute period of the trial to both the young people was short, extending scarcely over the first three weeks of Vincenzo's stay at the palace, while there were as yet no strangers there, or only a stray one or two. The end of July brought an influx of guests, which went on without any solution of continuity to the end of the season. Rose's time was in consequence much occupied, Vincenzo's society much in demand, and there were no opportunities for *têtes-à-têtes*.

The Signor Avvocato was repaying, by this hospitality, the many debts of kindness which his elevation to the knighthood of San Maurice and Lazare had entailed upon him. Foremost on the list of his invitations stood his relations and old friends in Turin, including his new one, Signor Onofrio — who, however, had declined going to Rumelli on the plea of business; then his friends of Ibella, comprising most of the functionaries there, the Intendente at their head — all of whom had called to congratulate him on his new honours; and after them, the mayor of this place, and the parson of that, who had performed the same civility, and so on. Of course, this mighty array of guests were not asked in a lump, but in driblets of six or seven at a time; to which if we add chance visitors, we arrive at an average of no less than ten persons enjoying at one time the hospitality of the palace; and a cordial, unceremonious, plentiful hospitality it was, worthy of a true knight of old. It rarely happened but that the company should be more than doubled on Sundays by arrivals from Ibella and Rumelli, Don Natale for certain among these last. We do not see young Del Palmetto figuring in any of these gatherings, for the very peremptory reason that he had long ago left the castle in high dudgeon: in fact, he had gone away immediately after he had been given to understand that Miss Rose (to use Barnaby's metaphor) "was no bread for his teeth." And so the *villeggiatura* went on happily through the usual months, until the time came for Vincenzo and the few visitors who had lingered to the last also to take their departure. After breakfast of the morning previous to Vincenzo's departure, the Signor Avvocato had a long, confidential talk with his godson, chiefly about the probable epoch of his being employed, the nature of the employment, and its locality. On these two last points, Vincenzo could throw no light whatever, but volunteered to inquire, if an opportunity should present itself naturally for so doing: as to the first question, he could only repeat, what he had already told the Signor Avvocato when in Turin, that the minister had expressed his positive intention of employing him as soon as he should have taken his degree.

"Ah! and in May next," said the Signor Avvocato, "you will be just turned three-and-twenty, an age when a youth begins to know a little what he is about. At the end of five or six years at the longest, we may reckon on your having got something very fine — a first-class Intendenza, let us say, or a secretaryship; — I don't mean of State," added he, smiling at his own wit; "you must be a deputy before you can be that — but the secretaryship of some embassy. You will be then twenty-eight or twenty-nine, exactly the fit age to marry. By-the-bye, Rose consents of course?"

"Consents to what?" asked Vincenzo.

"To what? — why, to marry you!"

"To know that, I must have asked her and..."

"And you have not?" resumed the Signor Avvocato. "What the deuce! Do you expect me to make a declaration for you?"

"That is a trouble, I think, I can spare you," said Vincenzo, "if you only give me leave."

"Give you leave! Have I not been giving you leave every day during these whole three blessed months?"

"I beg your pardon, sir," said Vincenzo: "you have more than once, it is true, kindly alluded to a possible happy consummation of something that was wished for, but what that something was you always left in a mist; and could I, on the strength of such obscure hints, consider myself freed from the strict promise of silence which you had exacted from me in Turin?"

"Well, perhaps not," said the Signor Avvocato; "I give you credit for unusual prudence at all events."

"In which I give you fair warning I shall not persevere *now*," said Vincenzo coaxingly, and rose to go.

"Where are you going?" asked his godfather, quickly.

"To pray the daughter to ratify the father's consent," returned Vincenzo.

"Dear me — what a hurry you are in all at once!" said the Signor Avvocato, with a slight degree of vexation.

"My time here is short — only twenty-four hours left: I must make the most of it," replied Vincenzo, and hastened away.

The old gentleman watched him depart with a very rueful countenance; had he dared he would have forbidden him to go — forbidden him to speak; he lacked the courage to do so, after what had passed between them. His good heart had betrayed him, in the impulse of the moment, into being more explicit than he had intended to be; and thus, in a twinkling, was lost all the advantage of his temporising policy of months and months.

Vincenzo, having sought in vain for Miss Rose indoors and in the garden, bethought himself of her favourite retreat, the belvedere, already so often mentioned, and took the shortest way thither, through the avenue of walnut trees, which he had scarcely entered before he espied Rose coming towards him from the other end. Vincenzo hurried on, and the two were face to face in a few instants.

"Good morning, Miss Rose! I came here in the hope of finding you."

"Did you?" said Rose, with a little surprise. "Well, here I am."

"I have something to say to you," began Vincenzo.

"I am listening," said Rose, not without a little flurry of expectation.

"I think I shall say it best if we walk on," said Vincenzo.

"As you like," said Rose, and moved on by his side.

Be it chance or design, he led the way down the avenue. "Are you charitably disposed?" asked he, after a short pause.

"I think I am," said she, with a half smile.

"Because," resumed Vincenzo, "I am going to plead guilty to a great presumption."

"That is the last sin I should ever have suspected you of: it must be one of very fresh date."

"On the contrary, it is one of my very oldest and most inveterate; and it dates, as far as I can remember, from the first day I saw you."

"As old as that — you alarm me!" said Rose, trying to smile. "What a dissembler you must be, to have hid it so long from me!"

"Have you then never guessed that I — I ... loved you, Rose?"

She blushed scarlet, and said, "Is that your sin of presumption?"

He looked at her and bowed his head.

"But there is no sin in that. Are we not desired to love our neighbours as ourselves?"

"Yes, but the love I speak of is of quite another kind; it is, to begin with, of a more passionate nature; it is exclusive and interested, so much so that . . ."

A shout from behind stopped the definition short; the young lady and gentleman turned round and saw the Signor Avvocato hobbling after them. However unseasonable the interruption, there was nothing for it but to go and meet the old gentleman.

"Six years hence — six years hence, remember,"

cried the Signor Avvocato, as soon as he could make himself heard.

"What is to be six years hence, papa?" asked Rose.

"Why, the wedding to be sure," said papa.

"The wedding?" repeated Rose, in unfeigned surprise.

The Signor Avvocato stared at her in utter perplexity, then at Vincenzo, then at her again, and at last said, "Yes, the wedding — that is, if you agree to it."

"Agree to what, papa?" cried Rose.

"Zounds! as if you didn't know," exclaimed her father, losing all patience; "if you agree to marry that young man by your side, — I speak plain enough now, I hope."

Poor Vincenzo blushed up to the very roots of his hair, less at the statement itself than at the prosaic way in which it had been made. Rose did not look alarmed, or shocked, or even embarrassed. She simply said, "How could I know if nobody told me?"

The Signor Avvocato turned a significant eye on Vincenzo.

"You left me no time," returned his godson, with a little testiness. "You seem, after all, quite determined to make the declaration for me; will you be so good, at least, as to complete it?"

"Complete it — how?"

"When any one presents a petition, he expects and hopes for an answer, does he not?" said Vincenzo.

"Ah! well — true — you are right. Well, Rose my dear, now is the time to make up your mind."

"Is it?" said Rose archly "I will some day during these next six years," and she ran away.

For the first time in his life was his godfather's company a bore to Vincenzo — not that it was an obstacle to his following Rose, and pressing her for an answer — he was in no mood for that: the sort of game at cross-purposes to which chance had lowered what was to have been the solemn effusion of his heart of hearts, had told too painfully upon his feelings, to leave him liberty of mind enough, or indeed the inclination, to urge his suit just then; but to have to listen to that prosing, and for form's sake to make some kind of answer, while longing for silence and solitude, was, to the young man, a real trial. At last the Signor Avvocato felt the necessity of rest for himself, so returned to the house; and Vincenzo, under the pretext of having some visits to pay in Rumelli, released himself from further bondage. A solitary walk of a couple of hours did much towards dispelling the gloom that had gathered over him, and Rose's smooth brow and smile full of promise, when he met her at dinner, completed the cure.

The Signor Avvocato, contrary to his wont, was very active and busy during the rest of the day; he had manifold directions to give his daughter, manifold commissions for Vincenzo to execute. He insisted on going out with them for a walk five minutes after having complained of being tired. In one word, the poor father did his best to keep them asunder; and, to a certain extent, succeeded in the attempt. But all the trouble he gave himself and others could not and did not prevent the young couple from occasionally exchanging confidential whispers, by which, to judge from appearances, they arrived at an *entente cordiale*. At least Vincenzo's face, when he left on the morrow, was not that of a rejected suitor, nor Rose's that of an unrelenting beauty.

The Signor Avvocato kept his room the whole of that day, so worn out was he by his extraordinary exertions of the day before.

CHAPTER XXVII.
The Interrupted Definition Concluded.

A WEEK, two weeks passed. Rose was as silent as a tomb — Vincenzo was gone away for six months. All being thus arranged for the best in this best of possible worlds, what could the Signor Avvocato do, but sink again on his soft couch of procrastination, and lull himself to sleep on it?

Little thought our Fabius Cunctator that an enemy to his repose lay in wait for him at Ibella. Yes, he was no sooner settled there comfortably for the winter, than no less a personage than the Signor Intendente waited on him, and asked point-blank for Miss Rose's hand. Had the Intendente asked him for his purse or his life, the good easy gentleman could not have been more startled. To say *no* to anybody cost him an effort at all times: *à fortiori* to say *no* to the head authority of the province, and that at a minute's notice, was a herculean task indeed. He lashed himself up to it though: but in his fear of offending, in his eagerness to soften the blow, he wandered into a maze of explanations, got entangled by his own words, and made a nice mess of it.

The *amour propre* of the Intendente being mightily wounded by what he perceived to be nothing but a beating about the bush, he had the bad taste to insist on knowing on what grounds a man of his rank and official standing was rejected. The Signor Avvocato, at his wit's end, protested and reprotested that it was on no grounds personal to the Signor Intendente; far from it, he felt all the honour conferred on him by a proposal from so distinguished a person; were it in his power he would be only too happy, but .... as it was, he regretted to say he had nothing but grateful thanks to offer — circumstances existed .... early inclinations — young ladies would have their way nowadays; he begged to be spared the necessity of being more explicit. Upon this the rejected suitor retired in no very pleased mood, and the Signor Avvocato, after a sonorous ouf! of relief, said to himself aloud, "Rather than be worried with more applications of this sort, why, I'll marry them at once."

Not long after D. Natale called on the Signor Avvocato on some parish business. "By-the-bye," said the old priest, "I am glad to hear that we are soon to eat *confetti*, sugarplums," (an idiom tantamount to saying "We are soon to have a wedding").

"Who is to be married?" asked the Signor Avvocato.

"No use playing the Indian," retorted D. Natale: "such discretion is ill-advised towards an old friend like me, when all Rumelli and Ibella are in the secret. Then you know that I always liked the boy, thought highly of him. You will have a good bargain in him for your son-in-law."

The Signor Avvocato's features fell — he was beginning to understand the allusion.

"And mind," ended the priest, "it is old D. Natale who is to give the blessing — I'll never forgive you if I don't."

"All Rumelli and Ibella are in the secret!" thought the Signor Avvocato. "How can they know?"

Obviously enough, they knew from an indiscretion of the Signor Avvocato himself. When, in the eagerness to gild the pill for the Signor Intendente, he had let fall the expression "early inclinations," it was much the same as if he had said, in so many words, that Vincenzo was to be his daughter's husband. For to no other could those words apply, but to Vincenzo or young Del Palmetto, with both of whom Rose had, to a certain age, been brought up. Now, it being notorious that the young lady had rejected Del Palmetto, the "early inclinations" could only refer to Vincenzo. Undoubtedly, it was ungenerous in the Intendente to take advantage of an unguarded word, to sound the trumpet about this match; but the Intendente was piqued, and pique is never generous.

There yet remained a hope, that it might all be a fancy generated by that weakened brain of D. Natale. The matter, though, was worth inquiring into. If there was any foundation for D. Natale's assertion, Barnaby would be sure to know; but, then, to question Barnaby was to create the evil, if it did not exist. No, it would not do to apply to Barnaby. Giuseppe was the man — he could be trusted. And forthwith, the dairyman who brought the milk to the Signor Avvocato's townhouse, and to market every day, was charged with a message summoning Giuseppe to Ibella. Giuseppe came.

The Signor Avvocato evinced the greatest anxiety to learn whether the late frost had done any injury in the nursery of young mulberry-trees, and being reassured on that point, had many other items about which to ask and to be enlightened. At last came the P.S.: —

"And how do you amuse yourselves up there in this weather? I hear there's plenty of idle gossip going on, eh?" — Giuseppe was not aware that there was any particular gossip going on in Rumelli.

"I was told," went on the Signor Avvocato, "that a report had got abroad about my daughter being engaged to be married. Has it reached your ears?" — The report mentioned by the Signor Avvocato had reached Giuseppe's ears.

"And pray, is it said to whom she is engaged?" — The name of Signor Vincenzo had been mentioned.

"Was such a rumour generally current?" — Pretty much so.

"And in the town also?" — As to that Giuseppe could not answer.

"And is any particular time assigned for the wedding?" — The coming Michaelmas was spoken of, said Giuseppe; who did not deem fit to add that, according to another version, the marriage was to take place as soon as Signor Vincenzo had finished his studies. Giuseppe was a born diplomatist, and confined himself to the strictly indispensable. In all likelihood he had never heard of the famous *"pas de zèle,"* but he acted up to it.

The Signor Avvocato, when left alone, rubbed, and rubbed again, his partially bald pate. It was pretty certain, that what was the common talk of Rumelli could not but be the talk of Ibella. There was little risk, he perceived, in sounding Barnaby. Barnaby was therefore summoned, and subjected to a cross-examination. His evidence was the counterpart of Giuseppe's, with only this difference — that he was as positive and incisive in his assertions as Giuseppe had been cautious and guarded. Was such a rumour rife at Ibella? Bless his heart! nobody talked of anything else. The whole town applauded the Signor Padrone's choice. It would be a general disappointment if the wedding were delayed till Michaelmas, as some folks said. For his part, Barnaby hoped and trusted that the moment Vincenzo had passed his last examination, the mine would explode — the sooner the better. The dear young ones had been on the rack long enough. See how they were pining away. As for Vincenzo, he was mere skin and bone . . . .

"How do you know? You haven't seen him for more than two months."

Barnaby, ignoring the interruption, went on: "And the blessed Signorina! Why, she is only the shadow of her former self: the bloom has left her cheeks — no smiles on her lips . . . ."

"What stuff are you talking?" cried the Signor Avvocato. "Rose is as fresh as a . . . . rose, as plump as a quail, merry as a bird . . . ."

"Is she? Well, suppose she is; but wait another six months, and see then what she will have shrunk into. Forewarned, forearmed: marry them at once, I say, or you'll rue it."

The old gentleman's heart misgave him, that no effort of his could long retard an event, upon the speedy consummation of which public expectation and Barnaby were bent. This impression, like most others, would have faded and died out in course of time, had not that terrible monitor, Barnaby, mounted guard, so to say, to cherish its existence. Barnaby displayed, in this office, the ingenuity and implacability of a Red Indian. Every action of his, however trifling — his very silence — conveyed either a warning or a reproach to his master.

Presently, this latter's anxious incubation entered a second phase, and one far more creditable to his feelings. Was he justified, even though he could do so, in delaying the union of the young couple so long? This new view of the question was suggested to him one day by Rose's unwonted paleness and somewhat drooping appearance. Could it be the beginning of that shrinking into nothing which Barnaby had prophesied? Rose was as brisk and cherry-cheeked as ever on the morrow, and the fond father laughed himself out of his fears; which, however, did not prevent his relapsing into them, and being overcome by a new qualm the next day, supposing he chanced to see his daughter looking vacantly before her, lost in a deep reverie. Rose, contrary to her habit, had become of late addicted to reverie. Ninety-nine out of a hundred fathers in the same predicament would have questioned their daughter, tried to ascertain the state of her feelings, and then determined upon some course of action; but so plain and obvious a method implied a set purpose, and consequently an effort of will, to which his wavering and procrastinating nature could not bring itself.

If he had only some one to consult, by whose counsel he could feel it safe to abide! But among all his friends in Ibella, there was not one to whose judgment he deferred. That most confirmed of blunderers, Barnaby, he utterly distrusted; Don Natale was past giving advice; the ex-Intendente of Ibella was gone. *That was a man you might trust with your eyes shut* — a man who, for prudence, foresight and decision, had not his match. While thus bemoaning his isolation, the bright idea flashed through the irresolute gentleman's mind, that the friend he so much missed, was not after all, either bodily or by letter, out of his reach. This friend was at Genoa, and Genoa was not at the end of the world. He would go, by Jove, and pay him a visit — that he would.

This ambitious programme, delayed as usual from day to day, from week to week, dwindled into the modest one of a letter — the writing of which was deferred of course, to a more convenient hour, begun, left off, taken up again, again discontinued, and .... at last completed. The answer came by return of post — we give it literally: —

"My dear friend, — Barnaby is right: marry them at once. I am of opinion that in all dubious cases you would do well to trust Barnaby's instinct, and act upon it — no beagle scents the hare more surely than he does what is right to do. A girl of near twenty too young to be married! Fiddlesticks! If you can do it to-day, don't wait till to-morrow. It will be best for all parties: for her, whose heart and mind will expand under the influence of a larger mind and heart — for him, whose powers in the hard struggle before him will be increased tenfold by love and happiness — for you, whose old age will be the sooner gladdened by a cluster of lovely little Roses, lisping out 'Grandpapa.' I regret that a world of business prevents me from saying more. I have tried, as you see, to make up for quantity by quality — In great haste, yours ever affectionately, —."

This letter was the wand which broke the spell. To read it, and grow as impatient as he had been hitherto slothful to conclude this match was for the recipient one and the same thing. With the intuitive consciousness of his weakness, the Signor Avvocato lost no time in putting between his new resolve and the possible recurrence of fresh hesitations, the unpassable gulf of an accomplished fact — that is, accomplished as far as the case admitted. He ran in hot haste to his daughter, read her what he thought fit of his friend's letter, and asked her point-blank if she had any objection to being married soon — sooner than he had once intended — next June, for instance. Rose, very naturally, was out of breath at such an unexpected question. Indeed, papa must remember that it was neither for him nor for her to fix a time: it was from another quarter that any pressing on that point should come.

"Humbug!" cried papa; "you well know that Vincenzo would not have waited till now to press the point but out of obedience to me."

"I cannot have him hurried, "insisted Rose. "Oh pray, papa, don't put me in such a false position!" Poor Signor Avvocato! to meet opposition from the very quarter where he looked for support. However, still under the influence of the Genoa letter, he held to his point. He would have the marriage in June, on the First of June, or not at all. Rose might trust her own father, that he would not do anything derogatory to her dignity — she must leave it all to him. Rose was afraid to say more, and the Signor Avvocato, following his own inspiration, wrote thus to Vincenzo: —

"MY DEAR VINCENZO, — I have, in my turn, to ask for a *Sanatoria;* as to your granting of which, truth to say, I feel very little uneasiness. For reasons of my own, which would be too long to give in writing, and which shall be communicated *vivâ voce,* I have *taken the liberty* of fixing upon the First of next June to be your wedding-day. By that time you will be a doctor *in utroque* of a full fortnight old. Just send a line by return of post, to let me know whether you approve and ratify the above arrangement; and believe me, my dearest godson, in haste, but very affectionately, "YOUR GODFATHER."

This letter duly sealed and addressed, word was sent to Barnaby, through Rose, to get the chaise ready and then come to his master. We have forgotten to say that the family had just returned to the palace with the spring; the fluctuations given in outline had taken up the whole of the winter.

"Here's a letter for you to take to the post in Ibella," said the Signor Avvocato; "it must go by to-day's post, mind."

"It shall," said Barnaby, taking the important despatch. "By-the-bye," added he, scratching his head, "suppose I am asked, which I certainly shall be, about the time . . . . ?"

"Haven't you got your watch?" interrupted the other, with a little chuckle.

"It isn't that — I mean what time is this blessed match to be, about which everybody is talking and speculating?"

"Ah! the marriage. Well, if anybody asks, say the First of June."

"Not difficult to say," answered Barnaby a little resentfully; "but when the First of June comes, and there is no match —"

"But there will be."

"There will not."

"Will you take a bet on it, Barnaby?"

Barnaby almost poked his nose into his master's face, the better to scan its expression. "Are you in earnest, sir?"

"I am," replied the master; "the letter you have in your hand is to inform Vincenzo of the precise day."

Barnaby looked at the letter spell-bound, made for the door, rushed back, twirled round and round again as if bent on giving himself a vertigo; and, having by these evolutions recovered his lost power of articulation, said at last — "Bravo! you are the worthy son of Signor Pietro, bless his soul!"

"Thank God! for once I have succeeded in giving thee satisfaction, old grumbler," said the Signor Avvocato, good-humouredly; "we'll see how long it lasts. Now look sharp with the letter."

Barnaby looked sharp, and so did Vincenzo, who came early the next day, the bearer of his own answer. What was its tenor we needn't doubt: and as to the spirit in which it was given and received, that was clearly legible in the traces of deep yet happy emotion, imprinted on the countenances of godfather and godson, when, after being long closeted together, they sallied forth in quest of Rose. The young lady, repeatedly sent for by her father, had not been to be found in doors nor out of doors.

"We will hunt her up, unearth her, though," said the Signor Avvocato in high glee, rolling his ponderous bulk down the stairs with all the alacrity of which he was capable. The chase was neither long nor difficult, thanks to Barnaby, who put them on the right track by dumb show. Rose was inspecting the young mulberry-plants in the nursery-ground — an out-of-the-way place behind the garden — with the close attention of a person meditating a purchase. "Here is the runaway — come along," cried the old gentleman in his merriest tones; and, putting Rose's hand into that of Vincenzo, he added, feelingly, "God bless you, my dear children, as I bless you from my heart! I know she will make thee happy, Vincenzo, and if thou ever makest her shed a tear . . . ."

"Oh! I should be a monster if I ever did," protested Vincenzo, energetically.

"Thank thee — thank thee for these blessed words; their warmth does me good! Adieu."

They stood face to face, hand in hand, alone: and there and then, for the first time, the long-sealed fountain of his love gushed forth in passionate jets. He told her how his whole life had been but a continuous act of adoration: she the sun and joy and pride of the poor infant-peasant, when they strolled the park together — she the secret thought and the consolation of the adolescent's long years of bondage in the seminary — she the strength of the youth struggling hard for university honours! Ah! but for her image to prop him up, but for her approval to deserve, how many times would he not have sunk under the trial! She his all in all in the past, in the present, in the future!

This he told her as they moved on, still hand in hand, under the blue canopy of heaven, amid the thousand subdued voices of Nature awakening under the breath of the early spring — this and much more, which we need not repeat. Lovers are terrible hands at idealizing. Had Rose been a saint descended from on high to lift him up — a common mortal — to share half of her celestial bliss, he could not have spoken and felt more highly of her, more humbly of himself. True love is always humble, and then his was saturated with gratitude: do what he would, could he ever pay off the balance of the immense debt he owed to father and daughter?

Sweet must be the odour of the incense burned at one's feet by the person one loves, for Rose to accept of Vincenzo's without protest. She did though, and looked on serenely calm and happy as he spoke, just as a saint might do in receiving homage at the hands of a common mortal.

"Poor is the lot," pursued Vincenzo, "which I can offer you, my Rose — so poor, indeed, to my wishes and to your deserts, that I should scarcely dare to ask you to share it, did not I feel so immensely rich in love, tenderness, and devotion — oh! so rich, as to feel sure of making up to you for all its short-comings. I know, for instance, how painful will prove the separation from your father, though only for a time."

"Oh! painful beyond what I can express," exclaimed Rose; "but cannot it be averted? Is it absolutely necessary?"

"Absolutely, I grieve to say," answered Vincenzo. "You know that when I get my degree, I am to enter, as agreed upon with your father, on an official situation under Government; and from that moment I shall be no longer my own master, but entirely under the orders of the minister, my patron."

"That I understand very well," said Rose, "if you accept of a situation: but what necessity is there for your seeking any?"

"What necessity, love? But I must work; every one must work, and make himself useful in this world."

"Papa does not work," objected Rose.

"Yes, papa does to a certain extent, though now nearing that age at which man is entitled to rest. Papa sees to the management of his estates, gives legal advice to those who ask it from him, and then his leisure hours he devotes to the study of music — he is far from idle, you see."

"Well, I allow all that, but could you not help papa, and find besides some useful occupation for yourself here?"

"To divide with your father the tasks to which he is quite equal alone, would be the same on my part as to accept of a sinecure. The little I could do for him would fall short indeed of my powers of activity, and also of my legitimate ambition."

"Ah! ambition," said Rose, "is the natural enemy of love."

"Not in me — not in me," protested Vincenzo with warmth; "my ambition is part of my love. I possess none of those advantages which men most prize, neither birth nor fortune. I am a mere cypher, and I must myself give this cypher a value. The name you condescend to wear must be an honoured one, and I will make it so."

"And if I am content with you as you are, and don't care for anything else?"

"Bless you, sweet soul! for saying so!" cried the enraptured lover, kissing her hand most passionately; "but even your gentle wishes cannot release me from the duty I owe to you, to your father, to myself, to the world. Would you have it said of me, with any appearance of reason, that I have sought a rich heiress in order to live in plenty and idleness?"

"Oh! who would ever be so wicked as to say so?"

"How little you know of the world, Rose dear! Who would say so? — the envious, the scandal-mongers, and their name is legion. No, no, darling of my soul; let me do what I think right, and aid me to do it. Bad as a separation is, do not allow your imagination to picture it worse than it is. Not for the world, not for my eternal happiness, would I urge upon you a sacrifice too hard for you to bear. Wherever we are, you see, we shall always be within easy reach of Rumelli. Piedmont is but a nutshell, and covered all over with railroads. Then, you know, I am to have regular leave of absence; and once a year, at least, we shall be able to come and stay some time with your father: he, on his side, will pay us occasional visits, and take you back with him whenever you choose. What do you say, Rose?"

The words were so sweetly spoken, that they sounded like a caress. He was seated by her side in the belvedere, both her hands in his, his black eyes plunging into her violet ones. There was an ineffable charm in the gentle earnestness of his tones and looks. Rose felt conquered, if not persuaded. "If it cannot be helped," she said at last, "why, then, it must be as you wish."

"Thank you — thank you!" said Vincenzo, sinking his lips into the plump rosy hands his own held willing prisoners — then looking up again into her eyes, he added: "It is so sweet to ask so gracious a giver, that I am greatly tempted to present another petition."

"And what may that be?" asked Rose.

"Simply to humour a love-whim of mine. There exists a custom in England which I much admire, and would fain adopt. A newly-married couple there, almost as soon as the ceremony is over, disappear from all gaze profane, and start away, alone, on what is termed their wedding-tour. Let us do the same. Let me enfold you in the cloud of my love, and have you all to myself for a little while."

"I would willingly say yes," said Rose; "but perhaps papa —"

"Your father is already my confidant, and will not object if you do not."

"Well then, I do not; where shall we go?"

"To Turin first — then to Genoa, to look at the sea, if you like."

"Oh yes, that will be charming."

"Then to Florence — '*Firenze la bella!*'" continued Vincenzo.

"Shall we go to Rome?" asked Rose.

"Rome is very, very far," objected Vincenzo.

"Oh! do let us go to Rome — I would rather go

there than anywhere. I do so long to kiss the Pope's foot, and go up the *Scala Santa* on my knees."

"But, indeed, Rome is too far," again observed Vincenzo, "and then there's the malaria in the summer months."

"Never mind the malaria."

"But I must mind it, dear. Only think, if you were to catch the fever — the mere idea makes me shudder. Your father would never forgive me, and with reason; nor could I ever forgive myself. Rome is quite out of the question for the present. We must put off our journey thither to some future winter."

"What a pity!" exclaimed Rose.

The conversation was brought to a close by a series of angry shouts from Barnaby, who came to summon them to dinner. Barnaby cried shame on them for keeping the Signor Padrone waiting: they knew the Signor Padrone was so particular as to his meals. Barnaby was too happy not to fret and fume at something or somebody.

Vincenzo started for Turin by the earliest train on the morrow.

CHAPTER XXVIII.

A Happy Pair.

Towards the middle of May in the year 1854, Vincenzo went through his last examination in dashing style — and scarcely a fortnight afterwards, that is, on the First of June, he led his betrothed to the altar.

The marriage was celebrated with all the pomp and circumstance of which a marriage admits. Turin sent no less than seven representatives to the ceremony, among them Signor Onofrio; and all the bigwigs of Ibella, with the exception of the Signor Intendente, who pleaded indisposition, were present; and so was Rumelli *en masse*, of course. Vincenzo could have well dispensed with nine-tenths of all this *éclat* and publicity — they jarred with his quiet and simple tastes. But the Signor Avvocato had set his heart on doing the thing grandly; and then Rose was so pleased with all the arrangements, that the bridegroom could not but be so for her sake. Rose was splendid in natural beauty as in adornment — her toilette was dazzling — connoisseurs said it might have suited a princess. An ill-repressed murmur of admiration followed her steps, as, leaning on her father's arm, she walked up the nave of the parish church to the high altar, the point of attraction of all eyes. The Signor Avvocato wore, for the first time, the Star of St. Maurice and Lazare in diamonds, ordered expressly for the occasion.

The service was read, and the benediction given to the young couple by old Don Natale, who further attempted to deliver a little speech of congratulation — (the third he had addressed to Vincenzo in public, the first dating twelve years back). But, as everybody expected, he broke down most pitiably at the second sentence — a failure which proved, after all, a success, inasmuch as the part of the congregation nearest to him, infected by his melting mood, burst into tears and sobs. Conspicuous among the chorus of weepers and sobbers stood Barnaby — Barnaby, as black as a drop of ink in his new suit of sables, and white cravat; Barnaby, whose naturally distorted features had reached, under the pressure of emotion, the *beau idéal* of ugliness. Extremes meet, and, next to the bride, Barnaby was the great attraction of the day. Impossible to look at him in his black coat without laughing outright.

At one o'clock P.M. fifty-one guests sat down to table in the large hall on the ground floor. Two bands of music, that of Rumelli and Ibella, were in attendance outside, and played during the repast. We say nothing of the fare — it consisted of every delicacy that money can buy, and culinary science improve; and as to wines, the cellar of the palace was celebrated throughout the province. The dinner went through all the legitimate stages of *crescendo*, from the subdued buzz during the soup to the simultaneous explosion of every voice at the dessert.

When the entertainment had reached this climax, the health of the *sposi* having been drunk and re-drunk, and drunk again *sine fine*, the bridegroom whispered to the bride, and cautiously withdrew. Rose, on the first convenient opportunity, followed his example, and went, unobserved, to change her bridal attire for a travelling dress; she then joined Vincenzo and Onofrio, who were waiting for her in a dark passage leading to a door opening out into the back premises. At this door was stationed a spring cart, which had served in the morning to bring from Ibella a load of elegantly elaborated edifices of pastry and confectionary, fruits of all kinds, and ices. It had an awning of thick striped canvas, and curtains of the same stuff closed it in all around, in order to protect the delicacies it contained from the heat of the sun and the dust of the roads. Into this vehicle Onofrio handed Rose, then Vincenzo, and, carefully closing the curtains, bid them good-bye.

The driver led the horse by the bridle, and the cart jogged away unobserved through the avenue, and down the road to the turning below Rose's belvedere. Here was waiting the Signor Avvocato's chariot and pair, with Giuseppe as coachman. Seizing a favourable moment, when there was no one in sight, the newly-married couple alighted, and hurried into the carriage. They were both so nervous and afraid of detection, that, but for Giuseppe, they would not have seen Barnaby waving a farewell to them from the belvedere, and weeping like a mermaid.

The scheme of the cart was of Vincenzo's own concocting, and he was not a little proud of it. Had it been a question of elopement, he could not have fenced it in with a thicker hedge of precaution and mystery. Nor had he been a whit too careful, if we take into consideration the amount of opposition which a course so contrary to all precedent could not have failed to meet with from the bridal party, had it transpired. Rose lent herself to Vincenzo's whim with infinite complaisance and good humour. They reached the station in full time for the last train, and an hour before midnight were safely lodged at the Hotel de Londres, at Turin, where the bride's luggage, thanks to Vincenzo's forethought, had preceded them.

Besides the natural eagerness, common to every lover under the sun, to have his beloved all to himself, Vincenzo had another motive for wishing to remove Rose from small local influences, and introduce her to a larger and broader current of ideas and feelings than could be found at Rumelli. Vincenzo had never shut his eyes to a fact, of which he had of late had ample confirmation — we mean the narrowness and lukewarmness of Rose's patriotism; and to enlarge and warm it, to bring it nearer to the level of his own, he trusted, rather than to any definite teaching of his, to the action of those thousand mysterious imponderables, which pervade the air of a large city, and constitute, as it were, the atmosphere of civilization. Not that Vinzenco wanted to make his wife a political character; all that he wished was, that she should be capable of understanding and sympathizing with a political man. Until a communion of feeling on this cardinal point was established between them, he felt that he could not call her quite his own. The trip to Florence had been devised to forward this purpose, to the attainment of which he anticipated no difficulty. His estimate of Rose's docility and good sense was, as we know, high. And what place was better calculated to open her mind and heart to the consciousness and pride of the Italian sentiment than Florence, the beautiful and *gentile*, the

Athens of Italy, the mother of Dante and Michael Angelo — Florence, the incarnation of Italian genius?

A better assorted or happier-looking pair seldom graced the arcades of Via Po, or the alleys of the public gardens; he, a head taller than she, fondly bending towards her his pale face, full of distinction and serene thought; she fondly lifting hers, all dimples, and lilies, and roses, up to his. Passers-by turned round to steal another peep of them; Vincenzo's fellow-students raised their eyebrows, and murmured as they lounged by, "Lucky dog!" Rose was lost in admiration of all she saw; the impression made on her by the long, wide, regular streets, the enormous squares, the mighty river, the affluence of people, the splendid shops, was the more interesting to Vincenzo, as it was a reproduction of that he had himself received six years ago.

They spent only a few days in Turin, but they were days well employed. Vincenzo played his part of cicerone conscientiously — not a sight worth seeing that he did not take her to see. Both Houses of Parliament, of course, were of the number. The Subalpine Parliament, in 1854, was a miniature likeness of the Italian Parliament of 1862. Almost all the States of Italy, Rome and Naples not excepted, had representatives there; men who had, many of them, tasted the salt bread of exile, been buried alive in the tombs of the Spielberg and the *Segrete* of Naples — men who had suffered in various ways in the name and for the sake of Italy, who were glad and proud of having done so, and were ready to do so again. Vincenzo pointed out some of these to Rose, and gave her a sketch of their lives. Onofrio, himself one of this noble band, introduced a few of these fellow-sufferers of his to the young couple, who heard from them stories, modestly and unaffectedly told, of narrow escapes, and hardships, and cruelties; of double irons worn and dragged for years and years; of heavy coupling chains never removed night or day.

The minister, Vincenzo's patron, paid the young bride a visit, and after saying many things very pleasant for her to hear, ended by giving her a smiling caution against any delusive hope she might harbour of having her husband all to herself for very long. There was another lady to whom Vincenzo also owed allegiance, and who would put in her claim to it within three months. Signora Candia need not blush so; she must be of a jealous disposition indeed, if she was jealous of "the country," for that was the lady, and no other, to whom he had alluded, and in whose service Vincenzo was pledged from the first of September next.

Genoa was their next stage. The palaces and the orange-trees of "La Superba" did not find much favour with Rose. She missed the space and the symmetry of lines which had struck her so much at Turin; but the sea made up to her for all deficiencies. They had rooms in one of the many hotels which overlook the port, and were never wearied of contemplating the new and ever-changing spectacle under their eyes. Rose declared she was in love with the sea. Vincenzo, too, was in love with it, but in a different way from hers. There mingled with his admiration of its versicoloured loveliness and majestically serene repose a sense of poetical awe of its mysterious immensity, and virtual uncontrollable force, when aroused to fury; that fury to which dykes and piers are like mounds of sand, and three-deckers cockle-shells. Whereas unimaginative Rose saw it hemmed in by the horizon, saw it beautifully smooth like a mirror, as it just then was; could not conceive it otherwise, and longed to feel herself rocked on its bosom. Why should they not go to Leghorn by steam, and thus escape the dust of the roads? Vincenzo emptied his quiver of classical arrows at *mare infidum*, but to no purpose; she laughed at Horace and his *triplex robur* with the perfect assurance of one who knows nothing of the sea, and just as much of Latin.

Vincenzo had obvious reasons for not leaving Genoa without visiting a patriotic memento which forms, and justly so, the pride of all Genoese, and that in particular of the populous and popular quarter of Portoria, within whose precincts it is by right situated. It consists of a slab of marble, commemorative of the event that follows, and which occurred in 1746. It would take too long to say what concatenation of circumstances had led to Genoa being abandoned by her powerful allies, France and Spain, and left to the tender mercies of Austria. Suffice it to state that the territory of the republic, and its capital, were in the occupation of thirty thousand Austrians. A squad of these soldiers, towards dusk on the 5th of December, 1746, were dragging through Portoria a large mortar, when the pavement gave way under the weight, and the mortar buried itself in the ground. Unable to raise it by their own efforts, the escort demanded the assistance of the neighbouring tradespeople and of the occasional passers-by, but to no purpose; seeing which the corporal had recourse to the Austrian argument, *par excellence*, the cane. Thereupon a lad of fourteen, an apprentice dyer, nicknamed Balilla, hurled a stone at the corporal's head, which knocked him over. In the scuffle that ensued one soldier was killed and seven badly wounded; the rest fled, to return backed by several hundreds of their comrades, who had, however, to beat a precipitate retreat from the stones, tiles, articles of furniture, boiling pitch and oil, thrown down upon them from the roofs and windows. This was the prologue to a fierce struggle, which extended over six days — from the 5th to the 10th of December — and which ended in the total rout and expulsion of the Austrians, with a loss of 1,000 slain and 7,000 taken prisoners. If ever there was a popular victory, this was one, fought and won as it was solely by the popular classes, who had not only a numerous, well-disciplined, well-fortified army to cope with, but the ill-will of their own Government to neutralize, a counter-government, head-quarters, leaders, arms, commissariat, &c. to improvise for themselves, and public order to maintain. To carry out this last purpose gallows were erected in the square of the Annunziata for the immediate accommodation of thieves caught *in flagranti*. And well might Giovanni Carbone, a young man of twenty-two, and one of the bravest combatants of the six days — well might he say to the Doge and Senate, when consigning to them the rescued keys of the city, "Here are the keys which your most serene lordships yielded so easily to the enemy; take care to guard them better in future, for we have redeemed them at the cost of our blood."

They went by sea after all — between the wisdom of Horace and the pouting of a cherry-lip, what man in love ever hesitated? — and a delightful passage it was: not a breath of wind, scarcely a ripple on the water. Who so happy and proud as the fair prophetess? Leghorn, after Genoa, had but little interest for our young tourists; so they pushed on to Pisa. They took only a peep of the fine old city, however, so impatient was Vincenzo to reach Florence. Rose was rather attracted by Pisa, particularly by the leaning tower; but what most tickled her fancy was a herd of camels which she saw in the environs, at the farm of San Rossore. They haunted her; she had never seen a camel before, except in a picture.

But her first impression of Florence was one of disappointment, owing partly to Vincenzo's imprudence in raising her expectations too high, and still more, perhaps, to a change of weather. Their arrival was saluted by a perfect down-pour of rain. Even the City of Flowers could not look otherwise than dingy and disconsolate under a heavy shower. It was short, as summer storms are; and, only a few hours later, when the married lovers went out for a walk, the sun shone gloriously, the birds sung merrily in the groves of Boboli, a delicious freshness pervaded the air. This magic change, however, wholly failed to dissipate the first unfavourable impression received by Vincenzo's wife. Rose was most tenacious of first impressions.

Vincenzo proceeded methodically, as his wont was — he devoted the first days to a general survey of the town, so as to make himself familiar with its configuration and distribution; he then took an Artaria, the Italian Murray, and began his rounds. We shall not follow him; the task of cicerone does not belong to our department; the description would be tedious to those who know anything of Florence, and entirely useless for those who do not. We will only say that which will be no novelty to anybody, namely, that our young couple met at every step with memories, names, and works, the mere mention of which thrills the hearts of five-and-twenty millions of Italians with pride and grateful reverence. Out of these noble names, and memories, and works, was to be elicited the spark which was to warm Vincenzo's Galatea into a new being. Young Candia had chosen for head-quarters a quiet hotel not far from the church of Santa Croce, and rare was the day when, either going to or returning from his sightseeing expeditions, he did not enter the noble pile and seek for inspirations at the tombs of Machiavelli, Galileo, Alfieri, Michael Angelo, and Dante. Vincenzo's system of tuition was simple and easy: he chose for his theme the most striking event suggested by the sights of the day — as, for instance, Pier Capponi's superb answer to Charles VIII., Ferruccio's death, the expulsion of the Duke of Athens, or such like; gave Rose a summary of it himself, and then in the evening read her an account of the circumstance as told by Villani or Machiavelli. Or, perhaps, taking his cue from a visit to the apartment of the Priori in Palazzo Vecchio, or to the hill of San Miniato, he would impress on Rose, and illustrate by apt examples, the great love of Dante and Michael Angelo for their country. (Everybody knows that Dante, previous to his exile, was one of the *Priori* of Florence, and that the fortress of San Miniato was strengthened with new ramparts and bastions by Buonarroti himself in the year 1529). Oftener still Vincenzo contented himself with reading to her such passages of the "Divina Commedia," Petrarca's political "Canzoni," Alfieri's tragedies, or Foscolo's "Sepolcri," as most forcibly embodied the sentiments he wished to instil into her.

All this Vincenzo did gently, discreetly, by driblets, be it understood. Of all things, he hated pedantry; he knew also how much Rose was equal to; and then he was in love — three infallible preservatives against becoming a bore. Even had he any disposition to become one, he would have lacked the time, so full was the share they took of the diversions and amusements that Florence afforded. The cool hours of the evening saw them oftener taking ices at the Cascine or at Boboli, at some of the theatres, or at a *conversazione*, than studying the history of their country, or of its great men, at home.

Rose listened to him and to his reading often with pleasure, sometimes with real interest, always with docility and an evident wish to humour him — never with an appearance of anything like a patriotic fibre vibrating within her. Far from finding fault with her for this, Vincenzo discovered plenty of reasons for her justification — her want of education, the narrow atmosphere in which she had lived, and so on — and he trusted for a change to the action of time. He felt grateful to her for the goodwill she evinced, for her invariably charming temper, for the easy way with which she put up with many little disagreeables inseparable from a stay in an hotel — grateful for the spirit of order she showed. Rose, according to the express request of her husband, was pursebearer, cashier, accountant; and it was a real pleasure to him to see the method, the clearness, the neatness with which she kept her accounts. On another also, and, in Vincenzo's eyes, capital point, she fully deserved, and he gave her, all praise: it was the simplicity of her attire. Rose, in spite of example, gave in to none of the eccentricities of fashion.

Late on a sultry evening they were sitting on the terrace, which was on the roof of the house. Florence, bathed in the mellow light of the moon, had a melancholy charm of its own, which went to Vincenzo's heart, and brought unconscious tears to his eyes. And, as he looked at it, and evoked its memories, his soul overflowed with enthusiasm, and he fell to indulging in a beautiful vision of the future, which came forth clothed in words of fire. He pictured an Italy independent, free, united — pictured the revival of its genius, its arts, its commerce, the increased splendour of its hundred cities. . . .

"With the Pope at its head," interrupted Rose, with a flash of enthusiasm quite new in her. Vincenzo looked at her, as if suddenly awakened, and knit his brows; but there was no tinge of impatience or displeasure in his answer, "Why the Pope, dear? Italy wants at its head some one capable and willing to draw the sword against its enemies; and the Pope cannot. He refused, you know, to declare war to Austria."

"Yet," persisted Rose, "did not Gioberti advocate the Pope's claims to be chief in Italy?"

"True; but he lived long enough to see his error, and to recant it in his last work. If there is ever to be an Italy united under one king, the *Re-galantuomo* is that king by right."

"Oh! Victor Emmanuel!" exclaimed Rose; "how can a country ever prosper under a king who has no religion?"

"Allow me to say, Rose dear, that your speech is uncharitable and ... inconsiderate. How do you know, and what has Victor Emmanuel done to justify your assertion, that he has no religion?"

"Do you ask what he has done?" was Rose's warm rejoinder; "have you forgotten that he has sanctioned the law against the priests?"

"Law against the priests!" repeated Vincenzo, his eyes wide with amazement. You must have dreamed of one, assuredly, my dear Rose: there never has been a law passed against the priests, nor so much as thought of."

"You are unfair, Vincenzo; you know very well what I mean — the Law Siccardi — the law to commemorate the passing of which a column was erected by public subscription."

"Do you know," inquired Vincenzo, "the provisions of the law you allude to?" Rose had, apparently, her reasons for evading the question, for, instead of answering it, she said, "I know the clergy regarded it as a spoliation, and resented it as an affront."

"True; but that only proves that they were angry, not that they were right in their appreciation of it. The clergy were not, could not be expected to be, impartial in their own cause."

"Do you mean to say that such men as Don Natale or Padre Terenziano could be influenced in what they said by mere partisanship?"

"Most assuredly they could, and were so, though, I have no doubt, in perfect good faith. It is difficult for the best of men to have a long-possessed privilege taken from them, and not feel their withers wrung. I myself, you see, only an ex-seminarist, one who had shrunk from being a priest, felt as a partisan in this very case." And he went on to tell her of his instinctive repugnance to the bill, of his attendance in Parliament to hear it discussed, of the light that had gradually stolen upon him, and at last of his entire concurrence in the principle and dispositions of the law.

That Rose was not convinced was clearly implied by the tone in which she said: "Well, that's your way of thinking."

"It ought to be yours also, if mine is right."

"And if it is not?" retorted Rose.

"If it is not," said Vincenzo, "convert me to yours. I ask for nothing better."

"I have no pretensions to converting you," said Rose, drily.

"Excuse me for saying that in that you are wrong, Rose. There can be but one legitimate way of thinking, as there is but one truth; and, if you believe me to be in error, it must be your wish, as it is your duty, to put me right; for how can we be united in the spirit, as we are in the flesh, if you do not?"

This appeal remained unanswered. Rose became all at once aware that it was late, and that she was tired, and left the terrace. For the first time since his marriage, Vincenzo went to bed with anything but a light heart, and he spent part of the night in upbraiding himself with having been harsh, — if not positively harsh, too stringent; at all events, he might have couched his remarks and arguments in gentler words.

On the morrow, there was a cloud on Rose's brow, the first that had overshadowed the serenity of her honeymoon. What lover worthy the name can see a cloud on the beloved features and not do his best to conjure it away? This Vincenzo did, and successfully, by redoubling all those little tendernesses and endearments, which say so pointedly in their mute language, "All that I care for is to be at peace with you." A dangerous way of mending little splits in the present, at the expense of large ones in the future. The reconciliation, in fact, rested upon a misconception. Vincenzo had been making amends for a real or supposed want of *form* in his strictures of the night before, whereas Rose had accepted his atonement as a recantation of their *substance*.

END OF VOL. I.

www.ingramcontent.com/pod-product-compliance
Lightning Source LLC
Chambersburg PA
CBHW030312240426
43673CB00040B/1141